Popular Culture and Popular Protest in Late Medieval and Early Modern Europe

MICHAEL MULLETT

CROOM HELM
London • New York • Sydney

© 1987 Michael Mullett
Croom Helm Ltd, Provident House,
Burrell Row, Beckenham, Kent BR3 1AT

Croom Helm Australia, 44-50 Waterloo Road,
North Ryde, 2113, New South Wales

Published in the USA by
Croom Helm
in association with Methuen, Inc.
29 West 35th Street,
New York, NY 10001

British Library Cataloguing in Publication Data

Mullett, Michael
    Popular culture and popular protest in
    late medieval and early modern Europe.
    1. Revolutions — Europe — History
    2. Europe — Politics and government
    I. Title
    940   D131
    ISBN 0-7099-3566-8

Library of Congress Cataloging in Publication Data

ISBN 0-7099-3566-8

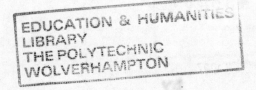
Printed and bound in Great Britain by Mackays of Chatham Ltd, Kent

POPULAR CULTURE AND POPULAR PROTEST
IN LATE MEDIEVAL AND EARLY MODERN
EUROPE

Music moves different people in different ways because if they are imbeciles or obtuse (like lowly shopkeepers and peasants) they will not receive as much delight as the others. People such as these — especially slow-witted women or other poor and simple little creatures — would do better to listen to blind men singing to the *lira*, the guitar or the whistle.

Whenever peasants listen to an ordinary preacher, as long as he shouts loudly and has a great thundering voice, he can let the conceits fall where they may and it matters little to them, for they regard him highly.

Severo Bonini, Discorsi e Regoli

For my students at the University of Lancaster

Contents

Preface

I am deeply indebted to Valerie Rudd, who spent a great deal of time and trouble in making her skilful translations from medieval French for me. I have benefited from numerous conversations with colleagues at Lancaster, especially those in the late medieval and early modern fields, in particular, Lee Beier, Bob Bliss, Sandy Grant, Marcus Merriman, Joe Shennan, John Walton and Austin Woolrych. A lot of the ideas in this book were discussed with my students at Lancaster, especially in a course I have taught jointly with Lee Beier. I am grateful for the insights I have had from my students, in essays, seminar papers and tutorials. My thanks are due to John Andrews, John Illingworth and the staff of the Lancaster University Library, in particular Thelma Goodman of interlibrary loans. Richard Stoneman of Croom Helm first suggested this book; my warmest thanks go to him for his constant support. As always, my wife Lorna has helped and encouraged. I must thank my sons, Gerard and James, especially for their forbearance on those occasions when I must have seemed somewhat preoccupied.

Michael Mullett
Lancaster

1

Introduction: Popular Culture and Popular Protest in Late Medieval and Early Modern Europe

This study is partly about popular protest in Europe in the later Middle Ages and the early modern period. We shall be dealing mostly with the fourteenth, fifteenth, sixteenth and seventeenth centuries. This forms the great age of European popular insurgency, a phase which opens in the fourteenth century and has a secondary peak in the sixteenth and seventeenth centuries. Europe — chiefly western Europe — is the focus of our study, concentrating on France, England, Italy, the Low Countries, Bohemia and Germany, and dealing with lower-class protest and insurrection in town and countryside, and the links that bound the protests of the lower orders in both urban and rural areas. At the very beginning, we shall need to spend some time in this introduction considering and establishing the importance of the town as well as of the country, and to underline the significance, particularly the cultural significance, of towns in what sometimes appears to have been an overwhelmingly rural society.

One argument in this book is that, with some exceptions, there was not a revolutionary, but only a reformist mentality underlying the lower-class protests of our period. Our lower orders — we shall attempt some definition of them below — often reacted forcibly, but pragmatically, to deteriorations in their living standards which they could blame on human agencies; they did not generally have alternative social structures to propose. It is true that there were movements like that of the Drummer of Niklashausen in Germany in 1476 which called for the complete equalisation of society. Such movements tended to be heavily influenced, or indeed created, by the ideas of religious visionaries and unofficial charismatics. There were also serious millenarian protest movements, drawing their inspiration from the eschatology at the heart of the Christian

1

message and envisaging the replacement of existing society by paradise on Earth. Some of the most serious movements we shall consider, however, either harnessed some social radicalism with political deference towards kingship, as did the English Peasant Revolt of 1381, or combined both social and political conservatism in programmes that aimed not to have existing society swept away but rather controlled by moral, and specifically Christian, values: such, broadly speaking, was the great German Peasants' Revolt of 1525. Popular protest used the assumptions and language of a phenomenon we shall attempt to define — popular culture.

We need some initial definitions of the popular classes (we shall be talking later about urban and rural elites) and we begin with that vast category known as the peasantry. Some historians, especially, perhaps, English historians, seem to encounter a little difficulty in defining the word 'peasant'. This difficulty may have arisen because England has lost its peasantry: perhaps a Frenchman would have less difficulty with the word *paysan*, an Italian with *contadino*, a German with *Bauer*. For the purposes of this book, the following definition of a peasant will be implied: a small-scale farmer directly tilling the soil for family subsistence and/or market production and normally owing certain financial and/or labour obligations in return for occupying the land. Not all rustic plebeians were peasants, of course: the countryside contained numerous artisans such as blacksmiths, and also, especially from about the sixteenth century onwards in such areas as the Netherlands and England, quite large numbers of people whose livelihoods came in whole or in part from rural industrial work, particularly in textiles. None the less, we shall use the figure of the peasant farmer as our archetype of the rural plebeian. The other section of our 'lower classes' comprises the urban lower orders. For our purposes, these are made up primarily of those townsmen and their families who relied mostly on wages, and sales of their manufactured and processed goods for their livelihood. Working peasants and townsmen, then, will be the main foci of our study, though we shall also take into account the more 'marginal' elements of urban and rural society — vagrants and the 'criminal classes'.

Incidentally, I assume that social class existed in the past. Some historians have quite persuasively argued that since the word 'class' was not used in the medieval and early modern periods, then class consciousness, and therefore class itself, did not exist, but only 'orders' and 'status groups'.[1] This seems to me to be akin to saying that the circulation of the blood did not take place before Harvey discovered it. I accept that 'status groups' dependent only partly on economic differentiation, such as the nobility, were predominant in subjective medieval and early modern social analyses. I would argue, however, that the status groups generally coincided with wealth and poverty and this means that objectively they at least resembled social classes, since class is based in the first instance on economic distinctions. There was in fact some class consciousness, and there was certainly class conflict.[2] Indeed, it is a theme of this book.

Such conflict had active insurgency as its most dramatic form of expression, and insurrection on a greater or lesser scale, from riot on individual estates to nation-wide rebellions, will be our main concern in dealing with popular protest. Action, concentrated and indeed violent action, formed the language of those generally denied constitutional means of self-expression. Increasingly in the early modern period, written manifestos appeared in revolts and gave them coherence: both the English Pilgrimage of Grace, 1536-7, and the German Peasants' Revolt of 1525, had a multiplicity of lists of grievances and demands. However, an apparently well-organised and exceptionally serious revolt like that of the English rising of 1381 lacked such a coherent literate formulation.

The truth is that the popular revolt was itself the method — no doubt clumsy, and generally unsatisfactory — of drawing attention to complaints. A revolt was often a kind of mobilised petition, directed at the king as an idealised arbiter, typically between peasants and lords. Most peasant revolts were defeated, at least on the face of it. Some popular revolts were, however, followed by some improvements in the condition of the lower orders, especially peasants. In many cases such improvements were doubtless inevitable, and might have come about anyway because of long-range demographic and economic factors. It is also possible, though, that when improvements came about in the wake of popular revolts, those gains might have been made because landlords and political authorities had been made freshly aware of the limits to which peasants in particular could be pushed. This was an underlying function of many popular revolts — to re-adjust, but not always to re-cast, society, often quite conservatively.

Yet we are forced to ask the question, if revolt was protest, why was revolt not permanent in late medieval and early modern Europe? I ask this question because some would see in the European social system of those centuries one massive apparatus of exploitation by lords and governments directed against peasants and workers. Part of the answer to my question is supplied by Braudel, who implies that there was indeed a continuous social war, through banditry and murder, in parts of Mediterranean Europe.[3] In addition, throughout Europe, and identifiably in Germany, there was deliberate unpunctuality, inefficiency and absenteeism over labour services, flight from estates, sabotage and arson of lords' property.[4] In much of northern Europe, too, there were periods of recurrent, and indeed endemic, revolt in certain countries and areas, if not quite a state of permanent revolt.

Such periods and areas include Germany from the late fifteenth century to 1525, and France from about 1580 to about 1640. Particularly in France in that period the lower classes were the victims of, and were responding to, aggression from landlords, from the state and from aristocracies fighting civil wars. Such intensified pressure, along with climatic deterioration coinciding with population increase, probably altered the terms of peasant existence from the tolerable to the intolerable. Depending on soil types, given reasonable weather, favourable population balances, hard work and good sized holdings, most European peasants could normally expect to feed their families more or less adequately, pay various reasonable dues to lord, church and state and perhaps even improve their houses, diets and general living standards.[5] They always tended to resent labour services, if only because these took them away from work on their own holdings and at the times they most needed to do it themselves. As we shall see, they tried to control community relations, weather, crops, sickness and death through religion, in the more extensive sense of that term.[6] The main determinants of their lives — weather and long-range population trends — were of course beyond any human control, though from the seventeenth century onwards, public authorities may have been instrumental in influencing population levels through checking illegitimacy, trying to guarantee food supplies and taking precautions against epidemics.[7]

Conversely, human intervention in peasants' lives, on the part of the state or of landlords, could also make hitherto tolerable situations insupportable. When the dues, labour services, estate obligations, rents and taxes that peasants paid were increased, when war was waged over their holdings, when access to supplementary food and fuel supplies in woods and waste land was curtailed, then a precarious hold on subsistence, or even on modest prosperity, was threatened or lost. Revolt was the result, and was a response to 'aggression' on the part of others. As we shall see, peasants were not fools. Each failed revolt, ingrained into the folk memory, must have acted as a warning of the risks of rebellion. Peasants in revolt were not generally revolutionaries initiating action but were largely reacting to changes introduced, to their disadvantage, by their social and political superiors — deleterious changes whose effects were exacerbated in periods of crisis and depression such as the first half of the seventeenth century.

There were times when revolt was indeed the outcome of absolute desperation. There was clearly a mood amongst the French peasantry at various times between the fourteenth and seventeenth centuries when they felt that revolt was the only way out of the sheerest misery.[8] There were also millenarian revolutions, like that in Bohemia in and after 1419, when peasants and workers took the offensive so as to destroy and re-cast society. At other times and in other places insurgent manifestos tell us two things about a widespread peasant mentality: first, there was a feeling that society was either basically benign or basically unchangeable; and second, that within society there was a line between justice and injustice which should not be crossed by lords or the state.

The concept of justice in society had been incorporated into the peasants' mental world as the effect of centuries of accumulated Christian preaching. The medieval Christian social ethic had its ultimate origins in the teaching of Jesus with its suspicion of wealth and the wealthy and its exaltation of the poor. From New Testament beginnings, developed especially by the medieval scholastic theologians, a social morality was built up. According to this morality, the virtues of justice and charity were supposed to be upheld in a Christian society which was seen as an organic whole, divided into estates, each making its contribution to the welfare of the whole. All forms of undue exploitation were foreign to this social balance. Lending money at interest was uncharitable, prices should be fixed according to the ability of the buyer to pay and the just rewards of the producer, and the rich had an inescapable duty to aid the deserving poor. Injustice occurred, not in the fundamental structure of society, which was created like all things by God, but when its equilibrium was upset by the acquisitiveness of any particular group or individual. Such social ethics were reflected in many of the manifestos of popular insurrections, as we shall see. They were implanted in the first place through a transfer from the social teaching of the Christian Church to the popular mind, chiefly through sermons.[9]

Marx thought that the medieval social order — to him basically

one in which the many served the few — was propped up ideologic-
ally by the social attitudes of the Christian Church,[10] and in its
essential structures, it was. This social order was, however,
legitimated by an ideological system — Christian doctrine — which
had its origins before the creation of the feudal order in a minority
sect alienated from the Roman world. Even when it appeared least
critical of the medieval world order, Christian theory offered some
critique of that order, some possibility of modifying it.

The medieval social system could be said to be morally acceptable, from the point of view of even the tamest theologians, when
in its everyday workings it balanced rights and duties. Whether it
was actually doing so or not was of course a subjective judgement
that would vary from individual to individual, but it would be too
simple to argue, as Marx did, only that 'the social principles of
Christianity . . . glorified the serfdom of the Middle Ages . . .'.[11]
Doubtless, with some Church spokesmen that would have been the
case, and all the apparatus of serfdom, including heriot taxes and
labour services, would be quite consistent with the moral rules that
society was supposed to observe. For others, some or all of these
features of manorial feudalism — for example, heriot payments to
the Bohemian reformer, John Hus — violated Christian social justice
and were repugnant to the word of God. Through intensive
preaching over generations, particularly by the friars, with their
gospel and example of holy poverty, Christian social teaching on
the need for some norms of justice and charity in human society
became embedded in popular consciousness, strongly influencing
protest movements, as we shall see.

Alongside the received teaching of the Catholic Church (which
itself, one must repeat, insisted that justice and charity must preside
over Christian society), there existed a more revolutionary
underground tradition. Friedrich Engels drew attention to its
existence:[10] it appealed to Scripture, especially apocalyptic Scripture; it tended to be nonconformist and heretical; and it made a
conscious social, as well as religious, appeal to the poor — as the
Fraticelli heretics did to the lower classes in fourteenth-century
Florence.[11] Clearly, medieval Christian social ethics did rather
more than just give moral support to a predatory social order.

This book deals not only with protest and revolt but also with
popular culture. In particular, we shall see how popular culture
influenced popular protest, not least in such areas as the timing,
organisation, language and symbolism of insurgency. The concept
of popular culture may require some explanation: indeed, even

some definition of 'culture' would be useful. At its most extensive, 'culture' can embrace ways of working, leisure, family life, all of the arts, religion, politics and learning — virtually everything which makes human life human. There is also a narrower definition, here taken from a slightly old-fashioned dictionary: 'cultivation: the state of being cultivated: refinement, the result of cultivation'. For the period we are considering, 'popular culture' accords rather more with the former, broad definition of culture, whereas its opposite, 'elite culture', tends to come rather closer to the given dictionary definition, and can even mean 'the fine arts', although popular culture can be restricted as a term to the arts used and enjoyed by the masses.

It has been argued that before the early modern period — before the Renaissance — whatever cultural divergences there were between status groups, there was also a common culture shared by all social classes in Europe. With the Renaissance, it has been claimed, two more separate cultures arose: one, 'popular culture', was conservative, but not un-changing, in many features; the other, 'elite culture', represented cultivation, and was subject to changes of style: Renaissance, Baroque, Classicism and Romanticism. Elite culture was recondite, expensive, academic and professionalised, largely purveyed by outstanding men who from the Renaissance onwards were increasingly individualised and celebrated for their genius. Elite culture was what we have come to know as culture *par excellence*. It included the 'better' sort of painting and sculpture, 'serious' music, exclusive theatrical entertainments such as court masques, as well as literature written in Greek or Latin and written works shaped by prescribed canons of taste and requiring education to be appreciated. Some random examples may help to illustrate our broad definition of elite culture and of how it differs from popular culture. Milton's *Comus*, Bach's cantatas, and Corneille's tragedies would seem to belong with elite culture, partly because the original form of their performance was exclusive, removing these works from the arena of mass participation.

In literature the form of expression dictated the extent of accessibility. Vernacular works written in the simplest language could command, and were intended to command, a wide audience of those able to read or able to hear popular works being read out: such works included the cheap pamphlets of the German Reformation and the English Civil War, along with ballads, chap-books, calendars and almanacs.[12] Other works might be written in vernacular speech, but had a restricted readership or audience because they were written in abstruse or erudite forms of a vernacular, being intended for a leisured, learned audience. The classic works of European political philosophy spring to mind as fitting into this category. We should also be aware of a large number of writings produced in Renaissance or post-Renaissance Europe which were written in Latin or Greek. These obviously had the narrowest market of all: even Erasmus's collection of proverbs, the *Adagia*, was a best-seller only in a restricted sense of the phrase.

By providing random examples, we can already begin to see some of the features of elite culture that make it different from popular culture — even if we define the two cultures largely in terms of 'the arts'. Elite culture is for a partly leisured and certainly a well-educated class, and that is why its appreciation involves some barrier of difficulty. In contrast, the songs, poems, stories and other artefacts of popular culture may appear facile, sensationalistic and meretricious — just as mass culture often appears to the supporters of educated culture today. Some of the barriers of technical understanding would be insurmountable: a Renaissance production of a Latin comedy in Latin would be closed off to the great majority of early modern Europeans. If we are talking of theatre, though, there could be other productions — characteristically, Shakespeare's comedies — where *some* level of appreciation, if not the fullest, would be open to an inclusive contemporaneous audience.

Similar issues present themselves with regard to the visual arts. The approved modes of early modern architecture were exceptionally academic, based on a classicism that became ever more intense almost right up to the nineteenth century. Yet some of the buildings that this architecture produced, especially the great churches, such as London's St Paul's and Rome's St Peter's, were seen and entered by thousands. Since so many eighteenth-century English people visited London — one in six, it has been estimated — and since many of them must surely have seen Wren's masterpiece, it is worth speculating for a moment on the visual effect of the massive contrast between the metropolitan cathedral and the still medieval style of almost all of England's parish churches at that time.

St Peter's, designed as a pilgrimage church, had some symbolic features that were surely intelligible to almost all Catholics: the colonnade embracing, like the Church, the world and the chair expressing St Peter's primacy. Other more recondite features of Bernini's symbolism were not so readily intelligible: how many, for example, would have realised that the baldacchino referred to the Church as the renewal of the Jerusalem Temple of old, with its

8

twisted columns? How many would have appreciated that the placing of a canopy (canopies were set up over living persons) above St Peter's tomb alluded to the idea that he was still present in the Roman papacy? Thus, in our period some examples of elite art and culture — if we make art synonymous with culture — were both closed off from popular appreciation, being difficult to interpret without prior instruction. Others were open to wide participation but were perhaps not fully accessible to all in their fullest meaning.

Peter Burke is a pioneer writer on popular culture in early modern Europe.[13] He notes that while there were already two cultures in medieval Europe, in early modern Europe they grew further apart, while proponents of elite culture became progressively removed from a popular culture which had earlier been more inclusive. Nevertheless, people with access to both cultures — 'cultural amphibians' — are always indispensable, not least as conveyers of insights from elite culture down to popular culture. It is, for example, an aspect of the impact of Martin Luther that is sometimes overlooked that he combined the intellectual insights of a don with the instinctive understanding of popular symbolism that came from his origins as the son of a peasant.

The conveying of messages from one culture to another was two-way: elite culture picked up signals from popular culture, as it did, for instance, in the response of the Church's central officialdom to popular demands for the canonisation of saints. However, when elite culture passed on messages to popular culture, it often passed on yesterday's messages. This was a process rather like Ariès's account of the way the poor in early modern Europe had for their clothes the hand-me-downs of the better-off — a usage made possible because, as Braudel said, Europeans, alone of human beings, had fashions in clothes.[14] The handing down to the lower orders of the discarded intellectual and artistic fashions of elites is well illustrated in the case of the heretical miller in sixteenth-century Friuli, Menocchio, in Carlo Ginzburg's *The cheese and the worms*. Menocchio obtains some of his ideas from a cheap second-hand book he has bought in the flea market stalls of Venice. In the sixteenth century, through buying or borrowing, he acquires the ideas of the fourteenth century.[15]

In religion, when scepticism and toleration became all the rage in the Enlightenment, people in the van of intellectual progress found that the masses retained much of the religious enthusiasm and the bigotry that had been fully shared, indeed partly inculcated, by elites in the age of the Reformation and the Counter-Reformation. In the late eighteenth century, enlightened English statesmen were attempting to demolish an arsenal of anti-Catholic legislation in England, Ireland and Scotland. They met savage resistance, notably in 1780, from London crowds whose inherited anti-Catholic prejudices had been, if not implanted, then certainly whipped up and played upon by the aristocratic founders of the Whig party a century before.

As for witchcraft, Ginzburg shows in *The night battles*[16] how educated inquisitors actually fostered a popular belief in witches in the late sixteenth and early seventeenth centuries. When upper-class belief in witches faded in the Enlightenment, the popular classes continued to hold on to a belief now classed as a superstition into the eighteenth century and well beyond.[17] It also seems that the approved theories of the middle ages that moral values should regulate economic conduct survived among the masses well into Adam Smith's age of purely economic laws. Certainly the belief of eighteenth-century English crowds that the price of bread should be controlled smacks of the medieval scholastic notion, passed on to popular audiences by medieval preachers and subsequently restated by sixteenth- and seventeenth-century English government action, that prices should be set by 'justice' rather than by 'market forces'.

The ideal of the 'just price' remained embedded in popular culture after it had been jettisoned by men of power and influence, and by a new school of economists. The demand for cheap bread was only partly an automatic response to the plight of the poor: one way for labouring people to make food cheaper is to demand higher wages, but in the eighteenth century such demands were voiced much less than the ancestral cry that the price and/or the size of the loaf should stay fixed. A coherent traditional idea, once given the most solemn assent by state and church, continued to exercise its sway over the popular imagination and indeed to occasion protest that was conducted with all the decorum that one would expect of the expression of a 'respectable' notion.[18]

Part of our task in this introductory chapter is to sketch a distinction — one that must be made, but not made too sharply — between town and country. Eventually, we shall superimpose upon that distinction another one, that between upper and lower orders (or classes). Later again we shall trace four main groups and examine some of the major cultural characteristics of each. We shall be giving a fair amount of emphasis to the town, as well as to the country, an approach that may need some explanation to justify it: indeed, given the apparent preponderance of the countryside in pre-industrial

Europe, we shall need to set out the claims of the medieval and early
modern town to be treated as either separate or in any way important. One argument of this study — perhaps an obvious one — is
that towns were the engines of change in culture, not least in popular
culture. Yet even as we try to establish the key importance of towns
and cities in our period, we must also be aware of the interdepend-
ence of town and country, and even sometimes their inextricability.
John Mundy, for instance, in studying the relationship of Toulouse
to the rest of the Toulousain in the middle ages, deals with the following facts: the endowment by Toulouse citizens of country
churches and monasteries; the control by urban nobles of country
estates; the presence in Toulouse of branches of rural religious
houses; the way the surrounding countryside followed Toulouse in
acquiring schools, colleges, doctors, notaries and political constitutions; and the essentially rural interests of the town dwellers.[19]
However, from Mundy's account it will appear that although country and town were interdependent, the town tended to exercise
leadership.

Such a leadership seems on the surface hard to accept, or at least
hard to explain. Was it not the case that the typical medieval person, with a few exceptions, was a tiller of the soil living in a village?
Surely towns, in a world of peasants, were of little consequence,
either numerically or culturally? By our standards, the towns and
cities of medieval and early modern Europe were indeed puny. One
modern city, Mexico City, has a population almost double that of
the country (Spain) which 'discovered' Mexico in the sixteenth century. When we look at the 'large' towns and cities of Europe at the
very beginning of the modern era, we can identify a category of
16 relative giants. One of these was in England, two in France, one
in Germany, seven in Italy, four in Spain and one in Bohemia. When
one of these 'giants', Florence, passed 100,000 inhabitants before
the Black Death, it was considered noteworthy, even a little shocking. Germany was less urbanised than Italy. There, the leading city
in size, Cologne had either 20,000 or 40,000 in the fifteenth century. To find a real urban demographic monster, one had to leave
the confines of Europe proper. Constantinople had about 400,000
inhabitants in the sixteenth century.[20] Today its size would place
it in the category of a moderate provincial city. By the same token,
in the fourteenth, fifteenth and sixteenth centuries, an unassuming
modern town such as Northampton or Swansea would have stood
out as a vast concentration of humanity.

If the medieval and early modern town was of insignificant size by present-day standards, it may seem unreal to talk of a distinct urban culture in our period of study. Most European towns were not of the order of magnitude of cities such as Florence, Cologne and Constantinople: the great majority were small or middling-sized market centres with populations ranging from as few as 500 to three, five, ten, fifteen or twenty thousand. The smaller towns in the group would have been little more than market villages. The population figures — they are almost always highly approximate — of the larger units need to be looked at, of course, in the light of the size of regional and national populations. Thus a city like early Tudor London, with an estimated population of 60,000, had some prominence in a national population of two-and-a-half millions.[21] Braudel actually suggested using a multiplier of ten so as to get rough modern equivalents of medieval and early modern demographic figures. If we were to use Braudel's multiplier on Leuschner's estimate of the population of pre-modern Cologne, we would get a city of about 400,000.[22] This is still not particularly impressive, either in modern terms or in terms of the late medieval and early modern population of the German lands at large. However, if we use this same multiplier on the population of Florence, the result is a pre-Black Death count of one million. This would certainly put the city in today's major league of Italian cities.

In the end, though, the leadership of cities in medieval and early modern European life was not entirely dependent on population figures. either absolute or relative. Even where population figures were not high, the medieval and early modern city possessed an unquestioned leadership. This leadership arose from the following factors: the traditional image of cities; their religious functions; their concentration of surplus value and educational provisions; their economic role; and their political functions. All of these factors came together to create an extraordinary intensity in urban life. This was the unquantifiable quality that Braudel was trying to convey when he wrote, with characteristic allusiveness, of the 'lively and original culture' of Cologne.[23]

Cologne possessed an aura that had nothing to do with its population size which, like that of any other major German city, was in statistical terms virtually an invisible element in the population of the German lands as a whole. One of Germany's three electoral archbishops, Cologne, or its prince-archbishop, played a leading role in the politics of the *Reich*. The question of its confessional orientation in the religious struggle of the German Reformation was an issue of great tension for the country as a whole. In the event, the city chose to remain Catholic, partly because of its material dependence on the Church. Although the archbishop himself lived apart from the citizens, who had struggled long and hard to free themselves from his overlordship, their daily lives continued to be dominated by religion and particularly by their great gothic cathedral. For Cologne, like several other European cities, was a holy place, with a special cult of the three Magi, and was the site of the reputed martyrdoms of St Ursula and eleven thousand Christian virgins. To add to its religious aura, Cologne also had a classical veneer: it had been founded as a forward post for the implantation of Roman civilisation in the northern world.[24]

Medieval and Renaissance Europeans lived with a sense of inferiority under the shadow of the essentially urban civilisations of classical antiquity. Seen from one point of view, the Renaissance is but the ultimate intensification of that sense of inferiority. The kind of words that were coming into circulation, for instance in post-Renaissance English, to describe manners, culture, order and government — 'polite', 'civilised', 'civil', 'civic', 'urbane', 'police', 'polity', 'politics' — all came from the Latin and Greek words for the city or the citizen: *urbs*, *polis*, *civis*. Cities such as Cologne provided direct physical links with this uniquely prestigious classical past. Zaragoza, for example, the capital of the Spanish kingdom of Aragon, preserved in its name the memory of its original dedication to Caesar Augustus; its imposing walls, along with the aqueduct in Castile's Segovia, were a vivid reminder of Rome's enduring architectural achievements.[25] As for London, Shakespeare reflected his contemporaries' belief that its Tower had been built by Julius Caesar.[26]

A particularly good example of a city that cherished classical roots (along with impressive religious credentials, as we shall see) was Milan, seat of the western Roman Empire in its later years.[27] What applied to Milan also applied with even greater force to Venice and Florence. Both of these claimed to be direct heirs of the Roman Empire. In emergent Russia, too, Moscow was acclaimed, from the fifteenth century onwards, as the 'third Rome', in succession to Rome itself and its equally subverted successor, Constantinople.[28]

As has been suggested already, the cultural prestige of cities as direct descendants of classical civilisation overlapped with their religious role. The religious function meant that citizens would expend their greatest artistic and financial resources on the construction not of secular buildings so much as cathedrals and great urban churches. Antwerp may strike us as a practical, hard-headed commercial centre of the sixteenth century, but its citizens celebrated its rise to prominence as Europe's leading port and banking centre by building the Continent's biggest parish church. The construction of Milan's cathedral over seven centuries must surely be Europe's most protracted building project.

The religious role of cities in Christian culture may owe something to the symbolic centrality of Jerusalem. It is true that cities could also assume an evil character, that of Babylon. In the writings of the medieval prophet, Joachim of Fiore (d. 1202), what was for Catholics the world's second most holy place, Rome, became the birthplace of the personification of evil, Antichrist.[29] Savonarola, the reformer of late fifteenth-century Florence, brought to a high pitch this suspicion of Rome. Yet Savonarola transferred the idea of the holy city from Rome to Florence, which, in his idealisation of the Tuscan city, fused sanctity with a heritage of Roman grandeur. For Savonarola, Florence was holy not so much because it owned holy relics but because its citizens had a collective messianic destiny. Like Florence, Venice also possessed both a Roman pedigree and holiness, having acquired, or to put it more bluntly, looted, the miracle-working body of St Mark.[30] Other great cities were also made holy by association with 'their' saints: Milan's secular historical prestige was enhanced by its association with the fourth-century bishop, St Ambrose (c. 334–97), a pattern of all bishops, and particularly of all bishops of Milan.[31]

The aura of sanctity that attached to a number of cities was supplemented by their more practical functions as centres of ecclesiastical government. When early Christianity was grafted on to the urban civilisation of the late Roman Empire, the Church's 'diocesan' organisation, like that of the Empire itself, became firmly centred on cities. The Christian religion itself spread out from urban nuclei. Examples are the large sub-diocesan Italian *pievi* parishes, the 'minster' centres (like York) in Anglo-Saxon England, and the missionary bishoprics on England's internal frontier with the Norsemen and on pre-medieval Germany's pagan frontier.[32] Something of the influence of towns as missionary centres can be seen in Schmitt's study of the Guinefort cult. The saint's venerated tomb was in the thriving city of Pavia in northern Italy, but his cult spread from there along a route of Cluniac abbeys, deep into France.[33]

Some of the most significant developments in the religious life of the Middle Ages confirmed the primacy of the city. The developments included the following: the building of the cathedrals; the enlarge-ment of episcopal authority and its concentration on the cathedral cities; the rise of the universities, in such cities as Paris, Padua, Bologna, Oxford, Prague and Cologne; the urban-based preaching of the mendicant orders of friars; and the siting of the Inquisition in such urban centres as Pamiers, Carcassonne or Udine. Perhaps because the Inquisition operated from its urban bases to control religion in the countryside, there may be a tendency to equate orthodox religion with the city and heresy with the country.[34]

A more satisfactory, if still generalised, statement of the case would be along the following lines. Heresy often originated in towns: for example, John Wyclif's heretical ideas were first propounded in Oxford in the 1370s and early 1380s and then taken up in Leicester and other towns in the English South and Midlands. To take another example, the Waldensian heresy seems to have originated in Lyon. However, towns were places of relatively close ecclesiastical supervision, and heresy, born in the towns, typically moved out into villages and hamlets. This happened with the ver-sion of Wyclif's ideas known as Lollardy, which became distributed throughout parts of rural southern England, and also with Walden-sianism, which found its enduring home in the Alpine valleys. Thus, in the dissemination of heresy, as in the earlier propagation of Chris-tianity itself, it was the towns that played the crucial initiating role. This religious centrality of towns and cities as places of religious mission increased in the Reformation, for example with the leader-ship of Geneva in the spread of the Calvinist Reformation.

After seeing something of the religious function of cities and towns, we may consider their economic role as agents of change, and to do this, we can use a contrast. It will be between one village of which we know a reasonable amount, Ladurie's Montaillou, and any typical large-scale medieval city — Florence, for instance. The implied contrast, between backwardness and progress, will certainly not be fair to all villages, for if Montaillou was primitive, it may have been exceptionally remote, and unusually static in its economic life. Archaeological study of one village in Yorkshire has revealed much more involvement with a national and international economy than we find amongst the villagers of Montaillou.[35] However, we shall take Montaillou as a paradigm *because* it may be an extreme example of slowness in the rural adoption of the cash economy and of the distinctive values that grew up in its wake. What we find in the work and economic life of this village is a primary concern with elementary and immediate subsistence. This meant the struggle for food, which was generally monotonous, for fuel, which was scarce, and for clothing, which was functional. A fully developed cash nexus was missing, in this village far from urban markets.

It has been said that for many peasants, cash was an extra (and to them somewhat irrelevant) 'crop' which they had to raise so as to placate landlords. Even many rural parish priests were perforce peasants for six days a week. The Montaillou economy, relatively undifferentiated, was one of usually adequate subsistence. There was a time lag in the adoption of the cash economy. The main centres of cash economics were, of course, towns, centres of minting, exchange and manufacture. Attitudes to work and money, as to work as a means of making money, were 'modernised' earlier in the towns than in the country. Amongst the commodities pursued by the villagers of Montaillou was leisure. They 'were not yet afraid of idleness . . . were fond of having a nap, of taking it easy, of delousing one another in the sun or by the fire. Whenever they could, they tended to shorten the working day into a half day . . . work in itself was not a source of earthly consideration . . .'[36] The culture of the villagers was made up largely of talk: either they talked a lot because they had a lot of time, or they made a lot of time for talk. In contrast, a glimpse of increasingly typical urban attitudes, for example in Italy in the high or later Middle Ages (we shall catch such a glimpse in chapter 2) indicates that time was already being valued and measured as the primary asset in the quest for wealth and success.

What Ladurie implies in his remarks about the easy-going attitudes of the Montaillou villagers is that they lacked what has been called a 'work ethic' — something that arose in the first place in towns because they presented opportunities for accumulation afforded by the greater intensity of the cash economy, the greater complexity of any economy lubricated by cash. The village economy of Montaillou certainly looks rudimentary. Freed by the flow of cash from the rigours of subsistence, the European towns of the Middle Ages added an enormous acceleration to the division and specialisation of labour. When these towns developed, or developed anew, in the early Middle Ages, they existed for trade. Then urban industry developed, the primary industry being textiles, in such centres as Ypres and Florence.

Gradually, urban industry came to display greater range and specialisation within the textile industry and in other forms of production. One of these was the embellishment of towns themselves through the building industry. New inventions and industrial techniques evolved, one of the most striking being that of printing. As both the cause and consequence of trade and industry, the medieval and early modern town attracted and produced a whole range of people who worked beyond mere subsistence. As was mentioned earlier, the craftsman — the miller, the wheelwright, the smith — was no stranger to the village, but he was essentially an auxiliary to fundamentally agricultural concerns. In towns there were workers promoting much more autonomous industry, though it still processed chiefly agricultural raw materials. There were specialised craftsmen of all kinds, possessing a bewildering display of acquired skills, most of them made obsolete by modern mechanisation: cloth shearers, bleachers, furriers, hatters, lace makers, wool carders, armourers, cutlers, smiths, needle makers, gunsmiths, locksmiths, millers, bakers, cooks, brewers, and so on. The archetypal skilled worker was the weaver. Like other groups of workers, weavers were supposed in folklore to have stock characteristics; in the weaver's case, he was well known for his leaning to heresy and puritanism. Perhaps it was the fact that he was able to talk, or even read, while he worked that made him so opinionated. Anyway, he was reputed a born dissident, in religion or in politics. He was to the fore in urban insurgency in such places as Florence and Ghent.[37]

Other craftsmen, such as dyers, finished the work of the weavers, those indispensable links in the textile chain. Within the textile industry, while groups of workers specialised in a branch of production, a whole town might specialise in the manufacture of a particular fabric, to which it often gave its name. Thus the rich 'lawn', from which were made the surplice sleeves of Anglican bishops, came from Laon, near Reims. 'Cambric', the fine white linen, came from Cambrai. 'Diaper' (d'Ijper = from Ypres) was the unbleached linen that we know today in the American name for a baby's napkin. 'Arras', the heavy tapestry used to curtain walls, was from the Flemish centre. There was not quite the same degree of specialisation in non-textile products: after all, the industrial revolution occurred in the nineteenth, not the thirteenth century. All the same, there *was* area specialisation: Cordova for leather goods ('cordwainer'), and Milan, not only Europe's leading armaments centre, but also, apparently, a city of hatters ('milliner'). Pre-revolutionary Paris specialised in luxury manufactures.[38] Specialisation of course also meant the simultaneous presence in one town of various trades and crafts. The guild organisation of the major medieval towns and cities mirrored this internal diversity and specialisation.

If ever the simple tri-functional model of medieval society —

priests, knights and peasants — fitted the reality of village sociology, it could never possibly accommodate the complexity of urban existence. In towns, even clerics tended to conform to the rule of the division of labour. The typical rural parish priest was a sacerdotal general practitioner. In theory, he was a liturgist, confessor, preacher, teacher, social worker, arbitrator and moral policeman. Many urban or urban-based clergy were, in contrast, allowed, largely through townsmen's patronage, to concentrate on one activity, especially that of preaching. St Bernardino, a vastly successful peripatetic preacher in fifteenth-century Italy, gave up other priestly functions such as hearing confessions (an activity that itself was being increasingly subject to professional specialisation) so as to concentrate on preaching. The godly 'lecturers' who proliferated in English towns in the Tudor period were full-time preachers, which gave them the added bonus of a canonical freedom from wearing the surplice, to which the puritan-inclined under Queen Elizabeth objected. The provision of urban preaching in Europe, often of a high professional quality, was characteristically financed out of bourgeois wealth and piety — the kinds of funds that made it possible for a city like Zürich to take on such a promising university graduate as Ulrich Zwingli as its 'common preacher' in 1518.

The same sort of resources of urban patronage that endowed preaching foundations such as the one at which John Hus preached in Prague in the early fifteenth century also fostered the arts. The Church was the primary artistic patron, with individual clerics wishing to see themselves as individuals featuring in pious works of art.[39] The further development of the portrait of the individual, especially in ordinary domestic surroundings, was strongly encouraged by urban bourgeois patronage — and also by the kind of urban bourgeois self-awareness that we shall examine more fully in chapter 2. Also in towns, superceding the rural monastic scriptoria, were the new printing presses, from the later fifteenth century and onwards — especially in such quality printing centres as Mainz, Antwerp, Venice, Lyon and Amsterdam. The arrival of the printing press set the seal on the urban domination of European civilisation.

Towns dominated their hinterlands, and those hinterlands might sometimes consist of whole realms. Part of this domination came about through the magnetic force of immigration into towns. Migrants came into towns and cities in different ways. Some came from far afield, others from near at hand. Some came in family groupings, others in waves from abruptly deserted villages, others as lone individuals. Some migrants came in hope, with resources, skills, ambition, to stay, to succeed; others came in despair, merely to survive or perhaps to die as paupers and transients. Urban pestilence actually enhanced the attractive force of towns. Of course we do not need automatically to equate pestilence with urban life: for example, while the Black Death in the fourteenth century ravaged thinly populated Scandinavia, its effect was much less catastrophic in well-regulated Milan. Yet towns, with their compressed populations and generally appalling standards of hygiene, were lasting foci of plague and other epidemic diseases.

To maintain or increase population levels, towns were massive importers of migrants. Eighteenth-century London, for instance, had a regular surplus of deaths over live births and consumed more people than it could itself produce.[40] Thus the typical medieval and early modern town was a killer of people. It attracted migrants and thereby controlled population levels in its neighbourhood: this 'neighbourhood' could be extremely extensive: strangers in medieval Florence, for instance, came from such places as Croatia and Dalmatia. Official urban attitudes to immigration were ambivalent. Hands, especially strong and skilled hands, were needed, particularly after visitations of the plague. There was at the same time a fear of starving migrants and of criminals, and strangers tended to be heavily represented in lists of detected criminals in towns. Venice showed clearly this ambivalence of city governments over migration. There were elaborate restrictions on entry into the city, but these were relaxed after the Black Death.[41] With or without regulation, towns continued to draw on rural human resources. Many migrants, apprentices and young people seeking work before marriage or a break from rural boredom, were relatively brief visitors. As transients, they would surely carry back with them some of the influences, habits and tastes of the town. Thus, for example, Wrightson and Levine write of the 'pervasive, multifaceted influence of London' on the villagers of Terling in Essex in the sixteenth and seventeenth centuries.[42]

The cultural magnetism of cities was underlined by their political centrality. Firstly, certain cities functioned as national capitals. Such cities broadcast the fashions and values of royal courts. Their dialects were accepted as the standard forms of national languages. They attracted litigants to their law courts. They passed on central government requirements to the localities, and they acted, notably in the case of London, as places to hold parliaments and estates, with London's role in this never again challenged after the Oxford parliament of 1681. All in all, cities were essential factors in welding dynastic amalgams into nation-states, with common habits and assumptions. Other major cities were politically important in their own right. These were not so much the great national capitals as self-governing entities, places that had their heyday before the consolidation of the great territorial states from the sixteenth century onwards.

Some cities governed not just themselves but dependent territories also. Florence, for example, assembled a small empire in central Italy before the end of the Middle Ages, and on a lesser scale, cities such as Zürich controlled quite extensive subject regions. In the Netherlands, the cities of Bruges, Ghent and Ypres dominated the politics of Flanders for at least part of the fourteenth century.[43] The German Imperial Cities were not as autonomous as were the leading cities of the Low Countries and Italy, but they formed a key element in the German political system. Cities such as Nuremberg and Augsburg increased their economic scope in the later Middle Ages. The Imperial cities (*Reichsstädte*) tended to be enthusiastic for the imperial-national ideal.[44] The German cities as a group played a vital role, especially in the decisive 1520s, in the adoption of the Lutheran Reformation in the country. The vision of cities as independent commonwealths was most fully realised in Italy. Venice, above all, was a European state in her own right, with a diplomatic weighting at the beginning of the modern era about the same as that of England or Portugal. Venice's economic resilience was formidable.[45] The city's continuing economic success and her social and political stability seemed to validate her republican-aristocratic constitution, which was unusual in a Europe of monarchies. In Italian city-states such as Venice and Florence foundation myths were invented so as to back up claims to possess sovereignty.[46]

The preservation of the autonomy of cities required their citizens to be as one. Many cities were surrounded by princes seeking to convert them into territorial states, or to swallow them up. Nuremberg, for instance, was steadily encircled by the princely state of Bavaria and then finally incorporated in 1806. Partly because of the ever-present threat to their independence, civic propaganda constantly stressed the need for internal unity. In German cities such as Strassburg in the Reformation period the ruling magistrates put brakes on rapid religious change so as to avoid divisions amongst the populace.[47] Earlier, in Florence under Savonarola's leadership, developing a major theme of the city's collective ideology, civic concord was held up as the highest good. Yet Savonarola was himself a kind of party leader, in the city which gave to history the *Parte Guelfa*. In the dictionary, the word 'party' is equated with 'faction'. 'Party' and 'part' (= 'something less than the whole') both come from a Latin root (*pars*) which in turn gives the verb *partiri*, to divide.

The word 'party', then, has unmistakable connotations of division. Now parties may be majority parties or minority parties; they may aspire to represent the interests of the rich or the poor or the in-between, a region or a religion, or they may even claim to speak for some vast 'national interest'. In truth, though, and by definition they must seek to promote the interests of particular groups. Thus the formation of parties became the central dilemma in the political life of medieval and early modern cities. The ideal of the city was one of unanimity, the reality one of faction; and faction meant weakness and vulnerability, as cities in the sixteenth century faced their greatest challenge, that posed by renascent territorial states. Arguably, the existence of faction is a (or *the*) primary reason that cities were not able to withstand the challenge, the main reason that they were eventually absorbed by and into monarchical states: for instance, the legacy of faction in Florence after Savonarola certainly helped usher in the Medici restoration which from the early sixteenth century converted the erstwhile free commune into at best the headquarters of a territorial principality.[48]

Though disastrous, party politics was unavoidable in city life, partly because of economic diversification and the presence of competing social classes. Indeed, the existence of party was built into the very ways that some cities had freed themselves from episcopal, baronial and royal overlords in the earlier Middle Ages. This earlier process of liberation was most fully evident in those parts of Italy, Germany and the Low Countries where, in the Middle Ages, urban economic life was strongest and royal power weakest. Indeed, the communes, notably in thirteenth- and fourteenth-century Flanders, played a vital role in *ensuring* the weakness of royal power. Internally, in the quest for communal liberty, alliances might be formed between members of one or more social classes against feudal overlords. In a typical progression, however, we find wealthy patrician families gradually monopolising political power and excluding from it both non-patrician bourgeois and also working craftsmen, journeymen and labourers.[49] New coalitions arose between these excluded elements, against urban patriciates.

In the case of Toulouse, Mundy shows how a territorial prince used the population at large against the entrenched oligarchy in the city.[50] Cities, then, were the scenes of complex and shifting conflicts and alliances between social classes for the control of government. Such control was necessary since it allowed those who exercised it to regulate prices, wages and above all, the apportionment of taxes to the advantage or disadvantage of groups. It is the intensity of social and political struggles in the late Middle Ages that gives so much interest to the urban scene. Some of the most interesting new developments in medieval political thinking, including civic humanism, originated in the cities, and it is true to say that the ideas of so creative a political thinker as Thomas Aquinas (c. 1225–74) were conceived with reference to civic political society — even though his background was that of a rural noble. We might even go so far as to say that modern politics, and republican and even democratic politics had their distant origins in the medieval European city.

As we have seen, in the economic field too the medieval city was the harbinger of modernity, not least in sowing the financial and psychological seeds of eventual industrialism. The culture of medieval cities also pointed to the future — to universal literacy and a rational, 'post-magical' outlook. Eventually, all traces of an autonomous rural culture were extinguished in western Europe, though not until our own century in some parts.[51] Cultural conquest — 'acculturation' — can be a protracted process and the cultural imperialism of cities, which has finally triumphed in our own day was well under way before the end of the Middle Ages; printing was probably its most potent weapon. Almanacs, political and religious pictures, cartoons, chap-books, pamphlets and ballads, produced in towns, would find their way, often on the backs of pedlars, into villages and country shacks.[52] It is interesting, for example, that when the nineteenth-century French peasant girl, Bernadette Soubirous, saw the vision of Mary at Lourdes, she saw her in a form originally imagined by a seventeenth-century urban artist. Murillo's version was reproduced in many copies, and was the model for a statue in Bernadette's country parish church.[53]

Along the same lines as artistic influence, information and news were disseminated from the city to the country. Collections of English gentry family letters provide examples of the flow of books, news and gossip from metropolitan relations to country cousins and spouses back home; indeed, the standard 'letter from a gentleman of quality [or members of parliament] to a friend in the country' became a conventional form of press and propaganda in the eighteenth century.[54] Country churchmen who had been to a seminary or university would try to keep in touch with an urban *alma mater*.[55] Then, as cities took their place in the leisure revolution of the eighteenth century, towns became more than ever the centres for the recreation of the prosperous classes. (This was before the Romantic preference for the wilderness reversed the holiday pattern.)

Perhaps enough has been said in the foregoing to establish, in the fields of amusement, information, art, politics, religion and economics, the importance of medieval and early modern towns as objects fit for study and, indeed, playing a leading role, though in an overwhelmingly rural world. We should have before us an image of medieval and early modern cities as powerhouses of cultural change. Certainly, both 'popular' and 'elite' cultures were constantly re-charged from urban batteries, and in addition any offensive by elite against popular culture in early modern Europe can be seen largely as part of the conquest of the country by the city.

In our next chapter, we will attempt a rough four-part sketch of the main European social groupings in our period, and try to identify some of the cultural characteristics of each grouping. In Chapter 3 we dwell on one group, the peasantry. We shall see that for much of the time the peasantry was simply taken for granted, occasioning comment chiefly when in revolt: and indeed part of the aim of peasant revolts was to make people take notice of peasants. By looking at some of those peasant revolts, we will see how revolts emerged out of the assumptions built into peasant culture and how the collective rituals and religious symbols of villagers formed the language of insurgency. In Chapter 4, shifting back towards towns, we shall investigate the influence of those most effective cultural communicators, preachers, by singling out a few examples. In our concluding chapter we shall examine the conditions of life in the Reformation era that began the modern period of European history. It will be argued that religious change in that era was genuinely rooted in popular culture and that the Reformation and the Counter-Reformation were by no means simply imposed by elites on the peoples of Europe.

Notes

1. For example, Perez Zagorin, *Rebels and rulers 1500–1660* (2 vols, Cambridge University Press, Cambridge and New York, 1982), vol. 1, p. 61 ff; see also the discussion by Armand Arrianza, 'Mousnier and Barber: the theoretical underpinning of the "Society of Orders" in early modern

Europe', *Past and Present*, vol. 89 (1980), pp. 39–57.

2. R.A. Hilton, *Bond men made free. Medieval peasant movements and the English rising of 1381* (The Viking Press, New York, 1973), pp. 130–1.

3. Fernand Braudel, *The Mediterranean and the Mediterranean world in the age of Philip II* (trans. Siân Reynolds, 2 vols, Collins, London, 1972), vol. 2, p. 735. Hilton writes of a 'continuous Jacquerie' in the Kingdom of Naples: *Bond men made free*, p. 111.

4. Günther Lottes, 'Popular culture and the early modern state in sixteenth century Germany' in Steven L. Kaplan (ed.), *Understanding popular culture. Europe from the Middle Ages to the nineteenth century* (Mouton, Berlin, 1984), pp. 153–4.

5. For example, Sarah M. McKinnon, 'The peasant house: the evidence of manuscript illumination' in J.A. Raftis (ed.), *Pathways to medieval peasants* (Papers in Mediaeval Studies 2, Pontifical Institute of Mediaeval Studies, Toronto, Ontario, 1981), pp. 301–9.

6. Carlo Ginzburg, *The night battles. Witchcraft and agrarian cults in the sixteenth and seventeenth centuries* (trans. John and Anne Tedeschi, Routledge & Kegan Paul, London and Melbourne, 1983), p. 24 and *passim*.

7. See, for example, R.B. Outhwaite, 'Dearth and government intervention in English grain markets, 1490–1700', *Economic History Review*, vol. 34 (1981), pp. 389–406; John Walter and Keith Wrightson, 'Dearth and the social order in early modern England', *Past and Present*, vol. 71 (1976), pp. 22–42; Paul Slack, 'The disappearance of plague: an alternative view', *Economic History Review*, vol. 34 (1981), pp. 469–76; Peter Laslett and Karla Osterveen, 'Long-term trends in bastardy in England', *Population Studies*, vol. 27 (1973), pp. 255–86.

8. See the discussion of rebellion and 'pure misery' in Hilton, *Bond men made free*, pp. 116–17.

9. Works on the social doctrines of the medieval Church, and the ways in which they were communicated to lay audiences, include the following: Drostan Maclaren, O.P., *Private property and the natural law* (Aquinas Papers, 8, Blackfriars, Oxford, for the Aquinas Society, 1948), p. 5 and *passim*; Jacques Melitz and Donald Winch (eds), *Religious thought and economic society. Four chapters of an unfinished work by Jacob Viner* (Duke University Press, Durham, North Carolina, 1978), pp. 85–99; Alexander Murray, *Reason and society in the Middle Ages* (Oxford University Press, Oxford, 1978), p. 333; Ernst Troeltsch, *The social teaching of the Christian Churches* (trans. Olive Wyon, 2 vols., George Allen & Unwin, London, Macmillan, New York, 1931), vol. 1, pp. 370–1; J. Gilchrist, *The Church and economic activity in the Middle Ages* (Macmillan, London, 1969), p. 52 and *passim*; R.H. Tawney, *Religion and the rise of capitalism: an historical study* (Holland Memorial Lectures, 1922, John Murray, London, 1926), p. 58.

G.R. Owst wrote that the 'preaching, not merely of the friars, but of other orthodox churchmen . . . was ultimately responsible for the outbreak of the Peasants' Revolt': *Literature and the pulpit in medieval England: a neglected chapter in the history of English letters and of the English people*, 2nd revised edition (Blackwell, Oxford, 1961), p. 304.

10. Karl Marx and Friedrich Engels, *On religion* (Progress Publications, Moscow, 1972), pp. 33, 74.

11. Marvin Becker, 'Heresy in medieval and Renaissance Florence. A

Introduction

comment', *Past and Present*, vol. 62 (1974), pp. 153–61.

12. Margaret Spufford, *Small books and pleasant histories. Popular fiction and its readership in seventeenth-century England* (Methuen, London, 1981), ch. V.

13. Peter Burke, *Popular culture in early modern Europe* (Temple Smith, London, 1978), *passim*.

14. Philippe Ariès, *Centuries of childhood. A social history of family life* (trans. R. Baldick, Vintage Books, New York, 1962), p. 59; Fernand Braudel, *Capitalism and material life 1400–1800* (trans. Miriam Kochan, Weidenfeld & Nicolson, London, 1973), pp. 227–36.

15. Carlo Ginzburg, *The cheese and the worms. The cosmos of a sixteenth-century miller* (trans. John and Anne Tedeschi, Routledge & Kegan Paul, London and Henley, 1980), p. 28 ff.

16. Ginzburg, *The night battles*, p. 86.

17. P. Guskin, 'The context of witchcraft: the case of Jane Wenham (1712)', *Eighteenth-Century Studies*, vol. 15 (1981), pp. 40–55.

18. E.P. Thompson, 'The moral economy of the English crowd in the eighteenth century', *Past and Present*, vol. 50 (1971), pp. 76–136, and esp. p. 132. Thompson deals in this article with seventeenth-century official price controls as part of a tradition of regulative economics which Adam Smith dismissed as backward superstition. For the medieval background, see Owst, *Literature and the pulpit*, pp. 352–61.

19. John Mundy, 'Village, town and city in the region of Toulouse' in Raftis (ed.), *Pathways to medieval peasants*, pp. 141–90.

20. Fernand Braudel, *Civilisation and capitalism, 14th-18th century. Volume I. The structures of everyday life, the limits of the possible* (trans. Siân Reynolds, Collins, London and New York, 1981), pp. 51–2. For the fourteenth-century figures, see Robert S. Gottfried, *The Black Death. Natural and human disaster in medieval Europe* (Collier Macmillan, London, Free Press, New York, 1983), p. 37.

21. Keith Wrightson and David Levine, *Poverty and piety in an English village. Terling 1525–1700* (Studies in Social Discontinuity, Academic Press, New York, 1979), pp. 3–4.

22. In the fifteenth century, Leuschner claims, Cologne reached nearly 40,000 inhabitants: Joachim Leuschner, *Germany in the late Middle Ages* (North-Holland Publishing, Amsterdam, 1980), p. 7.

23. Braudel, *Civilisation and capitalism*, vol. 1, p. 52.

24. Joachim von Elbe, *Roman Germany. A guide to sites and museums* (Philipp von Zabern, Mainz, 1975), pp. 183–226; Jean-Pierre Cuvillier, *L'Allemagne médiévale. Naissance d'un état* (Payot, Paris, 1979), p. 407. For Cologne's importance as one of Europe's four principal pilgrimage centres, see Bernard Hamilton, 'Prester John and the three kings of Cologne' in Henry Mayr-Harting and R.I. Moore (eds), *Studies in medieval history presented to R.H.C. Davis* (Hambledon, London and Ronceverte, 1985), pp. 177–91.

25. Zaragoza, with its two cathedrals, its cult of Mary 'del Pilar' and of St James, and its numerous martyrs, was a place of profound holiness: *Enciclopedia de la Cultura Española* (5 vols, Editoria Nacional, Madrid, 1963), vol. 5, pp. 709–10.

26. *King Richard the Third*, Act 3 Scene 1.

27. Pietro Verri, *Storia di Milano* (2 vols, Florence, Sansoni, 1963), and for a particularly appreciative tribute to Milan — 'il paragon di Roma' — vol. 1, pp. 21–2.

28. Edward Muir, *Civic ritual in Renaissance Venice* (Princeton University Press, Princeton, New Jersey and Guildford, Surrey, 1981), pp. 55, 66, 68, 72; Dmitrij Tschizewkij, *Russian intellectual history* (trans. J.C. Osborne. ed. M.C. Rice, Ardis, Ann Arbor, Michigan, 1978), pp. 92-4.
29. Richad Kenneth Emmerson, *Antichrist in the Middle Ages. A study of medieval apocalypticism, art, and literature* (Manchester University Press, Manchester, 1981), p. 61.
30. William H. McNeill, *Venice. The hinge of Europe 1081-1797* (Chicago University Press, Chicago, Illinois and London, 1974), p. 244.
31. For the conversion of Milan, the second capital of the Counter-Reformation, into a ritual site, see the fascinating collection by Adele Buratti *et al.*, *La città rituale. La città e lo stato di Milano nell'età dei Borromeo* (Franco Angeli, Milan, 1982), esp. pp. 50-3, 90-6.
32. Rosalind and Christopher Brooke, *Popular religion in the Middle Ages. Western Europe 1000-1300* (Thames & Hudson, London, 1984), pp. 82, 97.
33. Jean-Claude Schmitt, *The holy greyhound. Guinefort, healer of children since the thirteenth century* (trans. Martin Thom, Cambridge, Cambridge University Press [Cambridge Studies in Oral and Literate Culture 6] and Paris, Maison des Sciences de l'Homme, 1983), pp. 102-4.
34. For the way the friars conducted a mission to the towns, and a mission to the country based on the towns, see D.L. D'Avray, *The preaching of the friars. Sermons diffused from Paris before 1300* (Oxford University Press, Oxford and New York, 1985), pp. 30-1, 39, 41, 217-18, and references to the literature on p. 30, notes 2 and 3. For examples of rural (not urban) heresy, see Norman Tanner (ed.), *Heresy trials in the diocese of Norwich 1428-31* (Camden Fourth Series, vol. 20, Royal Historical Society, London, 1977), pp. 26-7.
35. J.G. Hurst, 'The changing medieval village in England' in Raftis, *Pathways to peasants*, p. 58.
36. Emmanuel Le Roy Ladurie, *Montaillou. Cathars and Catholics in a French village 1292-1324* (trans. Barbara Bray, Scolar Press, London, 1978), p. 339.
37. It has been estimated that there were at least 4,500 weavers in mid-fourteenth-century Ghent: Henri Pirenne, 'The Low Countries' in C.W. Previté-Orton and Z.N. Brooke (eds), *The Cambridge medieval history* (Cambridge University Press, Cambridge, 1936, reprinted 1964), vol. 8, p. 336.
38. George Rudé, *The crowd in the French Revolution* (Oxford University Press, Oxford, 1959), pp. 15-16.
39. Jan van Eyck produced some highly individualised studies of churchmen in pious attitudes. For his Virgin and Child with saints and Canon van der Paele, see Max J. Friedlander, *From Van Eyck to Bruegel* (2 vols, Phaidon, London, 1969), vol. I, plates 16 and 17; for his best-known 'bourgeois' portrait, Giovanni Arnolfini and his wife, plate 20.
40. For the question of population increase and decrease in early modern cities, see the debate between R. Finlay and A. Sharlin in *Past and Present*, vol. 92 (1981), pp. 169-80.
41. Braudel, *Civilisation and capitalism*, vol. I, p. 71.
42. Wrightson and Levine, *Terling*, p. 79.
43. David Nicholas, *Town and countryside. Social, economic, and political tension in fourteenth-century Flanders* (De Tempel, Bruges, 1971), p. 12 and *passim*.
44. Leuschner, *Germany in the late Middle Ages*, pp. 166-74, 177.
45. Domenico Sella, 'Crisis and transformation in Venetian trade' in

Brian Pullan (ed.), *Crisis and change in the Venetian economy* (Methuen, London, 1968), pp. 88–105.

46. Muir, *Civic ritual*, part I and p. 66.

47. Carl C. Christenson, *Art and the Reformation in Germany* (Studies on the Reformation, ed. Robert C. Walton, vol. II, Ohio University Press, Athens, Ohio and Wayne State University Press, Detroit, Michigan, 1979), p. 82.

48. J.N. Stephens, *The fall of the Florentine republic 1512–1530* (Oxford University Press, Oxford and New York, 1983), pp. 42, 155–6, 254–5.

49. A good concise account of the sort of processes being outlined here can be found in Jonathan W. Zophy (ed.), *The Holy Roman Empire. A dictionary handbook* (Greenwood Press, Westport, Connecticut, 1980), pp. 429–30 (for Strassburg).

50. Mundy, in Raftis (ed.), *Pathways to peasants*, p. 166.

51. Schmitt, *Guinefort*, pp. 162–3.

52. Burke, *Popular culture*, pp. 72–3.

53. Hilda Graeff, *Mary: a history of doctrine and devotion* (2 vols., Sheed & Ward, London and New York, 1963), vol. 2, p. 94.

54. *Historical Manuscripts Commission: Kenyon* (HMSO, London, 1894), pp. 29, 105–9, 357.

55. Dr Victor Morgan vividly captured the nostalgia of Cambridge-educated clerics for the university in a conference paper at York in 1984; one of these parsons wrote of his Devon parish, 'a place of deep contentment, but so far is banishment'. I am indebted to Dr Morgan for permission to quote.

2

Social and Cultural Groupings in Late Medieval and Early Modern Europe

In this chapter we shall delineate and distinguish the salient cultural characteristics of four more or less artificially constructed groups within late medieval and early modern European society. These groups — urban and rural, upper and lower, classes — do not conform to the standard medieval sociology of three orders: for example, I shall not be regarding clergy as a separate social category. However, the three-orders model is useful not least in that it postulated that society was fundamentally a unity. This may help to remind us that our identification of groups does not mean that any one of them was completely insulated from any others. Regionalism (and civic identity) were strong unitive forces and meant that, for example, in the important cultural area of speech, there was a tendency for gentry, nobility and even monarchy in at least some parts of pre-industrial Europe to share the vernaculars of their social inferiors.[1]

Cultural differences between classes were also blunted by the fact that before the Enlightenment virtually all shared some kind of Christian belief, though it had different accents in different social classes. In towns and cities cultural distinctions were blurred by the absence of residential segregation of inhabitants before the nineteenth century — though this could cause class conflict through highlighting differences of wealth.[2] In our period, however, rich and poor continued to occupy a good deal of common cultural territory. A recognised archetype of cultural amphibianism on the part of members of the upper classes is Florence's Lorenzo de' Medici (d. 1492). Unofficial ruler of Florence, Lorenzo was at home both in the learned civilisation of the Renaissance and in the popular carnivals and entertainments of the streets. Of course his popular style was part of the politics of condescension. Yet in Florence and in other cities like it there was a strong sense of common interest and common culture, reflected in the very word for the urban society — commune. There was constant cross-culturation between the social classes. Savonarola, for instance, led a faction, yet it was a faction that was also a cross-section of Florentine society, with aristocrats, artists and *literati* linked to the common people.[3]

An ideal of social harmony was also upheld throughout rural Europe, through the bonds of obligation, service, deference, mutuality, hospitality and charity. Patronage and clientage linked gentry and nobles to dependents further down the social scale. It has been claimed, for example, that the fourteenth-century English heretical theologian, John Wyclif, was rescued from a humble rural background and launched on an academic career through gaining the attention of his overlord, John of Gaunt.[4] There was much common ground between rural nobles, especially the poorer sort of nobles, and commoners. We can say this despite what we know of tension between lords and peasants. Indeed, there were occasions when nobles and gentry joined in peasant protests — most spectacularly in the German Peasants' Revolt. Many country noblemen were almost indistinguishable from at least the better-off peasants around them. Love affairs sometimes crossed social barriers.[5] Manners, before the rise of a new code, especially of table manners, from the sixteenth century onwards, were inclined to be universally rough. However, attempts had been made, and continued to be made, to give the European nobilities more polish and a clearer identification, in everything from cleanliness to speech.[6]

Despite our awareness of cultural blurring between our strata, we shall try to show in this chapter that each of the four groupings had some indentifiable hallmarks. Our groups are, in the random order in which we take them, nobles, peasants, 'bourgeois' and urban lower orders. In discussing noble values, we shall consider the main sub-divisions of nobility; the place of metropolitan courts in noble life; the ambivalence, expressed in the pastoral literary genre, about court versus country life; the unitive noble code of chivalry and its supercession by the code of courtier-gentleman; and the insistence on caste. When next we turn to look at the peasantry, we shall try to examine, with particular attention to the Middle Ages' central religious rite, the Mass, what Christian 'religion' meant to peasants; how much they understood of it; how it in fact made up a substantial part of their 'culture'; and how it was also the means they used to try to control the world and regulate and pacify their communities and ultimately seek to have human society directed in their interest along what they saw as Christian lines. From peasantry we turn to the better-off elements in urban society — numerically tiny elements, no doubt, but important harbingers, it will be argued, to modernity, since some of their cultural and psychological traits seem to point to our world. In our final section, we will say something about urban groups below the 'bourgeoisie' — ranging from craftsmen and other workers to the very poor and the criminous.

We begin with a group which, like all the others, was bewilderingly sub-divided and variegated, nobility. A deliberate effort was made in the Middle Ages to equip the European nobilities with a code of ideals. This was the knightly code of chivalry, transmuted in the Renaissance into the ideals of the courtier and the gentleman. If we spend a little time looking at nobility in the context of the codes of the knight and the gentleman, it is not because the European nobilities had no other values but those encapsulated in those codes. For instance, the part played by the nobilities in the religious life of Europe is incalculable (and chivalry itself contained important Christian ingredients). Noble families played leading roles as patrons of church benefices, appointing clerics and often taking over the richer benefices themselves. They endowed religious houses with land and spent vast sums on masses and prayers for the departed.[7]

Nobles were also sometimes indispensable in sheltering dissidents from Catholicism and in allowing new religious forms such as English Lollardy[8] and French Calvinism to take root within their areas of influence. The Hussite Reformation in fifteenth-century Bohemia is a particularly striking example of indispensable noble patronage. We should pay particular attention to the role of noble and royal women in promoting religious change, especially in the sixteenth century. However, while not overlooking the part played by religion and other elements in the mental world of noblemen, we shall concentrate on the code of chivalry and its derivatives, because chivalry, which extended to kings, was distinctive to those essentially (but not entirely) hereditary and landed elites that we call noble.

In defining nobility, a starting point must be the lordship of land. Nobility, however, was not entirely rural: there were 'civil-service' nobilities and, especially in Italy, essentially urban aristocracies. Yet we shall regard noblemen, with their wealth, power and titles derived from landed estates,[9] as basically rural. They tended, though, and increasingly from the end of the Middle Ages onwards, to gravitate towards cities and royal courts, where the opportunities to perform military and political services and receive commensurate rewards were to be sought. (We shall also see, however, that the literary mode called pastoral, a form of rustic nostalgia, probably expressed some ambivalence on the part of nobilities as between court and country life — almost a collective resentment at the court's irresistible magnetism.)

If we do not make 'nobility' and 'rural' entirely synonymous, neither will we try to make of nobility an entirely secular estate. There was a conventional but not very useful medieval distinction between a 'first estate' of all clerics and a 'second estate' of all nobles. That ranking and distinction were invented by clerical writers and reflected clerical *amour propre* rather than reality. Instead of accepting that notion of two estates distinguished by the presence or absence of holy orders, we are going to place senior clerics somewhere alongside the lay aristocracy. This was more or less done in England which sensibly ignored the continental separation between first and second estates and merged both bishops and lay peers in the House of Lords. This made sense because for one thing senior churchmen tended increasingly in our period to be recruited from the lay aristocracy itself. European noble and princely families frequently cornered certain bishoprics, major and minor. France's Cardinal Richelieu put his first steps on the ecclesiastical ladder by taking his family's virtually proprietary bishopric of Luçon and the Bavarian Wittelsbachs came to establish a family stranglehold on the diocese of Liège.

This tendency included England, at least before the Tudors put a stop to it: late medieval English bishops included noblemen such as Bourchier and Courtenay, as well as a scion of the House of Lancaster, Cardinal Beaufort. The rough alignment between senior churchmen and nobles was underlined by the habit of addressing the former with titles derived from secular feudality — 'my lord', 'your grace' and so on. Such prominent churchmen tended to have responsibilities, sizes of household and entourage, incomes, patterns of expenditure and even aptitudes — including military aptitudes — similar to those of the lay aristocracy from which often enough they sprang. From the time of Bishop Odo of Bayeux in the Norman Conquest of England to that of Bishop von Greiffenklau in the doughty defence of his bishopric of Trier during the German Knights' War in 1522, individual bishops showed that they could fight at least as well as any knight: England's Cardinal Beaufort, mentioned above, set out on an armed crusade against the Hussites in Bohemia.[10] All in all, then, our category of nobility should include the prelates of the church.

As well as extending our concept of nobility to take in the upper clergy, we should point to an internal division (one that applied, *mutatis mutandis*, throughout Europe) of the lay nobility into two sections: an upper nobility of dukes, marquesses, counts and the rest; and a lower nobility made up of knights, squires and gentry generally. The higher nobility tended, rather more than the lower nobilities, to be European in range. Indeed, through linguistic and cultural cosmopolitanism and through the possession of estates and relatives in several lands, some noblemen easily traversed national boundaries, in the psychological as well as the physical sense. Such a one was William of Orange in the second half of the sixteenth century. Indeed, Orange, with his German origins and his estates in France and the Netherlands, belonged to a sub-division of the European aristocracy, the Franco-Burgundian nobility, that took little account of national demarcations:[11] perhaps, then, there is some oddness in the fact that such a cosmopolitan headed a national liberation movement, the Revolt of the Netherlands. On the other hand, the Prince of Orange's most redoubtable foe in the Netherlands conflict, the Prince of Parma, was equally a figure on an international scale: an Italian magnate taking service with the crown of Spain in the Netherlands theatre.

Senior noblemen, then, often operated in a European dimension. Men from the lower branches of nobility might also take service, especially military service, in Europe at large. Generally speaking, however, there was a tendency for the poorer and humbler members of the European nobilities to live out their lives, and play any part in public life, on a national, provincial or even merely parochial level. Within these lower branches of nobility itself there were gradations. On the higher slopes of the junior nobilities there were individuals and families whose incomes and pretensions put them near a par with the higher nobility. Such people could legitimately claim major roles in national politics. Thus in England, for example, parliamentary representation in the House of Commons was dominated by the upper gentry, the tier in status, wealth and social relations closest to the titled peerage. Below these were substantial squires, and below these again a sort of parish gentry who, in education, wealth, culture and aspirations may have been only a cut above farmers.

On the Continent, there were similar internal rankings within the status group. In Russia, Czar Nicholas I commented on an aristocracy that ranged 'all the way from the steps of the throne almost to the peasantry'.[12] In Spain, there was a world of difference between a duke of Medina Sidonia or of Alba — men who qualified almost automatically for the highest posts under the crown — and a poverty-stricken village *hidalgo* with nothing to boast of but his name and hardly anything to do but sleep.

To the great nobles belonged the international stage, in fields such as diplomacy, though not exclusively, of course. In the national politics of individual countries too, it was the 'great men' who exercised the initiative, who set the tone of court life. The magnates were by tradition the companions and proper advisers of kings, and in England a popular conservative sense of propriety was affronted in the 1530s at the importation of 'new men' into the king's council. Thus the rebels in the Pilgrimage of Grace demanded 'the purifying of the nobility, and to expunge all villein blood and evil councillors against the commonwealth from his Grace and his Privy Council of the same'.[13] Socially, the great nobles were the natural associates of kings, a point underlined by the derivation of one of the titles of nobility, that of count (English, earl) from the Latin word for a companion. A ruler such the Emperor Charles V seems to have shown more real warmth to a great noble, the Prince of Orange, than he did to his own son.

Such social bonds were strengthened by the knighthood that kings and nobles shared. French coronations borrowed from the ceremonial of knighting, and in the sixteenth century Francis I of France saw the achievement of knightliness as one of his main aims.[14] Because the social distance was so narrow, great nobles might change from being the companions of kings to becoming their rivals for kingship. In the Wars of Religion in sixteenth-century France, the greatest nobles, the Houses of Guise and Bourbon, were putting in their own bids for the throne. One of them, Bourbon, won. His grandson, Louis XIV, found it prudent to re-assert distance rather than conviviality between kings and peers. No serious threat could surely come from nobles who were valets to, rather than companions of, the king. Nevertheless, whether as near-equals or as submissive dependents, nobles belonged at court. They would own or rent expensive properties in capital cities.[15] They were simultaneously the ministrants of ceremonial in such trend-setting courts as Brussels, Madrid or Versailles and arbiters of fashion in capital cities from Naples to London and from Paris to Vienna. Royal courts, their rituals and their architecture, were developed with ever-increasing elaboration from the sixteenth century onwards. From one point of view, nobles were their natural denizens.

Yet the nobleman, usually having some provincial base, however remote, however dull, however hopeless, could almost have personified the rift that became a major literary, cultural and (at least in England) political theme. The theme was the clash between court and city on the one hand, and country life on the other. The polarisation was heavily moralised. 'The Court' stood for sophisticated overindulgence, promiscuity, ambition, deception, irreligion, dissipation, treachery, dissimulation, and the sudden ascents and descents of men and women. 'The Country' came to represent modesty, frugality, stability, fidelity, contentment, candour, piety and chastity. The pastoral mode, going back at least to Horace, was the literary underpinning for the kind of moral preferences summed up in this indifferent, but none the less typical, piece of English anti-court verse:

> Not Courte but Countrye, I do judge,
> Is it wheare lyes the happyest lyfe,
> In Countreye growes no gratynge grudge,
> In Countreye standes not sturdye stryfe,
> In Countreye *Bacchus* hath no place,
> In Countreye *Venus* hathe defecte, . . .

The poem has plenty more of the same, including praise for the country's 'godly lyfe' and 'vertuous exercyse with joye'. The smarter urbanites might have expressed surprise at the absence of Bacchus, or for that matter of Venus, from the rustic idyll, but the poem, as with the better versions of the genre by Spenser and Pope, was not supposed to be a realistic portrayal of country life but was a conventional literary performance. The man to whom the poem just quoted, praising country life, was dedicated, 'My Cobham' (Sir Henry Brooke, Lord of Cobham), was no shrinking rural violet but in fact English ambassador to one of history's most debauched, treacherous and worldly courts, that of France between 1579 and 1583.[16] Nevertheless, the rural ideal clearly did have an appeal to aristocrats, no matter how courtly or urbanised, whose first homes were country estates. Royal orders, like those of Charles I of England, to courtiers and would-be courtiers to return to their estates conformed to nobilities' own code of essentially local leadership. In different periods the ruling aristocracies of Venice and England took their flights to the country. They made sure, however, that they kept their urban options open, and with art, the exercise of power and creature comforts, enjoyed all the advantages of city life in their villas and stately homes.

The pastoral mode, we may say, perhaps expresses some of the ambivalence of those most likely to be drawn to court about the lifestyle, risks and values summed up in the very word 'court'. Another largely literary genre, expressing, creating the cultural values of the European aristocracies, at least in the medieval period, was that of chivalry, knightliness. Nobility was by definition a coterie, and its code of chivalry was therefore expressed partly through the rituals of exclusive chivalric clubs — orders of chivalry — centred on courts. Most national nobilities had at least one of these courtly associations. Perhaps the definitive one was the order of the Golden Fleece. It emerged in the ultra-formal court of Burgundy in the luxuriant late Autumn of chivalry at the end of the Middle Ages.[17]

From this Burgundian tradition emerged the emperor Charles V, the master of vast areas of Europe in the first half of the sixteenth century. Historians have sometimes puzzled over the nature of Charles's motor of action. Was he motivated by Catholicism, or by a sort of ancestor worship, by family dynasticism or by the vision of a world empire? The Emperor was no doubt influenced by all these, but chivalry also played its part in his outlook. Perhaps his acceptance of a personal challenge to single combat from Francis I does not in fact indicate the primacy of romantic knightliness. After all, the issue and acceptance of the invitation, based on a characteristically chivalric desire to avoid the 'emission of Christian blood', did not result in any actual duel. On the other hand, this apparently anachronistic incident does indicate the strong survival of knightly values in these rulers.

Perhaps the place of chivalry in the life of the sixteenth century's most powerful ruler is best seen in some of the political iconography of Charles V, and in particular in two portraits by Titian. One is a quiet, reflective work. The world emperor has laid aside his pomp and is dressed in the plainest black Spanish style. He is devoid of ornament, except, that is, for the collar of the Golden Fleece. The other portrait is in more triumphal mood. It is one of the most successful artistic celebrations of late chivalry — Titian's equestrian portrait of Charles as a victorious crusading knight after his triumph over the Lutherans at Mühlberg. The painting, deliberately archaic and also something of a retrospective on Charles's career, sets out some of chivalry's abiding values: total dedication to a cause, gravity, individual valour, solitude, *machismo*, superb horsemanship, hardihood, defence of religion. Chivalry also embraced the ideals of courtesy, protection of the weak and defenceless and respect for women. All these ideals were set out in such works as the Arthur and Charlemagne cycles, the durably popular *Amadis de Gaules* and

35

later works such as Tasso's crusade epic, *Gerusalemme Liberata* and Ariosto's space fantasy, *Orlando Furioso.*[18]

These were some of the main chivalric scriptures. They proclaimed a set of ideals that were difficult to realise and often violated, not least in the dealings of knights and nobles with the lower orders. In the early sixteenth century, for example, German knights behaved as if they believed that they had the right to pillage their subordinates in order to keep up their living standards as nobles.[19] To take another example, historians have pointed to the contradictions in the conduct of England's Black Prince in his campaigns in France in the fourteenth century: there was limitless courtesy to his French peers, but atrocity against the humbler inhabitants of Limoges.[20] Despite the ideals of chivalry, there was indeed a good deal of brutality on the part of knights, nobles and their followers towards the lower orders, especially peasants, and above all in wartime. When they got the chance, peasants took ferocious reprisals which are recorded, for example, in the accounts we have of the Jacquerie and the German Peasants' Revolt.[21]

With all its contradictions, chivalry took a long time to die. Indeed, it underwent a kind of revival in nineteenth and early twentieth-century England.[22] In the sixteenth century, however, it started to become fashionable to deride chivalry, as Cervantes did in *Don Quixote.* One of chivalry's most important exhibitions, characteristic of its deliberate rashness, the tourney, became understandably unpopular after the death of Henry II of France in a joust in 1559: kings were too important, or the consequences of their premature deaths too calamitous, to lose them in knightly horseplay. A new ideal of humanity borrowed some of the trappings of the knight, but turned him into the gentleman and the courtier. This combination was depicted in Baldassare Castiglione's *Book of the courtier* (*Il libro del cortigiano,* 1528). The new courtier-gentleman had had, perhaps, to adopt some of the survival mechanisms which, as we shall see, had been evolved by urban and bourgeois groups, especially in Italy. Castiglione's ideal man was careful, prudent, cultivated, educated, watchful, discreet, ambitious for advancement but never revealing his ambition. He was more anxious to avoid disgrace than to gain reputation, more anxious to utter clever words than to do great deeds. In English literature there is an echo of Castiglione's courtier in *Hamlet,* with the canny advice that the courtier-politician Polonius gives to his son on the virtues of prudence, caution, forethought, silence, balance and discretion. To become the courtier, the knight assumes a more 'bourgeois' hue.

The appearance of the courtier as an ideal type was a major event in the growing divergence of popular and elite culture. Indeed, in Castiglione's work there is an earnest discussion on the wisdom of retaining the old Italian rustic custom of mingling gentlemen and peasants in holiday athletics. One of the most revealing lines in the dialogue — revealing, that is, of the new, calculating, *prudent* outlook of the courtier — is the comment 'I can not see what a man shall gaine by it.' However, another problem appears in this debate: 'For no comparison is there made of nobleness of birth, but of force and sleight, in which thinges many men of the countey are not a whit inferiour to gentlemen, . . .'[23] Any difficulty in this area could be solved by the simple expedient of not wrestling with peasants unless one was sure to win. However, difficulties were not so easily avoided as this in fields such as politics where the well-born could not indefinitely guard a monopoly against up-and-coming base-born rivals with brains and training. Facing up to the fact that royal courts, not country estates, are the places where fame and wealth are won, *The courtier* is a manual aiming to show men of rank how to gain the favour of rulers by sharpening their wits and improving their education — since rank and chivalrous behaviour alone might no longer be enough.

Another recourse, though — *not* the one adopted by Castiglione — was to stress ever more heavily noble birth as in itself a sufficient warrant for privilege. There was no let-up in early modern Europe in the production of family histories, coats of arms and family trees. Some of the last-named were of unbelievable antiquity, going back at least to Noah and the Ark. Awareness of ancestors was a vital part of the psyche of medieval and early modern nobles. The underlying belief was that a man had worth through the rank of his forebears. To us it seems a strange notion and its strangeness — even its absurdity — comes across in Philip of Spain's remark that he was a greater man than his father because he, Philip, was the son of an emperor, whereas his father was only the son of a duke.[24] The insistence on the claims of genealogy may be interpreted as part of a flight from a world in which knighthood and nobility, without ability and education, were no longer automatic passports to power, wealth and fame.

After looking at some of the values and attitudes of those who by tradition exercised the leading roles in European society, we come next to examine some features of the mental outlook of our second, infinitely larger group of rural humanity, the peasants, those whose labour supported the rest of society. We shall identify peasants'

beliefs and attitudes under an extremely broad heading, that of
'religion'. In doing so, we are by no means implying that only
peasants were 'religious': Christian piety played its part in noble
life and was a major component of both chivalry and the pastoral
form. Later, we shall investigate something of the place of religion
in the lives and values of our two main urban groupings. However,
our discussion of peasant religion will give us an opportunity to see
just how extensive a meaning 'religion' could have in pre-secular
Europe.

At its most extensive religion could be a way of representing
society, or at least community. As well as being a way of saving souls
for an after-life of bliss (or rather, avoiding eternal damnation)
religion was supposed to fulfil functions that today we use science,
technology, medicine and police to perform. The scope of 'religion'
was certainly much greater than just good conduct and belief, or
simply official, orthodox Christian belief. Today, for example,
farmers spray crops to ensure good harvests. In peasant society in
north-east Italy in the sixteenth century, adepts called *Benandanti*
purported to wage nocturnal battles against witches to achieve the
same sort of results.[25] Again, when today we want to cure a sick
child, we call the doctor. People in the Dombes, north of Lyon, over
several centuries would take their sick children to the shrine of a
miracle-working hound-saint, Guinefort. There were obviously
elements in the beliefs underlying these practices that lay outside
Christian doctrine as strictly defined. The *Benandanti* insisted that
they were waging a crusade on behalf of the Christian faith and
the Christian community. The Inquisition, seeking to instill a more
'correct' version of Christianity, did not agree and directly associated
the *Benandanti* with witchcraft.

The pilgrims to the shrine of Guinefort were invoking the aid
of an approved saint, but they also assimilated this saint to a story
of a faithful hound mistakenly killed after he had slain a snake (or
wolf) to save a child.[26] It is not necessarily the case that such beliefs
preserved under an appearance of Christianity the remnants of pre-
Christian cults. Rather, popular beliefs and practices were constantly
being elaborated to deal with the exigencies of daily life. Indeed,
as we will see, the official worship of the Catholic Church itself
encouraged the use of prayers to influence nature and the workings
of the human community.

We shall turn, then, to see first how peasant 'religion' operated
so as to sustain community. For peasants, the village church and
its rituals played the same kind of role, that of implementing

solidarity, as was played by the chivalric orders mentioned above, by the unitive ideology of the ideal Christian city and also by urban guilds and religious confraternities. Most European villages were reasonably well settled communities. This does not mean that villagers never moved. Looking at the Essex village of Terling in the sixteenth and seventeenth centuries, Wrightson and Levine have found hectic mobility in and out of the place.[27] Again, in a study of marriage patterns on the estates of Ramsey Abbey in the late Middle Ages, Judith Bennett finds that about one-third of marriages took place between peasants from different villages — even though most of these were within reasonable walking distance of one another.[28]

We need not take the above cases as evidence of an invariably high rate of inter-village mobility throughout the whole of our period or across the whole of Europe. The rate of mobility in Terling was much higher than that prevailing in the French village studied by Emmanuel Todd.[29] In the French village the lower degree of geographical mobility yields a higher density of kinships than in the English case — and kinship, the more extensive it was, as we shall see in a moment, played a major part in fomenting violence. Many — perhaps most — peasants in our period and our area of study lived out most of their days (perhaps after moving around more as youths) in ancestral communities as small as a dozen houses but usually numbering a few hundred souls.[30]

The more immobile, the more insulated, the more immune from urban influences it was, the more a village was likely to permit the formation over generations of quite extensive kinship lineages, making claims on the individual, requiring his loyalty, summoning his support in inter-kin feuds, demanding his defence of his kin's 'honour' in static, tradition-bound communities where that concept was likely to be important. Ladurie's *Montaillou* shows a community in which people's lives and loyalties were dominated by the *domus*, the family home.[31] This is not to say that all peasants in all villages were necessarily members of vast 'extended families'. These certainly existed,[32] but, as we have said, probably in more insular villages where low levels of population mobility allowed them to take root and flourish. However, whether their families were extensive or nuclear, most villagers lived in families, each of which competed with other families and each of which was 'the basic unit of production, consumption, property holding, socialisation, sociability, oral support and mutual economic help'.

We might add to the above list protection, insurance and

compensation. Bossy has shown how enduring was the primitive concept of 'satisfaction' for wrongs done to an individual. Perhaps the concept was not quite so primitive, since the threat of revenge was the individual's best protection against being wronged. Those who were to demand the satisfaction, or wreak the revenge, were the kin of the person harmed.[33] Stone may be colouring the subject overmuch when he describes the pre-modern family as a kind of murder gang bent on vendetta: 'the family that slayed together stayed together'.[34] Nevertheless, Professor Stone's view does show how the likelihood of lasting violent conflict in villages was multiplied by the obligation on individuals to take upon themselves the quarrels of their kinfolk and other close associates.

Whereas the relative economic and demographic immobility of the stereotyped medieval village made feud more likely by allowing large kin groups to become entrenched, economic change and economic differentiation made a different contribution to the likelihood of discord. If there ever was any such time when all peasants were on much the same economic level as the villagers of Montaillou broadly seem to have been, it was over with the alternation of rural prosperity and recession in the high and late Middle Ages. That cycle, plus the ever-greater penetration of the cash economy, allowed some villagers — the thrifty, the forceful, the industrious, the ruthless — to exploit changing circumstances. The widespread abandonment of direct demesne farming and, in times of rural depopulation, the search by lords for tenants, permitted the fortunate to better themselves, sometimes at the expense of fellow peasants. In particular, differentiation of peasant wealth, reflected above all in the varying size of holdings, allowed some villagers to emerge as creditors, others as their debtors.[35] This on its own created tension. As Bossy shows, lending money at interest was viewed as an absence of charity, even an act of hostility.[36] Differences of wealth also incited theft in villages, thus creating another train of discord and violence.

One way or another, opportunities for inter-personal and inter-kin conflict abounded in peasant communities.[37] The need for its elimination was absolute, and religion, rather than police, performed the literally vital function of limiting the potential for violence, partly through subordinating kin to community by making people feel that all of their Christian neighbours were their kinfolk: 'blood brothers'. The alternative to such restraints on discord and violence was, hypothetically, a pursuit of endless revenge, surges of economic envy, that might end in community suicide. Indeed, religious institutions, especially those set up to suppress heresy and witchcraft, could actually help people destroy their neighbours and thereby, ultimately, their communities: in Sicily from the sixteenth century the Inquisition provided a handy weapon for furthering vendetta.[38] Villages were fragile enough to be destroyed, if not always in the sense of physical extinction, then at least in the sense of negation as working, co-operating societies.

True, some villages needed harmony more than others. In the shepherding village of Montaillou, people and families went their own way to some extent. There were even two different religions in the place. However, in arable, open-field villages, a high degree of agreement was vital. Many decisions, especially those to do with planting and harvesting, had to be taken in common. In France, the late Middle Ages were the heyday of the village tribunal, the *communauté*.[39] Such bodies were essential to the successful functioning of villages. The threat to them from landlords' and princes' law was a major fear in the minds of German peasants at the time of the Peasants' Revolt.[40] Peasants needed their local community bodies for the unceasing tasks of reconciliation.

'Religion' played an even more important role in this. Its function in reinforcing solidarity meant that religious diversity could hardly be tolerated. French people, whether Catholic or Protestant, at the time of the Wars of Religion, were appalled at the prospect.[41] This was because religion was not a private set of opinions but a way of getting on — or not getting on — with one's neighbours. This in turn required religious unanimity. George Fox, the Quaker missionary, was firmly evicted as an invader from the introverted island village of Walney (off the north Lancashire coast) because on a visit there in 1652, he threatened to detach one of the villagers from the community by making a convert of him.[42] The violence of English villagers — some of it ritualised — towards invading Methodist missionaries in the eighteenth century can be explained partly by the same fear of discord arising from dissent.[43]

Religious ministers were themselves fully conscious of the part played by religion in instilling peace — allowing for the paradox that even the threat of religious diversity could cause great friction. The Catholic Mass was a sustained prayer for peace. In its place, the Swiss Reformer Zwingli sought to use the Holy Communion as a rite of solidarity in congregations.[44] Let us stay for a moment, though, with the idea of the Mass as a rite of peace. Its central theme is peace between man and God, previously estranged by sin. Something of that estrangement remained, and sins still needed to be forgiven. However, all sins, even private ones, were in some sense offences against the community as well as against God, so in one of the introductory prayers of the Mass, the *Confiteor*, a prayer for forgiveness, the priest confessed his sins to God, the saints, 'and to you brethren'. There followed a short series of further prayers asking for the forgiveness of the priest's sins, a congregational prayer for mercy, and then a paean to peace between God and man, man and man: 'Glory to God in the highest and peace on earth to men of good will.'

When this theme of peace was restated later in the Mass, it was with an even greater emphasis on peace between men. In medieval Germany, as part of the Peace of God movement promoted by the Church, new prayers for peace were inserted before one of the Church's two sacraments of reconciliation, Holy Communion. These pre-eucharistic prayers were subsequently adopted by the Catholic Church everywhere:

> *Agnus Dei* . . . Lamb of God, You who take away the sins of the world, . . . grant us peace; *Domine, Jesu Christe, qui dixisti Apostolis Tuis: Pacem relinquo vobis.* . . Lord Jesus Christ, who said to your Apostles, 'Peace I leave you, My peace I give unto you': Look not on my sins but on the faith of Your Church and grant her . . . peace . . .

The search for peace which these words express — the word 'peace' recurs about a dozen times and is the most common abstract noun in the Mass — applied not only to the end of formal war, but also to harmony in everyday life, and even to the removal of anxiety.

Lay folk in the main received Communion, with its insistent message of peace only infrequently. Consequently, the custom developed of passing around congregations a peace symbol, the *pax*. In the over-developed chivalry of the Burgundian court, matters were sometimes held up as individuals courteously struggled to give the precedence of the *pax* to their neighbours. Somewhat less edifyingly, scuffles sometimes broke out in congregations as people strove to have the *pax* first, which was not exactly the idea behind the custom. However, this very contention for the *pax* underlines the need for that uphill struggle to tame combative people through a rite of concord, peace between such strife-torn people as our ancestors were being indeed a 'social miracle'.[45]

The integration we have been trying to trace between 'religion' and the social organism means that Christianity would be less amenable in our period than it is now to a definition as a set of objective propositions. Of course there were basic doctrinal propositions and they were *supposed* to be known by all baptised Christians, villagers and townspeople alike. Leaving for the moment the question of religion's instrumental role in such things as preserving villages as communities, we shall now turn to ask how much Christian doctrine was known, especially by the rural masses in the Middle Ages and the early modern period. I shall try to show that although medieval peasants were not theologians, there is no reason to believe that most of them, in most areas of settled Europe, did not know at least the rudiments of the Christian faith. Staying for convenience in our general area of the Mass, I shall take as a test of popular knowledge the understanding (which we may be able to test partly through reconstructing group behaviour) of a fairly abstruse topic: the miracle of the Mass, in which the Church taught that bread and wine were by Christ's words transformed into Christ's body, in a sacrifice of limitless benefit.

Before we come to that particular point, we must admit that in terms of widespread knowledge of a general list of Christian beliefs, there were undoubtedly great gaps, and large areas, especially on the remoter fringes of Europe, where parishes and dioceses were too unwieldy for the preaching of the gospel. The 'mission to Europe' on the part of the medieval Church and, with the Reformation, of all the various churches, could easily be disrupted, especially by war. When, for instance, the French saint, Vincent de Paul, began teaching the gospel, he had to start virtually from scratch in parts of France — doubtless a result of half a century of civil war.[46]

Yet the long didactic crusade went on and, indeed, reached a point of special intensity in the Reformation and the Counter-Reformation. The Protestant reformers concentrated on conveying knowledge of the Scriptures and on preaching. In Catholicism's Counter-Reformation, a campaign of catechetical instructions was launched in rural parishes, and in Sunday schools, from the sixteenth century onwards.

To return, though, to the Middle Ages, we are aware, sometimes too much so, of the practical limits on this sort of educational drive. We know, for instance, that peasants were overwhelmingly illiterate and their parish priests sometimes only semi-literate at best. To set against this, the long haul for an educated, even a graduate, parish clergy made strides in the later Middle Ages, and there were certainly parish priests who preached and taught.[47] Their efforts were boosted by the sensational preaching missions, across whole provinces or even countries, of such brilliant preachers as Vincent Ferrer and San Bernardino. In a more routine way, the specialist preachers of the orders of friars also supplemented parochial preaching provisions. Regular preaching tours, with the aim of imparting Christian knowledge to the rural populace, seem to have been common amongst the preaching orders. Savonarola undertook such a tour as a trainee preacher in the 1480s, when he preached with great success in the districts of San Gimignano and Brescia.[48]

From the case of Savonarola we might also obtain some idea of the content of sermons preached by 'professional' preachers like himself. Apart from his deep grounding in the thought of his Order's leading intellectual ornament, St Thomas Aquinas, and the profound influence upon him of the prophet Joachim of Fiore (d. 1202), like Abbot Joachim himself Savonarola constantly read and meditated upon Scripture. His lengthy sermon cycles, then, were chiefly extended oral instructions, by an accomplished and trained exegete on Scripture. Savonarola provides an excellent example of the preaching orders continuing the task of preaching Christian doctrine, and especially the Bible, to large audiences of ordinary people in town and countryside.

Those preachers who used theatrical and mereticious techniques to aid them in their task of popularising Christianity, of reaching out to, and in the process helping to form, popular culture, sometimes perhaps allowed the technique to overwhelm the message — or at least they did so in the eyes of their many critics amongst the reform-minded and the purists.[49] The kind of preacher who threw sandals to attract the attention of a slumbering congregant was also trying to attract the attention of an audience by raising a cheap laugh. No-one could touch St Bernardino for these tricks of the preacher's art — mimicry of regional dialects, funny names for love-sick girls and boys, a running dialogue with his self-appointed amanuensis, and so on.[50]

Such popularising contrivances were required to bridge the two cultures in medieval religion. On the one hand, there was an intellectual Christianity of great sophistication. Its approach was that of philosophy, its language was Latin — often a highly technical Latin — and it reached its highest point of development in the theology faculties of the universities. The peasant, if he remained a peasant, could never fully enter that world of academic theology. That does not mean that he was ignorant of Christian doctrine. Disputing earlier views about the prevalence of ignorance amongst the Lollard heretics of fifteenth-century England, Norman Tanner

writes of the coherence of their beliefs, notably of their beliefs in
an area which we have been using to test popular knowledge, the
sacraments, and especially Holy Communion.[51]

Official sacramental theology could indeed be highly intricate,
as with the concept of Transubstantiation accepted by the medieval
Church. The formula, resting on distinctions found in Aristotle,
was as complex as it sounds. Looked at from one point of view, it
was a philosophically satisfying way of expressing an underlying
belief — that Christ was truly and physically present in the
Eucharist. It was this latter belief that seems to have been readily,
indeed urgently, grasped by the bulk of medieval Christians. The
popularity of belief in the 'real presence' (as distinct from the
technical formula of Transubstantiation) is attested by the following
facts. Firstly, congregations were anxious to catch a glimpse in the
Mass of bread-made-God at the consecration. Secondly, priests
responded to popular demand, making multiple elevations of the
Host. Thirdly, people spread stories of Hosts that bled, like the one
at Wilnsnack in fifteenth-century Germany. Finally, lay belief in the
real presence stimulated a popular cult, originating in Belgium, of
the summer feast of the Eucharistic body of Christ (*Corpus Christi*),
that was taken up by the Church in a response to popular piety.

There has been, perhaps, some confusion between Transubstantiation and popular belief in the Eucharist as *Corpus Christi*. A critic
of Ladurie, Leonard Boyle, properly takes issue with Ladurie's belief
that the peasants of Languedoc understood Transubstantiation:

> it seems quite clear that everyone, Cathars included, knew well
> that in Catholic belief the bread and wine became the Body
> and Blood of Christ, but that they were equally aware that
> this was by Transubstantiation is not at all evident, nor even
> to be expected.[52]

Transubstantiation, then, was surplus to popular mental and
devotional requirements. Indeed, there was a definite tendency in
popular religion, and especially in popular heresy, to shy away from
academic ways of expressing religious faith. As we saw, Tanner found
that the Norfolk Lollards had a certain coherence of belief — but
it was the coherence of simplicity. A major tendency in popular
heresy was that of rejecting the elaborations of classic scholasticism.

Our appreciation of what the bulk of medieval people, especially
peasants, knew of Christian religion, and particularly of the central
topic of the Mass, might be enlightened by any insight we could

gain into how they behaved at Mass itself. Reverent behaviour by congregations at the rite in which official teaching proclaimed that God was made present would presumably indicate understanding of, and assent to, that (in some ways) complex teaching. Yet on the face of it, medieval people would seem to have behaved informally, if not irreverently, at Mass. Apparently, scuffles broke out in parish churches, people sat on the altar steps or squatted on the floor, nipped out at intervals to the wine shop, talked, laughed, scratched, hawked, coughed and spat.[53] They left the service as soon as they decently could, and used the premises for assignations, seductions, flirtations and sales.

None of this would be very uplifting by the standards of churchly decorum that we have at some distance inherited from the Reformation and the Counter-Reformation. As long-term educational movements, those processes successfully instilled 'proper', silent, reverential behaviour in church. That kind of behaviour may also be seen as the expression of a largely post-medieval preoccupation with oneself in reflective communing with God in church. Thus, for example, the kind of eucharistic devotion that gained ground in the Catholic Church between the appearance in the fifteenth century of the handbook *Imitation of Christ* and the Second Vatican Council in the twentieth tended to see Communion as essentially communing with God in silent reverence on a one-to-one basis. Changes in church furniture have both assisted and expressed these post-medieval alterations in attitudes to worship in church. Between them the Reformation and the Counter-Reformation put a lot of woodwork into European churches — the Counter-Reformation with its confessional boxes, the Reformation with its pews. As Bossy shows, our pews and benches express the privacy that post-medieval Christians came to seek in church.[54] In part, medieval people lounged around because they lacked divided seating; but perhaps they lacked divided seating because they were not divided from one another.

Yet the centrality of community is only part of the issue: so also is the evident familiarity that medieval people showed towards the sacred. The divisions that existed in the main medieval 'church service' — those of time and space — in fact confirm general congregational appreciation of the miracle of the Mass. The time division was between different phases of the Mass. The less formal phases were those parts of the service which belonged especially to the congregation as a human society. If ribald remarks were made when the notices, and especially the bans of marriage, were announced, that was, so to speak, where such remarks belonged. However, no-one but the most egregious blasphemer would have made catcalls at the solemn centre of the action, the elevation of the Host. As for worshippers leaving for the alehouse, Bossy insists that this happened *after* the elevation.[55]

To repeat, then, not all the Mass was equally holy, nor was the whole church equally 'sacred space': the chancel, occupied by the priest saying Mass, was distinguished from the more secular space of the nave. These demarcations, together with lay veneration of the Host, point to popular understanding of the 'eucharistic mystery' that was the Mass. Large-scale peasant endowments of Masses for the souls of the faithful departed indicate acceptance of the idea of the Mass as a limitlessly beneficial sacrifice.

Much of what we have been saying of 'peasant religion' is, of course, true of the religion of all or most social groups in Europe before the Reformation and the Counter-Reformation. That having been said, it is possible that peasants were less responsive to certain forms of religious change than were some other social groups. In particular, I have in mind changes in the direction of making Christianity more of a private experience, and less of a social bond. Such a change was heralded and epitomised in the fifteenth-century manual of piety, *The Imitation of Christ*. This work helped to intern-alise piety, and separate it from social concerns. That process of separation was alien to the integration of Christianity and social ethics. 'Learn to depise outward things, and to give thyself to things inward'[56] is not a precept making for a communal Christianity or the construction of a Christian social ethic. It is all the more appropriate, then, that the *Imitation* should have pointed to, and probably pioneered, a highly private approach to the Eucharist: 'That he who is about to Communicate with Christ ought to . . . Shut out the whole world, . . . remain in some secret place, and enjoy thy God'.[57] The *Imitation* had an enormous influence on Catholic piety in early modern Europe. Something of that influence can be seen in the abandonment of the *pax* in the Tridentine rite of the Mass: 'Shut out the whole world . . .'.

Perhaps the sixteenth-century reformers were trying to reverse the divorce between the Christian and the social that we see in the late medieval devotional movement that produced *The Imitation of Christ*. (It should be said, though, that the group which best represented the piety of which the *Imitation* spoke, the Brethren of the Common Life, was distinguished by its 'social work'.) While Luther believed that world and spirit were opposed, he also believed that the true Christian must not shun 'outward things', but rather must work with all his strength in his calling for the good of his neighbours. Yet the Reformation itself, if not the reformers, prevented the continuance of the co-ordination between Christianity and community, the co-ordination that was endangered by the spirituality found in the *Imitation*. Put another way, the emergence of variant Christianities in and after the sixteenth century, along with the individualism of spirituality already evident in the *Imitation*, made it ultimately impossible to maintain an agreed community Christianity or uphold a Christian social ethic.

'Peasant Christianity' was bound to be somewhat left behind by some at least of the new developments in devotion in the late Middle Ages and onwards, especially since these developments were set out in a number of manuals, of which the *Imitation* is only the best known, designed for private or small-group reading. The new spirituality we have been discussing may be seen as the religious expression of the rise of the individual to a new plane of importance in European life in the late medieval and early modern period. In the nature of things, peasants, or at least most peasants, would be the last to respond to the discovery of the individual and its accompaniment, the invention of privacy — processes pioneered, as we shall see, by urban and bourgeois elements. Peasant religion would at the very least take some time to catch up with the sort of pious cultivation of the self, in leisured privacy, that we see, for example, in the kind of almost conventual Protestantism adopted by Lady Margaret Hoby in Tudor England.[58]

As we have seen, the Christianity of the peasants was, and for a long time remained, deeply involved with a number of adaptations of belief and ritual invoking supernatural forces for social and material ends. These ends were: curing sickness in people and livestock; ensuring good harvests; and maintaining peace in communities. Prayers, rituals and customs to achieve concord remained popular in peasant communities. Traditional church ales — village parties held in church — were still held in some seventeenth-century English villages, despite puritan attempts at suppression.[59]

To return to the Mass, it was the clearest expression of a set of beliefs about the efficacy of prayer and rituals as means of controlling the world. The Mass was the ultimate miracle, the high point of belief that the supernatural constantly affected the natural. At its centre was a startling transformation: bread into God. From this, the Mass opened the way to other assumptions about the way that supernature changed the world around the worshippers. It did this in three main areas: persuading God to make nature benign; praying for the health of people; and making friends.

The development of votive Masses — Masses for special intentions — allowed congregations to pray for the means of their survival. There were Masses 'in time of earthquake', 'for rain', 'for fair weather', 'in time of cattle plague', 'to avert storms' and 'for the fruits of the earth'.[60] The Mass, together with these special Masses, provided ways of regulating the unpredictabilities of nature. Secondly, the Mass included prayers for the health of people 'for whom we offer, or who offer up to Thee, this sacrifice of praise for themselves, their families and friends, for the redemption of their souls, for the health and salvation they hope for . . .'[61] Thirdly, the Mass, as we saw earlier, was about peace and friendship.

It is true that the Mass could be distorted for purposes of enmity: by praying for an enemy, still alive, to have a speedy passage through purgatory, one could hope in effect to secure his death.[62] However, this *was* a distortion of a rite expressing concord. Indeed, there were particular votive Masses 'for concord in a congregation', and these were doubtless said when there existed acute discord within a congregation. However, every Mass was in fact 'for concord in a congregation'. Each one was intended to transform such a this-worldly organism as a parish or village. Thus the Mass preserved much of its character as an infinitely beneficial rite and prayer for securing largely temporal ends. It certainly confirmed the validity of the idea of using words and rituals to affect things by influencing God — the idea which also underlay such phenomena as the Flagellant movement in the Europe of the Black Death.[63]

It should be clear that we are speaking of a Christianity that was concerned with more, or matters other, than personal salvation in a world to come. There was extensive confidence in the interest taken by a pre-Newtonian God, not just in harvests and human health but also in social and political conditions on earth. God was viewed as not indifferent to social and political relations in *this* world. He set up kings, and decided the outcome of battles. In English Protestant and patriotic folklore, He not only destroyed the Spanish Armada but also, a century later, wafted the Protestant liberator William of Orange into a safe haven.[64]

The popular rebellions of the late Middle Ages and the early modern period actually show an increasing belief that God and His saints, especially Mary (as we shall see in the next chapter), were anxious to see society regulated by Christian principles of justice, summed up in the phrase of the German Peasants' Revolt, 'God's Law'. This phrase bespoke confidence in the existence of channels of communication between the social and the divine. The Mass was the epitome of a largely 'inner worldly' Christianity, not only one of personal redemption (this was vitally important) but also one of communal welfare, indeed of social redemption.

In describing peasant and popular religion of the period, we should allow for the existence of strong currents of anticlericalism, albeit selective. Some of this anticlericalism arose because many higher clerics could be classed with other members of the landed ruling class, as we saw earlier. In the English Peasants' Revolt of 1381, the Archbishop of Canterbury, Sudbury, and Hales, Lord Treasurer and Prior of the Order of Knights Hospitallers, were murdered by rebels.[65] Were these murders really acts of anti-clericalism, or would it not be better to regard them as the assassinations of leading members of a discredited social and political establishment who also happened to be clerics? Much resentment of the clergy was indeed social and economic, [66] and some of it sexual, in origin.[67]

To set against this picture of clerical unpopularity, we have much evidence of extensive generosity by parishioners to the clergy. The wills made in Forez in France in the fourteenth century, for instance, reveal a constant stream of gifts of money, food and wine to numerous priests.[68] The steady improvement of clerical chastity [69] probably helped improve relations between laity and clergy. As for economic conflict, many priests must have found it all too easy to be what many laity seem to have wanted priests to be: poor. Chaucer made his clerical ideal types, the parson and the scholar, 'poure'.[70] Such priests, like St Francis, followed Christ who was, according to the hymn, '*pauper, servus et humilis*', a poor humble servant. Through voluntary poverty, the early Franciscans, and later the Spiritual wing of the Order, approached a Christlike state by imitating not just Christ but also the other personification of poverty, the peasant St Francis, for instance, when seeking to express self-abnegation in dress, adopted for himself and his followers the rough, one-piece hooded cloak of the Umbrian peasantry.[71]

The first waves of Franciscans, in their attachment to 'holy poverty', made a tremedously favourable popular impact.[72] While 'proud prelates' might be vilified and murdered by mobs, poor priests could turn into popular heroes and tribunes. John Ball was the priestly spokesman for the English peasant insurgents in 1381, the monk Jan Želivský and the 'priests of Tabor' for the Hussite revolution in early fifteenth-century Bohemia, and Thomas Müntzer for the most advanced radicalism in the German Peasants' Revolt in 1525.[73]

In our discussion of the 'culture' of rural plebeians, we have considered it largely in terms of collective identity and religion, giving 'religion' a wide meaning and sometimes virtually equating it with 'culture'. Separation, analysis and distinction differentiate modern from medieval man. Culture becomes distinguished from cult, and comes to mean 'the educated cultivation of good music, literature and fine arts'. Heightened individual self-awareness may be the thing that most distinguishes modern from medieval man. If we could consider changes in the history of religious devotion to be self-propelled, without reference to social or economic change, or even as inducing change in other areas, we might say that the introspection evident in the late medieval 'new devotion' represented by its classic, *The Imitation of Christ*, made a major contribution to psychological modernity.

Modernity as used here refers to the ability to distinguish oneself fully from the mass, to be aware of oneself. We shall find pioneers of modernity in this sense amongst townspeople and, for want of a better word, 'bourgeois'. This again is another of our vast social categories and ranges from merchant princes and patrician oligarchs to families on or a cut above the craftsmen level. However, it is in some of the substrata within this stratum that we shall find the traits and values which I now wish to identify: these are self-consciousness, a sense of individual and of immediate family, anxiety, prudence as its antidote, ambition, diligence, respectability, seriousness and piety.

We know quite a lot about medieval bourgeois. This is because they wrote about themselves and indeed were historians of themselves. That in itself tells us about their self-awareness and also about their habit of keeping records and careful accounts, as well as their spare time, privacy and literacy. Anxiety has been identified as a major trait, settling in with the economic crisis of the mid-fourteenth century.[74] 'Prudence', as we shall see, was the antidote to anxiety. Ambition was focused on the individual and the family. In commercial bourgeois circles, in a high-risk economy, concern for a family's future may have arisen because of the entanglement of family with firm, disaster for the one leading to the extinction of the other. Preoccupation with the family was preoccupation with its future survival. Nobles would tend to project their families back into the past, bourgeois forward into the future.[75]

Della famiglia was written in the 1430s by the Italian humanist Leon Battista Alberti, a kind of self-made man of the professional bourgeoisie who overcame his origins as the illegitimate son of a Florentine exile to emerge as a successful and versatile expert and intellectual. His treatise bears comparison with Castiglione's work, discussed earlier, in that it is about how men can equip themselves for fame and wealth through improving themselves by education. Alberti addresses the youth of his clan, urging the boys to improve its prospects in the future: 'So I beg you young Albertis to go on doing what you have done; to procure the welfare, increase the honour, expand the fame, of our house . . .'[76] The themes are the familiar Renaissance ones of *gloria* and *virtù*, but they are focused on the family rather than on the individual and they at least seem to be related to confidence, growth, increase: '*increase* the honour, *expand* the fame . . .' — though it will soon be argued that the apparent optimism masks a fear of collapse, the alternative to expansion being elimination.

The Italian Renaissance city was indeed a fiercely competitive place, with incessant violence between the 'better' families jostling for prestige, wealth and power.[77] Aristocratic violence was, of course, also endemic, and the loss of life amongst English families in the Wars of the Roses is far from being a myth. Yet there was an air of security about the underpinnings of aristocratic power — established titles and real estate — that perhaps allowed both noble and royal families to bask in continuity. Of course, both royal and noble dynasties were aggressive land-grabbers, whether on the level of the Nevilles in fifteenth-century England or that of the Habsburgs on the international scale. Yet there would come a point when a noble or royal dynasty became more concerned with the *preservation* of reputation and possessions: for instance, the key to the statecraft of Philip II, as a kind of manager of the Habsburg family concern in the second half of the sixteenth century, was the *retention* of inheritance.[78] The Habsburgs became, after all, one of the more fixed features of the European firmament.

In contrast, close observers of the urban scene were fascinated by its quality of impermanence. Dante remarked — there was no closer observer than he of the urban kaleidoscope — that 'old families, like men themselves, must die', or as a Lübeck pastor in the sixteenth century put it, 'Among all the families of Lübeck there are not three or more in which there is a living member of the fourth generation'.[79] It is easy to see how this sense of impermanence came about. Despite all the Whittingtonesque myths about instant urban social mobility — 'town air makes you free' — there *were* opportunities for fairly rapid advancement in towns and they were made possible in part by the demise of once great urban houses. In the city of Dante, where 'old families . . . must die', even the main Medici line of Cosimo and Lorenzo died out quite quickly, to be succeeded in the sixteenth century by distant cousins.[80] Where great urban houses like this could simply run out, through impoverishment or reproductive failure or both, where the signposts of caste were relatively unfixed, men became anxious to preserve their families' positions. The anxiety seen in Alberti to 'increase' and 'expand' the family's fortune may have concealed a fear of the extinction that was for some the price of urban social mobility.

There was a way of heading off calamity, through the observance of 'prudence'. Philip II of Spain was known as 'the prudent', almost as if the term 'prudent King' contains an inner contradiction, a disturbance in stereotypes, as if we were to speak of 'the thrifty knight' or 'the lone peasant'. Certainly times or values had changed since one of Philip of Spain's Burgundian ancestors had been awarded (through the operation of the Brussels court propaganda machine) the accolade 'the bold' or even 'the rash'.

Of all the cardinal virtues, prudence was the one Alberti made his own. Murray has written of the rise of this rather secular attribute to the status of a Christian virtue, though he is primarily concerned with prudence as the quality of a rising political elite, whereas I should like to see it as part of the survival equipment of any bourgeoisie, in Florence, for example.[81] There is no need to labour the point that merchants should be prudent, so as to minimise risk, through the application of wisdom. Prudence arose from anxiety to avert catastrophe. The related virtues were self-restraint, good advice, forethought, discretion and planning, including the planned day. These themes, along with advice, like that of Alberti, to the young, to whom the future of the family was entrusted, are combined in Machiavelli's highly evocative description of the daily routine of a Florentine father of a family:

> dignified, responsible, sober. He passed his time worthily, got up early in the morning, heard Mass, ordered the day's food, and then saw to whatever business he had in town . . . [then] shut himself up in his study to balance and tidy up his accounts. Then he dined happily with his family and after dinner talked to his son, gave him advice, taught him how to live . . .[82]

Part of the orderly routine, the well-planned day of Machiavelli's bourgeois type is 'heard Mass'. Obviously, religion played its part in the lives of medieval and early modern urban bourgeois, although it is possible that they inclined towards a more private, more internalised, more literate, even more 'rational' religiosity than some of the forms we have already considered. I have in mind the kind of piety promulgated, for example, by Erasmus in the Northern Renaissance, or perhaps the kind of reflective Christianity favoured by the city fathers of Nuremberg on the eve of the Reformation, or even the sort of religion adopted in such German and Swiss cities as Strassburg and Zurich in the Reformation itself.

It may be that a more individual or family-based Christianity was made possible by quite high urban bourgeois literacy rates and also by middle-class habits of privacy alluded to by Machiavelli: 'he shut himself up in his study'. Before the Reformation, and in cities such as Venice after the Reformation passed by, a deep middle-class Catholic piety was combined with a degree of bourgeois anticlericalism. This must not be over-estimated. Years ago, with characteristic subtlety, Weber examined the points of contact as well as those of conflict between 'the city' and the urban clergy. There were political and economic collisions, and a latent conflict over economic values, but there was also a symbiosis between bourgeois and clergy.[83] In any case, before the end of the Middle Ages, in many cities ruling patriciates had put the clergy firmly in place. The unfalteringly Catholic patricians of Venice kept both the Inquisition and papal jurisdiction at a distance, and in cities such as Strassburg and Nuremberg the clergy were corporation appointees before the Reformation.[84]

In our list of 'bourgeois virtues' we included restraint. This did not only mean self-restraint: as we shall see in a moment in a study of crime in late medieval Paris, it included restraint on others. In Nuremberg before the Reformation an oppressive welfare state was operated by the same bourgeois oligarchy that controlled religion in the city. The dim view they took of their less self-disciplined fellow citizens was reflected in minute regulations of the city's life.[85] The eventual acceptance of Lutheran Protestantism by many German cities facilitated the control and promotion by urban patriciates of properly administered poor relief, education and public morals. In England, through partnerships between bourgeois town governments and puritan ministers, towns such as Leeds and Hull were turned into miniature 'godly commonwealths' before 1640.[86] It was not only the Protestant Reformation, though, which advanced this kind of discipline. In seventeenth-century Flanders, middle-class magistrates, fired with the spirit of the Counter-Reformation, tried to take in hand what they saw as a feckless and godless people.[87] In Venice, the Catholic activism of a middle class denied a role in government was channelled into charitable archconfraternities, the *Scuole Grande*.[88]

In the final section of this chapter, we shall be considering a grouping even more variegated than our other vast categories — a broad band of urban plebeians near the top of which were families indistinguishable from the lower bourgeoisie and, at the bottom, those sunk in beggary or involved in crime. We shall be spending a little time considering crime in particular, the main reason being (apart from the inherent interest of the subject) that crime control was a major area of encounter between rulers and ruled in which cultural collision, and the challenge of one value system to another, took place.

From criminals and vagrants up through labourers, craftsmen and merchants to patricians, all strata of urban society felt at least some of the impact of Christian religion whose omnipresence we have been noting elsewhere. It has been said of medieval Norwich, for instance, that builders put up churches as a matter of course and much as Victorian town developers erected public houses, as social centres.[89] In towns and cities throughout Europe, streets, districts, and political wards took their names from churches, especially those of the friars. While preaching formed a staple of urban public opinion, popular theatre originated in religious plays. The craft guilds were held in an embrace of collective prayer. Christian ideas formed the ideological basis for urban popular protest and agitation. Sometimes the nature of this agitation — as with the attacks on the Jews in the Rhineland towns and in Prague and elsewhere in the Middle Ages — will repel us. To argue whether these pogroms were economic or religious in origin is rather pointless. They fused two elements: hatred for money-lenders and of any groups who could be depicted as outsiders and scapegoats; and the influence of the friars in stirring up religious hatred of the Jews as descendants of the killers of Christ.[90]

A major feature of the mental make-up of urban crowds was a kind of social demonology. Urban crowds sought human villains to attack, especially those whose avarice — rather than impersonal economic forces — was seen as the cause of shortages and high prices.

London, Paris and Edinburgh were cities with histories of chronic religious rioting in which the victims of religious riot were people viewed as the causes of social distress. In London's Sacheverell Riots of 1710 the targets were Nonconformist bankers; in the Gordon Riots of 1780, well-off Catholics and the Irish as rivals for jobs.[91] In Paris in 1572 the predominantly Catholic populace massacred the Protestant minority. By straining the evidence, we could argue that there was a direct economic motive here: that the Parisian lower orders were conducting a class war against a Protestant 'bourgeois' element, held responsible perhaps for jacking up food prices. However, apart from the fact that there is certainly no automatic link between Protestant and 'bourgeois' as far as sixteenth-century France is concerned, it is important to see the real cultic ingredients in such pogroms, the Protestant minority being regarded as pollutants. On the other hand, even if we do not accept that high grain prices were the immediate cause of the 1572 Massacre of St Bartholomew, the Protestants were surely blamed for a widespread social distress exacerbated by the Wars of Religion.[92]

London, meanwhile, maintained a pattern of rioting in which religion was often a major element. Demonstrations in the eighteenth century against the emancipation of the Jews, the reform of the calendar and the dissection of criminals' corpses by surgeons all had powerful religious overtones. When we say 'religion', however, we must recognise once again that in our period the term means something much more extensive than just private piety. We shall find in it the indispensable ideological and emotional motor of popular protest.

We cannot leave our brief study of the urban lower orders (and of those who moved from country to town and from town to town) without some remarks on vagrancy and crime, which were closely related, at least in perceptions of them. Crime was not of course the monopoly of any particular stratum. However, we have more or less arbitrarily identified chivalry and gentlemanliness as the preserves of noble estates. We have equally arbitrarily associated collective religiosity with peasants, and rationality with bourgeois. With an almost equal degree of approximateness, we are now about to link crime largely with those driven to it by poverty. Part of our justification for identifying crime as the social hallmark of a particular social category — vagrants — is that contemporary 'respectable' opinion did just that. This in itself is a significant fact in the separation of cultures along class lines in early modern Europe.

In discussing crime, we shall consider the main forms: violence, fraud and theft. However, while violence was far from unknown amongst the lower orders, rural and urban, theft was their characteristic crime, because it generally arose out of poverty: its rate would shoot up, for instance, in a famine.[93] It followed that because a good deal of crime, especially rural crime, was a response by the poor to hard times, it tended to be un-planned, un-professional, incompetent, with the 'criminal' committing crime once or twice rather than regularly. Perhaps in this sort of thieving — much of it of food or of things that could be quickly sold to buy food — there was a distant echo of the moral theologians' ruling that a starving man may steal.[94] The major exception — allowing for rural banditry — to the generalisation that crime was amateur arose in some of the greater towns. Crime may happen when wealth meets poverty head on, as in 'court cities' such as London and Paris or in those southern European cities that had criminal quarters: Naples, Seville and Venice.[95] Patterns of crime in later medieval Paris are particularly well documented, thanks to the work of Geremek.[96] If we consider this city for a while we may learn something about crime, social control and the clash of value systems in cities in our period.

Cases investigated by Geremek give us invaluable insights into the existence of a criminal underground in the Middle Ages. They provide information about the locations of crime; we learn about the main categories of crime, which were theft (including information about stolen goods); and we can discern the organisation of professional crime and the existence of a conscious 'criminal culture' — one that was totally opposed to the 'bourgeois' values set out by Alberti and Machiavelli. To see this culture-clash in operation, we will examine the attitudes of the authorities, the crucial factor in defining crime. In particular, we will consider the association that was formed in the minds of urban rulers linking crime with vagrancy.

Firstly, the places where professional crime was likely to be carried on were, as we have seen, towns and cities, for crime was one of the specialisations and divisions of labour that urban life facilitated. In addition, as we saw earlier, cities were the generators of the cash economy — and cash and crime were made for one another. Within towns and cities — the larger the cities the more crime-prone — crime was likely to occur where people congregated — churches, including Notre Dame, fairs, law courts and other places where 'ordinary' citizens went. However, crime flourished above all in places where transients gathered — taverns, gaming houses (where crime was associated with an 'easy-come easy-go' attitude typical of our 'criminal culture'), and brothels. Above all, lodging houses, some of which may of course have had some or all of the functions of the other sorts of places on our list, bred crime: 'In the lodgings of Oudet le Doyen'; 'today in the Shield of France Inn in Mortarer Road'; 'he was staying in Paris in the Striped Quill Inn at the end of the rue de Sacalie'; 'in some hostel'.[97] The police obviously checked such places closely and often, partly because of the conviction, which we will examine, that crime and lack of fixed abode went hand in hand. Crime in lodgings sometimes had as its victims affluent landlords and landladies (though these might, as we shall see, also feature as accomplices and fences):

> Over a period of six weeks or so, during the daytime and the night, he took from the proprietress of the said inn her belt from beneath her bolster and from that removed a key, while she was sleeping in bed with which he unlocked a chest and took from it 120 gold florins . . .

Lodging-house theft was also facilitated by the custom of people sharing beds: 'Then the said prisoner while sharing a bed with a man took in his purse 16 Parisian sous and stole his doublet . . . others go to bed in some hostel with some merchant and . . . rob the said merchant . . . '.[98]

The main crimes of the criminal classes were theft and fraud, since murder, or even assault, are not really criminals' crimes. As we have already seen, there was some in-house burglary. However, theft, linked to the urban cash economy, was largely related to the money that people had about them and that they took to taverns, brothels and gambling dens. The 'cut-purse' was obviously a dexterous character, a real urban specialist, though given his apparent ubiquity it is odd that people did not think up a safer way of carrying cash than the detachable purse. Ready money, then, was the prime target — a marvellous, lightweight, untraceable medium. It was exchanged, without the discount on stolen goods, for precisely its value (though stolen money, as we shall see, was frittered away): 'he cut the purse of a woman in which there were seven *douzains* and an IOU . . . 98 gold crowns of the king's coin, 20 eagle crowns and 2 angels . . . 6 crowns from a Lombard . . . '. Next best to coin were personal ornaments and jewels and small objects fashioned from precious metals: 'a silver belt . . . jewels . . . a ring . . . a silver bucket and the chain with it which he melted . . . '. Holy objects made of precious metals were fair game — 'a chalice and a paten' — as well as relics, which could be just as valuable as bullion. Horses were great prizes, reminding us of the steady trade in stolen cars in modern cities.[99]

The other main type of offence was fraud. Sometimes this was loosely defined: 'being in the con racket (*de la pipée*) and of deceiving and defrauding the good people throughout the country . . . they lived by deceit . . . he spent his time by deceits . . . '. At other times, the frauds, often quite ingenious, are described in detail. We shall deal shortly with the 'criminal type', so for the moment we need only note that the 'conman' had to be plausible, perhaps aided by looks, a smooth tongue, charm, travel and experience.

Aware that fraud is the crime above all others that rests on a sort of complicity between victim and villain, we can peek through the door that human cupidity and stupidity throw open to the artist of the main chance:

> [they] rob the people by changing gold for coin or coin for gold or by buying some merchandise; others come, carrying and selling false ingots and false gems in place of diamonds, rubies and other precious stones; others play with false dice, loaded to their advantage and win all the money of those playing; others know subtleties of the games of cards . . . so that no-one can win against them . . .

For sage merchants too shrewd for the three-card-trick approach, the confidence tricksters adopted a more psychological type of fraud: 'others go to bed in some hostel with some merchant and rob themselves *and* the said merchant and have a man of their own to whom they give the booty and then they lament with the said merchant . . . '.[100]

The 'criminal type' varied somewhat according to the branch of crime (and bearing in mind that the stereotyping comes from the court records). Common characteristics (inherent or accredited) were: idleness and vagrancy; extravagance; licentiousness; varied (and frequently unpleasant) experience of life; for thieves, resourcefulness; for confidence tricksters, glibness; and for all types, a certain resilience and capacity for survival, until, that is, they landed in court and finished up on the gallows. Let us look in greater detail at these personality traits.

Idleness was thought by the authorities to be at the root of crime: 'they led an idle life . . . an idler, a vagabond . . . ruffians and wrongdoers, idle people of evil lifestyle . . . going from one country to the other without doing a job or working . . . idlers and vagabonds . . . '. Leaving aside any question as to whether these 'idlers' were the involuntarily unemployed, it is clear, and will become clearer when we investigate the association between crime and vagrancy, that by the fourteenth century, crime was partly defined in terms of the pursuit of a way of life that did not accord with the restraint, thrift, respectability, industriousness and sobriety increasingly valued by elites, especially urban elites. So the criminal was seen, for example, as unthrifty, congenitally extravagant, having to resort to fresh crimes because his booty slipped through his hands: 'he spent everything that is mentioned above . . . they did nothing but drink, eat and maintain great expenditure . . . '. The criminal was also seen as formidably licentious and promiscuous:

> Marion le Liourde, woman of the night . . . was living at St Denis de la Chartre and offering her body for the comrades' desires and pleasures . . . pillaging, ravishing women . . . they stayed continually . . . at a brothel where they led the filthy, vile and dissolute life of ruffians . . .[101]

Many arrested criminals had had ample, and often unfortunate, experience of life, made up of much travel and a pattern of being passed from hand to hand reminiscent of the classic picaresque novels.[102] In particular, many were displaced persons, ex-soldiers, the victims of war and other disruptions:

> . . . he said that while he was at the said inn, he purported to be from Melun because there was a war against the abbot of Rebais . . . these had previously been on the journey from Brantonne and had frequented the wars in various countries . . . He said that they . . . took money at will from the master of the battle and then they failed at their task and left the army and set to pillaging . . .

Part of the pattern of chequered experience was the fact that criminals came from all over the place: 'of Tournai . . . born in Crêpi in Valois . . . native of Lens in Artois . . . native of near Grammont in Flanders . . . native of Louvain . . . native of Valenciennes . . . '. It is perhaps worth noting that overcrowded, urbanised Belgium provided Paris with much of its underground.[103]

For the confidence tricksters, cosmopolitanism and some acquaint-

ance with noblemen and noblewomen were distinct advantages, as
they had been to one horse thief involved in a complicated scheme
to purloin the queen's carriages:

> he is a poor servant, serving the lords, knights and esquires
> of the realm, with whom he followed, frequented and stayed
> for 20 years, also journeying to Flanders, Germany, Languedoc
> and other places where they had been in the wars . . .

Personal attributes suitable to a thief, especially one who took high
risks in burglary and taking purses, included great presence of mind
and physical resource: 'and, this done, he lowered himself from the
window of the said inn using bed coverings'.[104]

Was urban crime professionalised and organised, did criminals
have leaders, and was there a conscious picaresque culture? The
evidence of Paris suggests that all of those features were indeed
present. 'Organisation' may have been loose — 'the company of
idlers, vagabonds and men of evil repute' — but some groups may
have had a more elaborate structure, with even a hint of parody
of the guilds — 'the comrades'. There undoubtedly were some
organised gangs and they had leaders: ' the chief or leader is one
Jehan Pellet, otherwise called Coquillon . . . Monnet Aillenault,
called the chief . . . these gentlemen call themselves the Coquillards,
that is to say the Companions of the Shell *(Coquille)*, who, as it is
said, have a king whom they call the King of the Shell' — parody
here also.

Besides these organisational structures, however rudimentary,
there was also an economic support system, doubtless largely
supplied by tavern- and brothel-keepers. Such people were hosts to
criminal communities, straddled the respectable and non-respectable
worlds and had the capital that allowed them to pay for stolen goods
before re-selling them:

> it is said that Jacquot de la Mer, keeper of the said brothel,
> knew them all, or the greater part of them; and what is more,
> that he is certainly of their estate and way of life; and so he
> hides them and sometimes helps them to do their deeds and
> to sell horses and other things wrongfully taken, as much for
> the gain he made in disposing of them as because it is apparent
> that he was sometimes a party to the booty from their
> deceptions.

Finally on this heading, it may already have become clear that urban crime was professionalised, at least inasmuch as many of its practitioners had never done anything else: 'the prisoner by his own confession, had been accustomed to stealing since his youth . . . '.[105]

Was there a conscious criminal culture? We have touched on aspects of this already in dealing with the 'criminal type'. Certain features of a criminals' code, such as honour, secrecy and *omertà*, seem to be lacking, and confessions and disclosures indeed abounded. There seems, though, to have been a feeling that criminals should have style, swagger and bravado: '[they] returned on horseback . . . well dressed and attired, well decked with gold and silver . . . '. We have already caught a glimpse of aliases, and there were already signs of that familiar criminal trait, colourful nicknames, 'Big Colin . . . the Stutterer . . . '. There was also a criminal patois, like the cant so lovingly recorded in England by Dekker: 'the said companions have between them a certain slang language and signs by which they can recognise each other . . . '. Finally, there was a kind of 'literature', Villonesque, haunting, rueful, fatalistic, painfully realistic:

Wind, hail, ice, my bread is baked.
I am a bawd, bawdiness follows me,
What is best? One follows from the other,
The one is worth the other; it's a bad rat, bad cat.
We love filth, filth delights us.
We defy honour, it defies us,
In this brothel where we hold our estate.[106]

Needless to say, the Paris authorities saw no romance or poetry in the criminal 'estate'. Crime was treated — *pace* Weber — not yet in a 'rational' way. Prosecutions were definitely *ad homines*, and certain categories of people, above all the mobile, as well as certain acts, were regarded as intrinsically criminous. Other categories of people, the settled, the respectable, were automatically almost exempt from prosecution: 'the son of a citizen cannot be questioned if there is no party for the prosecution.' Equality of people before the law was not much valued, and sentencing policy seems to us to have been capricious, illogical and non-judicial: 'considering there was no famine [a nod to the notion, seen earlier, that starvation exculpated theft], considering that the day on which he committed the said offence was Good Friday . . . and that the said Jehan

Lefèvre is aged 54 years, they all agreed that he should be hanged . . . '[107]

Presupposition of guilt was the norm, especially in the cases of vagrants. Already by the fourteenth century, 'masterless men', the workless and the mobile were singled out as probable criminals. Well before the end of the Middle Ages, the rulers of Europe's most important city were using criminal law for 'social control', especially the control of migration:

> of no fixed abode, brought prisoner . . . prisoners detained at Châtelet because they are vagabonds roaming the country and because they led an idle life and also because they were suspected of being in the con racket . . . an idler, a vagabond, without estate, not in the service of a lord . . . considering that the said prisoner has been on several occasions taken prisoner for many excesses and misdeeds and had been a vagabond, of wicked life and conduct, this prisoner was condemned by the said lieutenant to be hanged as a thief . . . many idle companions, generally called vagrants, were arrested in the said town . . .

The last-named group is particularly interesting since this case clearly shows the way that mobility was taken as virtual proof of crime:

> great suspicion was on them because at the feast of St John at Amiens and at the feast of St Peter of Corbie last past, some thieves cut many purses of the good people and committed many thefts from the merchants of which the said vagrants were suspected . . . '[108]

Our study of crime here has allowed us to investigate the sharpest possible cultural cleavage opening up between the value systems of two urban strata, loosely labelled the respectable — 'the good people' — and the disreputable.

The social, or rather cultural, groups we have tried to identify in this chapter are to a degree artificial constructs. This is partly because in all social groups there are elements at the top and bottom ends that shade into the groups above and below. Great merchants in early modern London could buy and sell landed gentlemen. Is there any point in labelling such individuals as 'bourgeois'? There were peasants, too, who were economically quite close to the lower gentry, and others who sank into vagrancy and crime. We could go on to consider the almost infinite gradations, complexities and mobilities of the kaleidoscope of human society. If we agree, however, that social categories are artificial, they can also have some use, not least in identifying some 'character traits' that perhaps attached to some groups more than to others. We go on in chapter 3 to focus on a category with whom we have already spent some time in this chapter, the peasantry.

Notes

1. For example, Giuseppe di Lampedusa, *The leopard* (trans. Archibald Colquhon, Collins, London, 1961), pp. 18–19.

2. Ibid., pp. 77–8, though see Emmanuel Le Roy Ladurie, *Carnival at Romans. A people's uprising at Romans 1579–1580* (trans. Mary Feeney, Penguin, Harmondsworth, 1981), pp. 216–17, 220–5.

3. Richard C. Trexler, *Public life in Renaissance Florence* (Studies in Social Discontinuity, Academic Press, New York and London, 1980), p. 413; Donald Weinstein, *Savonarola and Florence. Prophecy and patriotism in the Renaissance* (Princeton University Press, Princeton, New Jersey, 1970), pp. 125, 181, 186–7, 242.

4. Herbert Workman, *John Wyclif. A study of the English medieval Church* (2 volumes, Oxford University Press, Oxford, 1926, cited here in the reprint, 2 vols in one, Archon Books, Hamden, Connecticut, 1966), vol. I, p. 278.

5. Ladurie, *Montaillou*, pp. 163–4.

6. W.L. Wiley, *The gentleman of Renaissance France* (Harvard University Press, Cambridge, Massachusetts, 1954, cited here in the reprint by Greenwood Press, Westport, Connecticut, 1971), pp. 77, 82–3.

7. For an important aspect of noble piety, see Joel T. Rosenthal, *The pursuit of Paradise. Gift giving and the aristocracy, 1307–1485* (Routledge & Kegan Paul, London, University of Toronto Press, Toronto, Ontario, 1972), esp. ch. 2. For chivalry, see in particular Maurice Keen, *Chivalry* (Yale University Press, New Haven, Connecticut, and London, second corrected printing, 1984).

8. K.B. McFarlane, *Lancastrian kings and Lollard knights* (Oxford University Press, Oxford, 1972), pp. 194–5.

9. Alice Clark, *Working life of women in the seventeenth century* (George Routledge, London 1919, cited here in the new paperback edition by Routledge & Kegan Paul, London, Boston & Henley, 1982), p. 16.

10. H.R. Loyn, *The Norman Conquest* (Hutchinson, London, 1965), p. 95; Hajo Holborn, *Ulrich von Hutten and the German Reformation* (trans. Roland H. Bainton, Yale Historical Publication Studies 11, 1937, Yale University Press, New Haven, Connecticut, 1937, cited here in the reprint by Greenwood Press, Westport, Connecticut, 1978), pp. 181–2; G.A. Holmes, 'Cardinal Beaufort and the crusade against the Hussites', *English Historical Review*,

vol. 88 (1973), pp. 721–50.

11. C.V. Wedgwood, *William the Silent. William of Nassau, Prince of Orange 1533–1584* (Jonathan Cape, London, 1944), pp. 11–12.

12. Jerome Blum, *Lord and peasant in Russia from the ninth to the nineteenth century* (Princeton University Press, Princeton, New Jersey, 1961, cited here in the 1963 reprint), p. 349.

13. Anthony Fletcher, *Tudor rebellions* (Seminar Studies in History, ed. Patrick Richardson, Longman, London, 1968), pp. 120, 122.

14. Miss Pardoe, *The court and reign of Francis the First king of France.* (2 vols, Richard Bentley, London, 1849), vol. 1, p. 142; Richard A. Jackson, *Vive le roi! A history of the French coronation from Charles V to Charles X* (University of North Carolina Press, Chapel Hill, North Carolina and London, 1984), pp. 5, 6, 134–5.

15. Lawrence Stone, *The crisis of the aristocracy 1558–1641* (Oxford University Press, Oxford, 1965), pp. 394–8.

16. For Barnaby Googe's (c. 1540–94) *To Master Henrye Cobham of the most blessed state of lyfe*, see William Tydeman (ed.), *English Poetry 1400–1580* (Heinemann paperback, London, 1979), pp. 137–8 and 251. For attitudes to the Court, see Spenser's *Prothalamion*, and to the Country, Pope's *Ode to solitude*.

17. For example Richard Barber, *The knight and chivalry* (Longman, London, 1970), pp. 309–11.

18. Harold E. Wethey, *The paintings of Titian* (3 vols Phaidon, London, 1971), vol. II, plates 141, 142, 145, 146; Wiley, *Gentleman of Renaissance France*, pp. 116–17.

19. Gerald Strauss, *Manifestations of discontent in Germany on the eve of the Reformation: a collection of documents . . .* (Indiana University Press, Bloomington, Indiana, and London, 1971), p. 154 ff.

20. *The Chronicle of Jean Froissart . . .* Gillian and William Anderson (eds) (Centaur, London, 1963), pp. 131, 157.

21. For a vivid account of a vengeance killing in the German Peasants' Revolt, see E. Belfort Bax, *The Peasants War in Germany 1525-1526* (Swan Sonnenschein 1899, cited here in the reprint by Augustus M. Kelley, New York, 1968), pp. 118–31.

22. Mark Girouard, *The return to Camelot chivalry and the English gentleman* (Yale University Press, New Haven, Connecticut, and London, 1981).

23. Baldassare Castiglione, *The book of the courtier* (trans. Sir Thomas Hoby, Dent, London 1975), pp. 97–8.

24. H.G. Koenigsberger, 'The statecraft of Philip II', *European Studies Review*, vol. I, (1971), p.7.

25. Ginzburg, *The night battles*, p. 4.

26. Schmitt, *Guinefort*, pp. 70–3, 133.

27. Wrightson and Levine, *Terling*, pp. 79-82.

28. In Raftis (ed.), *Pathways to peasants*, p. 219.

29. Wrightson and Levine, *Terling*, pp. 85–7.

30. Braudel, *Civilisation and capitalism*, I, 61–2.

31. Ladurie, *Montaillou*, ch. 2.

32. John W. Shaffer, *Family and farm. Agrarian change and household organisation in the Loire Valley 1500–1900* (Suny Series in European Social History, State University of New York Press, Albany, New York, 1982), ch. 1.

33. John Bossy, *Christianity in the West 1400–1700* (Opus paperback, Oxford

University Press, 1985), pp. 4–5.

34. Lawrence Stone, *The family, sex and marriage in England 1500–1800* (Weidenfeld & Nicolson, London, 1977), pp. 95, 126.

35. For the subject of increasing differences in the sizes of peasant holdings, see B.H. Slicher van Bath, *The agrarian history of Western Europe A.D. 500–1850* (trans. Olive Ordish, Edward Arnold, London, 1963), p. 136. For the same phenomenon tied to money-lending, see Georges Duby, *Rural economy and country life in the medieval West* (trans. Cynthia Postan, Edward Arnold, London, 1962, cited here in the 1968 edition), pp. 254, 282–5.

36. Bossy, *Christianity*, p. 77.

37. Barbara Hanawalt, *Crime in East Anglia in the fourteenth century Norfolk gaol delivery rolls, 1307–1316* (Norfolk Record Society, vol. 44, 1976), pp. 16-17.

38. H.G. Koenigsberger, *The Government of Sicily under Philip II: a study in the practice of empire* (Staples Press, London, 1951), p. 163.

39. J.H. Salmon, *Society in crisis: France in the sixteenth century* (Ernest Benn, London, 1975), p. 30; Robert Mandrou, *Introduction to modern France 1500–1640: an essay in historical psychology* (trans. R.E. Hallmark, Edward Arnold, London and New York, 1975), pp. 90–4.

40. Peter Blickle, *The revolution of 1525. The German Peasants' War from a new perspective* (trans. Thomas A. Brady Jr., and H.C. Erik Midelfort, Johns Hopkins University Press, Baltimore, Maryland, 1981), pp. 80–4. For law enforcement by local communities in England, see J. Kent, 'Folk justice and royal justice in early seventeenth-century England: a 'charivari' in the Midlands', *Midland History*, vol. 8 (1983), pp. 70–85.

41. Natalie Zemon Davis, 'The rites of violence' in her *Society and culture in early modern France* (Duckworth, London, 1975, cited here in the edition by Stanford University Press, Stanford, California, 1975), pp. 152–87.

42. *The journal of George Fox*, John L. Nickalls (ed.) (Cambridge University Press, Cambridge, 1952), pp. 129–31.

43. John Walsh, 'Methodism and the mob in the eighteenth century' in G.J. Cuming and Derek Baker (eds), *Studies in Church history*, vol. 8: *Popular belief and practice* (Cambridge, 1972), pp. 213–27.

44. Jean Rilliet, *Zwingli: third man of the Reformation* (trans. Harold Knight, Lutterwoth Press, London, 1964), pp. 115, 215, 286, 310.

45. In the debate amongst social historians on long-term trends in violence, I incline to the views of Lawrence Stone put forward in his 'Interpersonal violence in English society', *Past and Present* vol. 101 (1983), esp. pp. 25–9. For liturgy and peace, see John Bossy, 'The Mass as a social institution', *Past and Present*, vol. 100 (1983), pp. 32–4, and John Bossy, 'The Counter-Reformation and the people of Catholic Europe', *Past and Present*, vol. 47 (1970), pp. 51–70.

46. Pierre Janelle, *The Catholic Reformation* (Bruce, Milwaukee, Wisconsin, 1963, cited here in the Collier-Macmillan paperback edition, London, 1971), pp. 242–3.

47. Bernard Hamilton, *Religion in the medieval West* (Edward Arnold paperback, London, 1986), p. 71.

48. Pasquale Villari, *Life and times of Girolamo Savonarola* (trans. Linda Villari, T. Fisher Unwin, London, 1896), pp. 84–6.

49. For a typical Lollard attack on the allegedly meretricious methods of the preaching orders, see Ann Hudson (ed.), *Selections from English*

Wycliffite writings (Cambridge University Press, Cambridge, 1978), p. 120.
See also Bernard Lord Manning, *The people's faith in the time of Wyclif* (The
Thirlwall Essay 1917; second edition, Cambridge University Press, Cam-
bridge, 1919, cited here in the reprint by The Harvester Press, Hassocks,
Sussex, and Rowman and Littlefield, New York, 1975), pp. 19–24.

50. Iris Origo. *The world of San Bernardino* (Jonathan Cape, London, 1963),
ch. 1.

51., Tanner (ed.), *Norwich heresy trials*, p.20.

52. In Raftis (ed.), *Pathways to peasants*, p. 134.

53. Jean Delumeau, *Catholicism between Luther and Voltaire: a new view of the
Counter-Reformation* (trans. Jeremy Moiser, Burns & Oates, London, 1977),
p. 197.

54. Bossy, *Christianity*, pp. 142–3.

55. Ibid., p. 68.

56. Thomas à Kempis, *The Imitation of Christ* (Collins, London, n.d.), p.
105.

57. Ibid., pp. 363, 365.

58. Claire Cross, *Church and people 1450–1660: the triumph of the laity in the
English Church* (Fontana Library of English History, ed. G.R. Elton, Fon-
tana/Collins, London, 1976), pp. 159, 167.

59. Alexandra F. Johnston, 'Parish entertainments in Berkshire' in Raftis
(ed.), *Pathways to peasants*, p. 337.

60. These examples are in fact taken from the post-medieval 'Tridentine' Mass, which incorporated and standardised medieval rites.

61. Bossy, 'Mass as a social institution', pp. 38–40.

62. Ibid., p. 46.

63. Robert E. Lerner, 'The Black Death and western European
eschatological mentalities', *American Historical Review*, vol. 86 (1981), pp.
533–52.

64. Clyve Jones, 'The Protestant wind of 1688: myth and reality', *European Studies Review*, vol. 3 (1973), pp. 210–22.

65. *The Anonimalle Chronicle 1333 to 1381*, V.H. Galbraith (ed.) (Manchester
University Press, Manchester, 1927, cited here in the reprint by Manchester
University Press, 1970), p. 145.

66. For some of the literature on anticlericalism, and especially on its
economic roots, see: Henry J. Cohn, 'Anticlericalism in the German
Peasants' War 1525', *Past and Present*, vol. 83 (1979), pp. 3–31; Eric J. Evans,
The contentious tithe. The tithe problem and English agriculture 1750–1850 (Routledge
& Kegan Paul, London, 1976), esp. ch. 2; Christopher Hill, *Economic problems
of the Church. From Archbishop Whitgift to the Long Parliament* (Oxford University
Press, Oxford, 1963), ch. V.
Ralph Josselin, the seventeenth-century minister of Earls Colne in Essex,
complained bitterly and regularly of the delays and reluctance of his parish-
ioners as regards paying their tithes: *The diary of Ralph Josselin 1616–1683*, Alan
MacFarlane (ed.) (Oxford University Press, London, for the British
Academy, 1976), pp. 135–7. Dr Houlbrook points to a rising volume of
refusals to pay tithes in early modern England: 'The decline of ecclesiastical
jurisdiction under the Tudors' in Rosemary O'Day and Felicity Heal (eds),
Continuity and change. Personnel and administration in the Church of England 1500–1642
(Leicester University Press, Leicester, 1976), pp. 245–6. Resistance to

payment of tithes tended to be stronger in towns, as in fifteenth-century London, where the disputes, though protracted, were free from bitter anticlericalism: J.A.F. Thomson, 'Tithes disputes in medieval London', *English Historical Review*, vol. 78 (1963), pp. 1–17.

67. For example, Simon Fish, *A supplicacyon for the beggers*, J. Meadows Cowper (ed.) (Early English Text Society, Extra Series, 13, 1871, cited here in the reprint by Kraus Reprints, Millwood, New Jersey, 1975), p. 6; Ladurie, *Montaillou*, pp. 154–9; Strauss, *Manifestations*, pp. 14–15.

68. *Testaments Foréziens 1305–1316*, M. Gonon (ed.) (Département de la Loire, 1951), pp. XI, 3, 9, 12, 16, 19, 21, 29, 31, and *passim*.

69. Bossy, *Christianity*, pp. 64–6; R.I. Moore, 'Family, community and cult on the eve of the Gregorian Reform', *Transactions of the Royal Historical Society*, 5th series, vol. 30 (1980), pp. 64–9.

70. *The Canterbury Tales by Geoffrey Chaucer*, N.F. Blake (ed.) (Edward Arnold, London, 1980), pp. 42–3, 51–3.

71. *Butler's lives of the saints*, Herbert Thurston, S.J., and Donald Attwater (eds) (4 vols, Burns & Oates, London, 1956), vol. 4, p. 24.

72. Rosalind B. Brooke, *The coming of the friars* (Historical Problems: Studies and Documents, ed. G.R. Elton, no. 24, Allen & Unwin, London, Barnes & Noble, New York, 1975), p. 204.

73. *The Westminster Chronicle 1381–1394* (L.C. Hector and Barbara F. Harvey, eds and trans., Oxford University Press, Oxford, 1982), p. 15; Charles Oman, *The Great Revolt of 1381* (Oxford University Press, Oxford, 1906, cited here in the new edition, with introduction and notes by E.B. Fryde, Oxford University Press, Oxford, 1969), p. 12. For a comparison of Ball and Müntzer, see M.M. Smirin, *Die VolksReformation des Thomas Müntzer und der Grosse Bauernkrieg* (Dietz Verlag, Berlin, 1956), pp. 322–3. For the social radicalism of Hus, and the more intense radicalism of Želivský, see their sermons in Josef Macek, *The Hussite movement in Bohemia* (trans. Vilem Fried and Ian Milner, Lawrence & Wishart, London, 1965), pp. 93–5.

74. Benjamin Z. Kedar, *Merchants in crisis. Genoese and Venetian men of affairs and the fourteenth century depression* (Yale University Press, New Haven, Connecticut, and London, 1976), pp. 81–90 and ch. 5. See also William J. Bouwsma, 'Anxiety and the formation of early modern culture' in Barbara C. Malament (ed.), *After the Reformation. Essays in honour of J.H. Hexter* (Manchester University Press, Manchester, 1980), pp. 215, 246.

75. Murray, *Reason and society*, pp. 90–4.

76. Leon Battista Alberti, *I libri della famiglia*, Ruggerio Romano and Alberto Tenenti (eds) (Giulio Einaudi, Turin, 1972), pp. 14, 249 and *passim*. For Alberti, see *Dizionario biografico degli Italiani* (in progress, Instituto della Enciclopedia Italiano, Rome, 1960–), vol. 1, pp. 702, 713.

77. Guido Ruggerio, *Violence in early Renaissance Venice* (Crime, Law and Deviance Series, Rutgers University Press, New Brunswick, New Jersey, 1980), ch. V.

78. Koenigsberger, 'Statecraft of Philip II', p. 11.

79. Murray, *Reason and society*, p. 1; Fritz Rörig, *The medieval town* (trans. Don Bryant, Batsford, London, 1967), p. 115.

80. Eric Cochrane, *Florence in the forgotten centuries 1527–1800* (University of Chicago Press, Chicago, Illinois, 1973), p. 14.

81. Murray, *Reason and society*, pp. 132–6.

82. From Machiavelli's comedy, *Clizia* in *The literary works of Machiavelli*, J.R. Hale (ed. and trans.) (Oxford University Press, London, 1961), pp. 84-5.

83. Max Weber, *The city* (ed. and trans. Don Martindale and Gertrud Neuwirth, Free Press, New York, 1958, cited here in the paperback edition by Collier-Macmillan, London, and The Free Press, New York, 1966), pp. 192-5.

84. For examples of civic restraints on the operation of the Inquisition, see: Henry Charles Lea, *A history of the Inquisition in the Middle Ages* (3 vols, Harper & Brothers, New York, 1888-90, cited here in the re-issue by Russell & Russell, New York, 1955), vol. I, p. 384, vol. II, pp. 249-53, vol. III, p. 195; also A.S. Turberville, *Mediaeval heresy and the Inquisition* (George Allen & Unwin, London, 1920, cited here in the reprint by Archon Books, London, and Hamden, Connecticut, 1964), pp. 169-70; see also Brian Pullan, *Rich and poor in Renaissance Venice: the social institutions of a Catholic state to 1620* (Blackwell, Oxford, 1971), pp. 44-5. For control of the Church by city states in Germany, see, for example, A.G. Dickens, *The German nation and Martin Luther* (Edward Arnold, London, 1974), p. 147.

85. Ibid., p. 138.

86. Claire Cross, 'The development of Protestantism in Leeds and Hull 1520-1640: the evidence from wills', *Northern History*, vol. 18, (1982), pp. 230-8.

87. Robert Muchembled, 'Lay judges and the acculturation of the masses (France and the Low Countries, sixteenth to eighteenth centuries)' in Kaspar von Greyerz (ed.), *Religion and society in early modern Europe* (The German Historical Institute/George Allen & Unwin, London, 1984), pp. 56-65.

88. Pullan, *Rich and poor*, ch. 4.

89. James Campbell, *Norwich* (Scolar Press, and the Historic Towns Trust, London, 1975), p. 22.

90. For example, James Parkes, *The Jew in the medieval community. A study of his political and economic situation* (Soncino Press, London, 1938), ch. 3; Jeremy Cohen, *The friars and the Jews. The evolution of medieval anti-Judaism* (Cornell University Press, Ithaca, New York, and London), pp. 238-9.

91. G. S. Holmes, 'The Sacheverell Riots', *Past and Present*, vol. 72 (1976), pp. 63-4; G. Rudé, *The crowd in history. A study of popular disturbances in France and England 1730-1848* (New Dimensions in History, John Wiley, London, 1964), pp. 62-3, 138.

92. Albert Soman (ed.), *The massacre of St. Bartholomew. Reappraisals and documents* (Nijhof, The Hague, 1974), pp. 4-5.

93. Hanawalt, *Crime in East Anglia*, pp. 12-14.

94. *New Catholic Encyclopedia* (17 vols, McGraw-Hill, New York, 1967), vol. XIV, p. 8.

95. Braudel, *Civilisation and capitalism*, pp. 504, 532.

96. Bronislaw Geremek, *Truands et misérables dans l'Europe moderne* (1350-1660) (Gallimard-Juillard, Paris, 1980), *passim*.

97. Ibid., pp. 29, 30-2, 52.

98. Ibid., pp. 29, 26-7, 52.

99. Ibid., pp. 23, 29, 30-2, 25, 50, 53.

100. Ibid., pp. 23, 33, 52.

101. Ibid., pp. 23, 33, 49, 50, 52, 30-2

102. For example, *The life of Lazarillo de Tormes. His fortunes and adversities* (trans. W.S. Merwin, Peter Smith, Gloucester, Massachusetts, 1970), *passim*.

103. Geremek, *Truands*, pp. 29, 50, 24, 29.

104. Ibid., pp. 33, 29.

105. Ibid., pp. 33, 39, 49, 24, 52, 53, 26–7.

106. Ibid., pp. 51, 52, 41.

107. Weber, *The city*, p. 183; Geremek, *Truands*, p. 39.

108. Ibid., pp. 23, 33, 50.

3

Language and Action in Peasant Revolts

In this chapter we shall be preoccupied with Europe's peasants, their assumptions and particularly their protest movements. We shall be dealing with peasants over great periods of time and distance, in which many generalisations will be subject to major exceptions. Having said that, the case of Germany, in its greatest peasant revolt, will provide a focus enabling us to anchor our generalisations. In the first place, we shall consider what non-peasant society in later medieval and early modern Europe thought of peasants, especially from the point of view of whether or not peasants could be considered capable of articulating grievances and of organisation. We shall find that there were two conflicting attitudes on the part of non-peasants towards peasants; by some, peasants were seen as mutely incapable of anything but field work, and by others viewed as being maliciously cunning. From the point of view of our own subject, it is quite important to establish the capacity of peasants for thought, expression and action on their own behalf, and we certainly need to dismiss the myth of the outside agitator inciting peasants to revolt. We shall find that peasants did indeed have their ideologues — often dissident priests — and their organisers, but that the stimuli for their protests lay in their own consciousness and culture, through whatever influences that consciousness had developed. Amongst the features of peasant consciousness and culture were an inherent collectivism and a fundamental conservatism, typically focusing on kings as secular redeemers. We shall include in our discussion peasant religion, especially as manifested in confidence about the material help available from powerful sacred figures, notably Mary in pre-Reformation Europe. In reviewing some features of popular culture, we shall consider how it yielded the attitudes, forms of expression, symbols, and times, seasons and rallying points for mass action. Amongst the traits of mass protest to be investigated are violence, carnivalesque themes, organisation and armaments. Finally in this chapter we shall contrast a model of conservative peasant protest with one of radical insurgency and see if we can account for the difference.

Before going into peasants' own attitudes, we might begin by looking at attitudes towards peasants, which are almost necessarily those of articulate elites, writers and artists. In the first place we might be struck by how little the peasant features in artistic and literary depictions, considering that peasants made up the over-whelming majority of the European populations. There are some medieval portrayals of peasants, often used to deck out scenes of the year's cycle and so on. Such details as we can pick out include the changelessness of the costume of the northern European peas-ant over centuries in which the fashions of elites underwent many changes. Even in the early sixteenth century, peasants could be depicted wearing the long hair and beards, and short tunic and hose of Germanic forebears.[1]

When we come to Brueghel's much more painstakingly observed Flemish peasants, however, they seem to have caught up with fashion and are wearing styles that recognisably belong to the second half of the sixteenth century — though without the upper-class decora-tions, such as ruffs, that made it impossible, and were designed to show that it was impossible, to do manual work. Brueghel's port-raits, initiating a Netherlands genre, are the most detailed and plen-tiful that we have of the mass of pre-industrial rural Europeans, so it is worth dwelling on them for a moment. It may indeed be that Brueghel's peasant series exemplifies some resentment felt by townsmen for farmers doing well in a time of high food prices. Cer-tainly Brueghel's peasants are far from starving and often they are shown gathering (as well as eating) plentiful and varied food and drinking deeply.[2] In work or play, they are never alone — a telling, if unconscious, appreciation of the incessantly communal nature of village life. Unlike the emaciated, tax-ridden farmers of Bour-bon France,[3] Brueghel's peasants are stocky and well-muscled. They have coarse features, homemade haircuts and faces that are, at least in many cases, undeniably vacuous.

It is possible, then, that Brueghel shared the traditional view of the peasant's basic stupidity. 'They stand', wrote an Italian observer, 'the week long in the fields without opening their mouths except to the animals . . . [they are] humble and gentle, with the good nature of the plough, and hoe and spade.'[4] It followed from this patronising analysis that the docile peasant was no more capable of insurrection than a spade, and that if protests were voiced they must be the work of outside agitators, inciting the fundamentally good-natured peasants. Such a view can be seen in the House of Commons Petition Against Rebellious Villeins, 1377;[5] in this, the gentry landlords dominant in the Commons complained of 'counsellors, procurers, maintainers and abettors' who seduced the peasants into withdrawing labour services.

It is indeed probable that peasants hired legal counsel to draft their grievances in proper form, but that is an entirely different thing from being led on by outside agitators. We could surely apply to many, if not most, peasant protests and insurrections what Professor Dobson writes of a group of Essex petitioners in the early fourteenth century: 'a group of peasants fully conscious of their common interests and remarkably skilled in presenting their grievances in an articulate legal form'.[6] Indeed, many contemporaries refused to believe that peasants were stupid. Alberti, for instance, had no illusions about peasant blockheads. Thus he wrote:

> It is incredible how malicious are these ploughmen who have grown up amongst clods. Their whole study is devoted to diddling you, but they never let themselves be caught out in anything. If they do make a mistake, it's to their own advantage; they'll try everything to get hold of your property . . .[7]

Alberti's words, then, form a rueful tribute to the peasant's acumen. Indeed, though the peasant was shut out from the higher culture, he was not necessarily without education. There was often some literacy. Waldensian heretics knew passages of the Bible in the vernacular and English rustic Lollards owned, or had memorised, tracts of Scripture.[8]

There was a popular culture of great richness whose main medium was speech. Proverbs, those conserved droplets of ancestral sagacity, belonged peculiarly to the peasants.[9] Stories took up much of their time and for the peasants of Montaillou conversation was their chief recreation and cultural activity. Verbal and argumentative aptitude, familiarity with custom, attention to details and knowledge of rights can be read into manifestos from various peasant revolts. Those manifestos also show the limitations of the peasant outlook — the intense localism, the concern with minutiae that could become trivial. Perhaps rhetoric and abstract theorising were best supplied by townsmen, such as the editors of the Twelve

Articles of Memmingen, Schappeler and Lotzer. It was the essential practicality of the archetypal peasant, his proverbial common sense, that led to his acceptance at certain times, such as the German Reformation, as the personification of the wisdom of the ordinary man.

All in all, the peasant could not be dismissed as a mere beast of burden, mute and tractable. J.R. Hale writes of 'a tenacious bloody-mindedness of which governments and would-be improving landlords had to take account . . . The voice [of the peasant] is violent, litigious . . .'. Professor Hale goes on to describe the peasant's 'endurance, his ability to work with others, his urge to collect land and stock his own . . .', and he concludes with a tribute to the typical peasant's 'generosity and humour'.[10]

Let us isolate from Hale's list of characteristics the peasant's 'ability to work with others'. This was built into the nature of peasant agriculture and technology, or lack of technology. It probably endowed the peasant with a basically communal rather than individualistic approach to life. This must not be sentimentalised: there was obviously fierce rivalry between households and much striving for personal betterment. In any case, if communal instincts preponderated in villages, they were dictated by the harsh self-preservation of the pack. Yet undoubtedly the sense of community identity existed, and it was celebrated in the congregational worship of country churches and marked in the fraternal invocations of their liturgies.[11] It was a feature of European village life both before and after the Reformation. The group mentality — the lack of individual consciousness — is revealed in the peasants of a village in the Lutheran duchy of Pomerania who formulated their doctrinal beliefs in the terms used by their leading farmer: 'I believe what Hans Hille believes.'[12]

The need constantly to get agreement on such things as the right times for ploughing and sowing dictated a strong consultative instinct, still detected by some observers of the behaviour of modern Russians, legatees of what was until recently the most overwhelmingly peasant society in Europe and western Asia.[13] In German villages before the sixteenth century justice seems to have been implemented consultatively, so that the imposition of law from outside became a major grievance of the Peasants' Revolt period.[14] When law and work — even the communal raising of houses in the English half-timber districts — were collective, a basis existed for collective politicisation.

It has already been hinted that peasants tended to think in a conservative (as well as a collective) way. As we shall see, not all plebeian or peasant rebellion was conservative in inspiration, but we are concerned for the moment with the origins of highly traditionalist attitudes in the majority of settled peasants. The way farming was conducted, by the next generation copying parents, was the primary factor in producing attitudes that resisted change. In seventeenth-century England, Gervase Markham wrote contemptuously of the countryman 'who only knoweth how to do his labour, but cannot give a reason why . . . more than the instruction of his parents or the custom of the country'; and John Aubrey commented that 'Even to attempt an improvement in husbandry, though it succeeded with profit, was looked upon with an ill eye'.[15] In fourteenth-century English peasant protests, lists of complaints took their stand on ancient custom and appealed to traditional sources such as Domesday Book and Magna Carta,[16] and it was the introduction of *new* forms of taxation — the Poll Tax — which was the immediate cause of the English Peasants' Revolt of 1381.

In the German Peasants' Revolt it was the novel demand of the Countess of Stühlingen that the peasants collect snail shells (apparently for her embroidery work) that pushed them over the brink into revolt. To generalise, then, we could say that attempts to alter the ground rules of village work and justice, dues, taxes and labour services, or sometimes religious innovation (especially in Tudor England) could ignite peasant conservatism into violent protest. In the field of law, in particular, an area in which change could be particularly injurious to peasants, they tended to take refuge in static concepts, such as the 'good old law' of custom — generally a set of rights and duties which they understood and over which they could exercise some control. The 'good old law' could be, and was, easily equated with God's law. 'Old law' and 'God's law' were frequently wedded to respect for kingship in a view of the social order that was essentially static.

In the course of the Middle Ages, peasant attitudes across Europe, probably through the preaching and teaching of the Church, seem to have become impregnated with the ideal of the three interdependent estates of society, each with its rights and duties. At the pinnacle of the social pyramid was the king. Popular fantasy clearly regarded kings as omnicompetent secular messiahs and especially as guardians of equitable law. The facts and the stories about archetypal kings — for instance the German Emperors Frederick I and II — created the most powerful political myth in European history, that of kingship. Charlemagne was a pattern for all kings, and great as he no doubt was, his greatness was magnified by legends of his total invincibility and of his leading a crusade in the Holy Land.[17] In England Henry II was reputed to be a king pre-eminent in justice; he was also vigorous and incessantly active, able simultaneously to conduct government business and hear Mass, the latter a reflection of the piety that was expected of kings and which, in Henry's case, was only enhanced after his murder of Becket.[18] In France the conceptual legacy of Charlemagne continued through Louis IX, himself becoming a pattern for kings. Louis's care for justice in particular strengthened the ideal of the king as being almost Christlike in his pastoral care of his subjects. The poet Ronsard echoed this idea in the sixteenth century, at a time when many Frenchmen felt that only forceful kingship could rescue the country from chaos: 'Les roys et les pasteurs ont le mesme estat de vivre.'[19]

The feats of great kings — their victories, their thirsts for justice — added, or should have added, layer by layer to the accumulating popular prestige of kingship. The question is, how do we know that the regalist propaganda developed by royal biographers, epic poets and various other publicists actually did its job and influenced the popular, and in particular the peasant imagination. Apart from knowing of kingship, what did common people know of kings, past and present, and what efforts, and how successful, were made to convey images of rulers to a mass public? In the first place, we have insights into the grip that monarchy exercised over the medieval and early modern popular imagination from peasant action and slogans. In France, the removal of the king, or his rumoured absence, was greeted with mass grief. The rising of the Pastoureux in 1251 and the Jacquerie in 1358 were provoked by captures, in the first instance imagined, in the second real, of kings of France. In England, the absence and then the captivity of Richard I are the backdrop for the activities of the rebel-outlaw Robin Hood, the righter of wrongs in the king's stead; in England, too, the slogan of the 1381 Revolt was 'King Richard and the true commons'.

One might add that according to popular expectations of kingship, the king ought to be of mature years — a point illustrated not only by the English rising of 1381 but also by two serious risings in 1549 during the minority of Edward VI. As we have seen, the king was also expected to be generally present in the realm, conceivably all the more so as the Crusade lost some of its allure before the end of the Middle Ages. The Habsburg rulers who dominated the sixteenth century, Charles V and Philip II, faced serious trouble in various of their dependencies because they could not, or would not, be on hand in those territories. The desire to have the king on hand is seen in its most acute form in attempts to seize his person, often out of the hands of wicked advisers or so as to set him right on real conditions as they were. It is generally true that medieval and early modern people were deeply concerned with securing the possession of important persons, dead or alive: hence the insatiable quest for relics and saints' bodies, and hence also the urgent attempts to regain the persons of kings after their capture in battle, as with John II of France after Poitiers. The wish to secure the person of the king for the people underlay the initial aims of Joan of Arc and of the English peasant insurgents of 1381: 'they would never let him loose for any consideration but would take him round with them through all England . . . and they would make him grant all their demands . . .'.[20] Perhaps enough has now been said to make the point that before the end of the Middle Ages, large parts of the European masses had been securely converted to the political religion of monarchy.

A related question remains to be addressed — that of what common people knew of politics and political personages, above all of kings. In England in 1376 the Commons expressed a wide-ranging protest against government mis-management at home and abroad and this, as Professor Dobson writes, 'undoubtedly encouraged the rebels to react even more violently five years later'.[21] Here Professor Dobson quite rightly assumes a transfer of political information from 'elite political culture' to 'popular political culture'. We might, though, explore further what access common people, those without acknowledged political rights, had to political information in general, and information about their rulers in particular.

On the face of it, the situation was not promising. Even had there been extensive literacy, newspapers did not get going until the seventeenth century, partly because of deliberate rationing of public information. English governments seem to have been particularly close-lipped. Indeed, we might be astonished at the way Tudor governments launched radical new departures in policy without any preparation whatsoever of public opinion. This was the case, for instance, with the issue of a new, quasi-Protestant prayer book in 1549 — a novel liturgy whose purpose the government took no trouble to explain, though in a highly sensitive area where habit dictates acceptance.[22] Tudor governments did not like discussion, least of all in matters of religion, where they made the most bewildering changes of any contemporaneous European state. In 1545

Henry VIII bewailed the fact that religion was being discussed at all, and in 1576 his daughter Elizabeth suppressed those doctrinal seminars, the Prophesyings.[23] English government was closed government, and alehouses were particularly suspect because they generated political discussion. However, the suppression of information created its own problems, notably those engendered by rumour: speculation was a major factor behind the Pilgrimage of Grace.[24]

Government suspicion apart, there were, of course, acute practical difficulties in distributing up-to-date news. A case of delayed news comes from the German *Bundschuh* period when a group of insurgents wishing to display their loyalty to Church and state are depicted exhibiting the coat of arms of a pope who had died and already been succeeded.[25] Yet whatever delays and shortages there were, political news *was* available and emanated in the first instance from towns and cities. Even in these favoured locations, the news could be stale, at least by our standards of instantaneous accuracy. For instance, it has been rightly pointed out that the rising in Naples in 1585 was encouraged by news of the difficulties that the Spanish crown was having in the Netherlands.[26] This might appear to be a good example of the urban populace's access to current affairs bulletins from distant parts — until we recall that in 1585 the Spanish recovery in the Netherlands was proceeding with unusual success, including the recovery of Antwerp. Perhaps better instances of the availability of news in cities comes from the Netherlands itself, where well-informed gossip supplied the market and provided highly subversive alternatives to official statements. When, for instance, Philip II's hated minister Cardinal Granvelle was dismissed in 1564, the regime tried to save face by announcing that the Cardinal had had to leave, *sine die*, to visit an ageing parent. The Brussels wits were not taken in: the sign 'house for sale' posted on the Cardinal's quarters showed an accurate realisation that the king's agent had been humiliatingly recalled.[27]

So much, then, for the availability in cities of political news, much of it certainly unapproved. We can, of course, assume the distribution of news, as of all other commodities, from town to country. Yet though states obviously did nothing to facilitate news that put government in a bad light, much energy was given to broadcasting favourable propaganda, and especially images of kings and queens. Coins, one of the oldest, remained one of the most effective ways of circulating portraits, more or less glamorised, along with the names and titles of rulers throughout their realms. Regal names were particularly attached to coins of the highest value, such as the French *Louis d'or* or the Austrian Maria Theresa *Thaler*, thus cementing an association between regality and the highest good. And if coins are portraits, portraits proper, especially with the advent of printing, could be produced and distributed in their own right as royal information and propaganda. Combining the themes of majesty and religion, and perhaps designed to correct an unfavourable public image of the monarch, the frontispiece of Henry VIII's Great Bible, ordered to be placed in parish churches, showed the king, at the head of the hierarchy of the realm, distributing the Scripture to a suitably grateful populace: 'God Save the Kynge' is the reaction, not entirely inappropriate, to this gift of God's word.[28]

Printed ballads conveyed even more enticing, even more intimate, insights into the doings of royal personages. A German *Volkslied* (a popular ballad) of 1491 makes available to a mass audience the details of the wooing by Emperor Maximilian of a Breton princess. The translation of this extended jingle by Professor Strauss perfectly captures the crashing awfulness of its rhyme scheme, and also the smirking prurience of its sexual innuendo. The Emperor commissions a knight to make his marriage by proxy:

> King Maximilian, with delight,
> Summoned a well-born, noble knight
> Of stainless honour, untouched by blame
> Herr Wolf von Bolheim was his name,
> And sent him off on embassy
> To claim his bride in Brittany,
> And, in King Maximilian's stead,
> In Church and in the marriage bed,
> Accomplish with the least delay
> The marriage, as is princes' way.[29]

Clearly, royalist soft-pornography has a long, if not honourable ancestry. However, ballads like *The Lady from Brittany* undoubtedly helped to convey to mass audiences impressions of kings and other rulers as actual people, well-known in some of the most intimate details of their private lives. Stories about kings thus entered the popular consciousness on all levels. One of the most widespread of such tales — an almost exclusively fictional genre, though — concerns the king in disguise who meets his subjects, sometimes leaving them a coin or other token without their knowing his identity. He is thereby able to hear their views without inhibition on their part:

Shakespeare uses the form in *Henry V*, and there are many other versions. The prominent place of kings and queens in the popular consciousness, sustained by some deliberate and forceful image projection, reflected hopes that there were at the head of human society benign and powerful figures, well disposed to the common people.

There was in pre-Reformation Europe and in those parts of Europe that remained Catholic throughout and after the Reformation another, indeed a supreme, queenly figure. She is mentioned and invoked in *The Lady from Brittany*, which appeals frequently to 'Mary, Queen of Heaven':

> Ave regina caelorum,
> O mater regina angelorum.
> Hail, queen of the heavens
> O Mother queen of the angels.[30]

Just as the vision of kings as familiar figures and as founts of justice was a factor helping to make much popular protest conventional rather than radical in its political character, so the cult of Mary, as a mother of earthly mercy, helped predispose many of Europe's masses to a conservative — specifically, a Catholic — viewpoint in religion. One says this advisedly, knowing, for instance, that in the Netherlands in the iconoclastic riots of 1566 images of Mary were prime targets for crowd violence. Yet in those riots the way Mary was addressed by name leads one to suspect that the crowd retained more than a trace of the ancestral belief that images of the Virgin were, or should be, powerful. If, for example, some participants in image-breaking riots were levelling a score against Mary for failing to do anything about conditions in the Netherlands in a time of acute distress, then this could be seen as a kind of inverted tribute to Mary's power. For Mary combined vast power with limitless benevolence, and the first fact to note about Mary in the Middle Ages is that she was viewed as a real and present figure — quite as real as any 'actual' ruler.

Late medieval Europe developed to a high degree a patronal system in which powerful men, in return for submission, extended protection through life's many perils. The Church's galaxy of saints mirrored the secular patronage networks. One needed vitally such celestial patrons, just as much as, if not more than, one needed terrestrial protectors. There was to begin with one's guardian angel, a personally assigned monitor. In addition, one might adopt saintly patrons according to one's name (the fashion of conferring saints' names at baptism grew markedly in the late Middle Ages), or according to the patronal saint of one's parish or of one's craft.[31] All saints were in a favourable position to intercede with God on behalf of a petitioner and their role paralleled that of addressing the king through some powerful noble or favourite.

No saint was nearer to God, especially through His son, than Mary, acclaimed in fact by the medieval Church as 'mother of God'. Using this concept, the Church also elaborated the Scripture's 'angelic salutation', the *Ave Maria* or 'Hail Mary' into a prayer begging the aid of Mary at the moment of supreme crisis: '*Sancta Maria* . . . Holy Mary, Mother of God, pray for us sinners now and at the hour of our death.' Given the medieval horror at the prospect of death unprepared for, but in view also of the likelihood, at least for many, of more or less sudden death, especially from plague, this prayer offered the most profound consolation. It was woven into a semi-meditative catena, the Rosary, which enjoyed a vast popularity in late medieval Europe.[32] So popular was the *Ave Maria* itself that its duration became a recognised way of measuring a brief space of time.[33]

The *Ave Maria*'s themes of salutation and petition are also seen in the prayer authored by Adhemar de Monteil (d. 1098) and St Bernard (d. 1153): '*Salve Regina* . . . Hail, Holy Queen, Mother of Mercy . . .'. This prayer, a classic of supplication, was incorporated into the afternoon prayer of vespers, in which an earlier composition, *Alma Redemptoris Mater*, by Hermannus Contractus (d. 1054) asked Mary to 'hear thy people's cry'. In anthems such as these the constant theme was the intercession of the Virgin Mary and her queenly power. Additional prayers included the *Regina Coeli* which again celebrated Mary's queenship and her mediatory powers, the *Memorare* of St Bernard — perhaps the high point of the patronal theme, the Litany of the Blessed Virgin, which emphasised Mary's influence (*virgo potens*), and the *Angelus*, a prayer which, again, was used to mark off time, and which particularly stressed Mary's motherhood of God. There is, however, a further element in the 'personality' of Mary, and it comes in one of the prayers alluded to above, the litany. Here Mary is addressed, among other titles, as *Consolatrix afflictorum*, 'comfort of the afflicted'.

This was indeed a major part of Mary's role, but its full poetry comes out when we realise that she was the object as well as the source of compassion. This is developed in the hymn, possibly by Pope Innocent III, which was incorporated in the Stations of the Cross, popularised by the Franciscan Order. This hymn, *Stabat Mater dolorosa* — the sorrowful mother standing at the Cross — powerfully evoked the agony of the sorrowing mother of the Crucified.[34] In the visual arts the same note is struck by the *Pietà* scenes, including Bellini's and Michelangelo's versions, Brueghel's *Procession to Calvary*, Grünewald's *Isenheim Altarpiece*, which we will consider below, and Niccolò da Foligno's work which, as Berenson wrote, evokes 'frantic grief'.[35]

Mary was both powerful and vulnerable. In her weakness she was the natural friend of the friendless, though in her power as mediatrix she was in an unique position to aid her petitioners. The theologians helped create a devotional mood in which the prayerful and the distressed 'resorted' to Mary: for as the theologians emphasised the power and justice of God, so Mary assumed ever greater importance as intercessor for sinful man at the throne of the Father — a mother, and a queen too — averting the punishment due to sins. One would emphasise here the great power of Mary as queen. There may even have been some association of ideas as between royal ladies noted for their care of the poor, such as Elizabeth of Hungary and Margaret of Scotland, and Mary as queen and fount of mercy. There was a popular tradition, encapsulated in the story of Queen Philippa and the Burghers of Calais, of queens interceding for mercy from otherwise unrelenting kings.[36] God was of course a king and as such the well-spring of justice, the supreme judge. The theologians described God as both totally just *and* totally merciful, but many people, including for a time Martin Luther, could not reconcile this justice and mercy. The infinite justice of God meant above all His righteous punishment for sins, a justice that perhaps was only to be moderated by the mercy dispensed by Mary. This changing theological accent helps account for the vast popularity of Mary in pre-Reformation Europe.

Historians of the veneration of saints have traced a tendency for the local saints of the early Middle Ages to make way for the 'international' saints. Mary was both. She was, of course, queen of heaven, a role that was celebrated in feasts and in representations of her Assumption into heaven and her Coronation. As such, she was universal. She was also intensely local, markedly in Italy, where both the Sienese and the Milanese made her their own. In Naples, Mary's special role as '*speculum justitiae*', mirror of justice, is evident in the cult of the Virgin of the Carmine, the icon of the Masaniello revolt of 1647.[37] Of course we usually think of Rome as a city dedicated to St Peter, but Mary was reverenced in the city's and Christendom's mother church, Santa Maria Maggiore, a basilica

founded, according to legend, on the precise instructions of 'Our
Lady of the Snows'. Outside Italy, and in northern Europe, the
English had a strong cult of Mary, with their own Marian pilgrimage
centre at Walsingham; the freshly liquefied milk of Mary which
Erasmus, to his derision, was shown there may perhaps be regarded
as a slightly pathetic, and certainly coarse, version of the cult of
Mary as mother.[38] Whatever Erasmus thought of mariolatry in
England, his own Netherlands exhibited the Marian devotion to a
high degree, and sometimes in an intensely localised form. The
Black Madonna of Antwerp was the object of the most splendid
public devotion but was also, as we saw above, a prime target of
iconoclasts in 1566.[39] In France, localised cults of Mary are evident
in the capital's Notre-Dame de Paris and in the Madonna of Le
Puy, itself an echo of Poland's national Marian icon, the Madonna
of Czestochowa.[40] In Germany, Mary was considered almost as an
informal national patron saint, '*Illuminatrix*, hope of our nation'.[41]
Certainly Martin Luther preserved some at least of the medieval
German devotion to Mary.[42] We shall see that in Germany, Mary's
functions in delivering secular assistance were strongly magnified.
Her task of re-asserting social justice is seen in the propaganda of
the Drummer of Niklashausen in 1476, with his claim to derive an
economic programme of equality from an encounter with Mary.
Mary in fact had two related undertakings as far as fifteenth-century
Germans were concerned: to restore the *Reich*, and to dispense
justice. As the fifteenth-century grievance poem, *The insolence of
Ecclesiastical Princes*, put it,

O Mary, without stealth,
Virgin and Mother, see your people's plight;
Let this poor poem find favour in your sight,
And help restore the empire to its might.

Thus Mary would heal wounded national pride, and indeed
restore the *Reich* itself when its own leadership, especially in the weak
imperia of Sigismund, Frederick and Maximilian, was unable to solve
the country's problems. This was Mary as the proper patroness of
the holiest political organisation in Europe, the German *Reich*. The
other involvement of Mary in German life was the one already
touched upon, that of ironing out social inequality. Thus, when the
Bundschuh was organised in the Speyer district in 1502, there was
a requirement that 'those who joined their organisation must first
say five *paternosters* with the *Ave Maria*'.

There are several ways of interpreting this requirement: as a cloak of religious respectability, as an initiation rite, as a password, or as a version of small confessional penances, ensuring that the participants were guiltless. Principally, however, this was a straightforward dedication to Mary, source of justice. 'They chose Our Lady, the Virgin Mary, and St John as patron saints.'[43] This selection is seen in the banners of the *Bundschuh* which show Mary and St John standing below the Cross of Christ.[44] This arrangement of figures, one seen on rood screens of churches throughout Europe, is also found in Grünewald's 1505 *Isenheim Altarpiece*, painted in the period of the *Bundschuh's* foundation. Despite the conscious verbal Lutheran inspiration of the Peasants' Revolt, much of the iconography of the *Bundschuh* was thoroughly traditional, not least in its Marian preoccupations. In the Crucifixion scene represented in the *Isenheim Altarpiece* and in the *Bundschuh* banners, Christ conferred universal maternity — and hence solicitude — on Mary for the whole human race in the person of St John.[45] Because its assemblage of figures was also seen on the rood screens which in parish churches gave pictorial representation to the meaning of the Mass, the *Bundschuh* banner could also be read actually as an allusion *to* the Mass, which, as we saw in the last chapter, was regarded of being of limitless benefit to the living and the dead, both spiritually *and* socially.

The central figure in the Crucifixion scene referred to is, of course, Christ Himself, and for all our talk of Mary we should not forget that Christ was invoked in movements of popular protest and reform. The *Bundschuh* rebels in Speyer, for instance, prayed 'in memory of the five principal wounds of Jesus Christ so that God might grant success to their endeavours' — a theme also found in the English Catholic revolts of 1536–7 and 1549.[46] This devotion to the Five Wounds expresses a widespread late medieval pious appreciation of the humanity of Christ *per se* — something found in the song-cycle, later incorporated in Bach's Passion Chorale, in honour of the wounded physique of the Saviour.[47] However, this meditation on the reality of the sufferings of Christ in His Passion, brought to its highest point in the *Isenheim Altarpiece*, could make of Christ — *pauper, servus et humilis* — both the source and the object of pity, champion and epitome of the afflicted.

All flags and banners need to be read. Even the *use* of a flag may tell us something about the cause for which it was used — as the flag of the *Bundschuh* tells us that auxiliary *Landsknechte* brought their military habits and customs into the cause.[48] For all its use of

Christian symbols, the *Bundschuh*, a movement that took its name and its identity from its banner, used an emphatically non-religious — indeed an apparently prosaic, but for all that, complex — symbol, the *Bundschuh*, literally the laced boot. It was the *Bundschuh* symbol and name that gave continuity to otherwise fragmented regional risings over a period of some years. People spoke of an individual *Bundschuh*, but they also referred to the *Bundschuh*, the permanent, if underground, movement.

Commentators such as Adolf Laube have done much to explain the meaning of the *Bundschuh* as a symbol, though perhaps they have not stressed sufficiently the note of irony, similar to that evident in the designation 'Poor Konrad', in the choice of this particular distinctly un-romantic symbol. The *Bundschuh* from which the movement took its name was the heavy, functional farm boot, impervious to either glamour or fashion and designed to cope, like its wearer, with the mud of German fields. On the most obvious level, its adoption signalled that the movement which it symbolised was made up of peasants — peasants, we might go on to say, who had no aim of renouncing, but only of re-adjusting, their condition as small farmers. The note of humour is a little lost on us, unless we perhaps try to imagine a farm labourers' strike with a wellington boot as its logo. The humour is of the same essentially sixteenth-century kind as that of the rebels in the Netherlands Revolt who, being contemptuously dismissed as *gueux*, beggars, thereupon defiantly took not only the name but also the insignia and effects of beggars.[49]

The robust humour of the *Bundschuh* emblem was of course quickly seized upon by the movement's enemies so as to confirm a clownish image of the peasants, something we will discuss a little later. The symbol was chosen in the first place, however, above all as an expression of unity. *Bund* is the German for a league; in all depictions, the boot's laces which drew it together are prominently displayed. 'Tied boot' fails to express all the connotations of *Bundschuh*, and 'union boot' is clumsy, but beween them these English versions convey the shades of meaning of the original, which was designed above all to express the co-operation that the peasant needed in his everyday life and above all in his acts of resistance. Then, as an expression of the dignity of labour — of which Martin Luther made so much in his writings — the laced boot had the same kind of force as the hammer and sickle symbol in modern socialist movements. Was it possible that the *Bundschuh* even had a religious meaning? It was in fact in some representations placed at the foot of the Cross in the Crucifixion scenes mentioned earlier, thus expressing the kind of ideas, voiced in the English Kett's Rebellion of 1549, that the commons were free 'through Christ's blood shedding'.[50]

We have seen so far that the symbolism of peasant insurgency favoured images of the shedding of Christ's blood, for instance the Five Wounds in the English risings and the chalice of Christ's blood in the eucharist in the Hussite Reformation in fifteenth-century Bohemia. The connections are quite easy to understand: Christ's blood shed for the redemption of the world, peasant risings begun for the renewal of society . However, we turn now from examination of the visual symbols of peasant insurgency to the peasants' articulate expression of grievances, chiefly in written statements.

Firstly, we need to be aware of their formal conventions. We find that in popular rebellions as far afield as the German Peasants' Revolt and the English Pilgrimage of Grace, the participants commonly resorted to a familiar format, that of an itemised list of grievances and demands. A kind of legal or notarial form was often favoured, sometimes with the various clauses being introduced with the word 'item'. In some risings a definitive set of articles might be accompanied by sets of regional articles, but the serial form tended to persist throughout.[51] Such a form is found, of course, in outbreaks of baronial opposition, in parliamentary statutes and in grievance lists such as the *gravamina* of the German *Reichstag*.[52] The manifestos of peasant revolts often began with an explanatory preamble designed to win support, along with a concluding peroration.[53] They also tended to include a great deal of detailed information, since the proclaimed purpose of many revolts was to describe actual conditions in the countryside. There also tends to be a convention of placing religious material first, as in the articles of the Pilgrimage of Grace.[54] This may be the outcome of pious convention or it may be a reflection of the actual order of priorities existing in the minds of participants.

In terms of content, by carefully selecting manifestos an historian could prove with equal assurance widely different propositions about peasant revolts. Thus, for example, an historian wishing to show that popular revolts were concerned with messianist rejection of existing society would produce sets of articles from the radical Taborite wing of the Hussite Reformation in Bohemia, whereas someone chiefly concerned to stress, as we have so far been doing in this chapter, the relative conservatism of peasant revolts, would concentrate on the main manifestos of the German Peasants' Revolt. Since for the time being I wish to emphasise this conservatism, I shall use the grievance lists of the German Peasants' Revolt to illustrate its essential moderation. Having said that, one must also realise that the German Peasants' Revolt itself had an important revolutionary and visionary element. On its broadest front, though, it was concerned with restoring German society without drastically altering, and certainly without destroying it. Was this because it was dominated by substantial villagers — village honourables — with a stake in the existing system?[55]

The classic statement of conservatism in the German Peasants' Revolt, and indeed its classic statement of purpose, is the document known as the Twelve Articles of Memmingen. Significantly, the Twelve Articles appeared on the agenda of the *Reichstag* meeting at Speyer in 1526, and Blickle shows how they brought into the cause all of the main elements of German life, not only peasants.[56] Indeed the Articles were intended as a manifesto for a rising of the whole nation. They were fully in line, in form and content, with the nationalist protests of the *Reichstag*, denouncing foreign, usually Roman, exploitation of Germans. It is clear that the whole of Germany was groaning under a sense of grievance and reform in the early sixteenth century.[57] It is also clear that the great mass of Germans was enlisted in the early stages of Martin Luther's calls for the renewal of the Church and the *Reich*.[58] The Twelve Articles have to be seen as part of these stirrings of reform, but also as part of an atttempt to maintain the unity of Germans as a people under protest. Thus, although in word and deed the Peasants' Revolt inevitably attacked nobles, it also invited them to participate, but since villains had to be found, the clergy was singled out, so that, as Dr Cohn shows, the German Peasants' Revolt was very much an anti-clerical revolt.[59] The Twelve Articles of Memmingen envisaged the whole *Reich* as a huge *Gemeinde*, a village assembly in which agreement was won through negotiation and compromise.

The articles therefore open with a greeting, closely modelled on St Paul's salutation to churches: 'Peace and the grace of God through Christ'.[60] This certainly reflects the strong Lutheran orientation to St Paul on the part of the Articles' editors, but this Pauline greeting is best seen as an eucharistic call to peace in a Christian congregation: the German nation as a *Gemeinde* in the sense of the word as parish. After an opening reference to Christ, the Articles turn to his antithesis, Antichrist. The great utility of this well-worn symbol was his combination of limitless malevolence with imprecision. When the Memmingen Articles hit out at 'many Antichrists', no element in German society — neither the bankers, princes, nobles, nor even the clerics — is mentioned by name or specifically excluded from the community of the nation. There was however a medieval heretical tradition, much used in the propaganda of the German Reformation, in which the pope and his minions — the enemy without — was the Antichrist.[61]

In point of fact the Memmingen Articles are more concerned with Christ than with Antichrist, and Christ at the expense of the now partially dethroned patroness of the German peasants, Mary. If Mary had occupied a throne of mercy because her son had sat in a seat of judgement, the Memmingen Articles now present Christ as the ultimate source of mercy and above all of concord: 'the promised Messiah, whose Word and life teach nothing but love, peace, patience and concord, so that all who believe in this Christ become loving, peaceful and of one mind'. Here Christ himself underwrites one of the strongest features in the mental make-up of peasants, the quest for concord.

There was a divisive potential — the clear Lutheran inspiration of the Articles. Even this, though, sustains the peasants' idealisation of community, through working on an idea of Martin Luther's — the congregational election of pastors — to evoke an idyll of the village community at one: 'it is the will and intention of us all . . . full authority for the whole community itself to elect and choose a pastor . . . '. Each of these collectivities was envisaged as united around its 'leader and pastor'.

The corporate spirit of village democracy (much modified in practice, however, by the leadership of village notables) breathes through the proposals of the Twelve Articles on ecclesiastical finance. Church wardens 'whom the whole community appoints' would pay over to priests, 'who will be elected by the whole community', a stipend 'according to the judgement of the whole community'. The procedure suggests not so much majority voting as carefully considered solutions arrived at when all were agreed, or at least placated. The actual subject of the clause in question — a lengthy one — on the tithe issue seeks to resolve, equitably and sensibly, one of the most painful problems in European agrarian history.[62] There are proposals for making sure that the minister, who is envisaged as a hard-working social worker and village guru, receives a just maintenance, and that any surplus remaining should be used for poor relief, federal taxation and the fiscal exemption of the poor.

If some of these ideas seem to be borrowed from Lutheran civics, especially the notion of a community chest, they are surely inoffensive, indeed laudable, tied up as they are with concepts of social fairness and the proper responsibilities of the subject. Moderation shines through in the consideration given to the rights of all claimants and there is a well-designed procedure for meeting the demands of the impropriators of tithes. All this sweetness and light, surely calculated to win maximum support, encountered occasional hurdles, especially over the notorious obstinacy of the German peasant. The iniquitous lesser tithe, for instance, a niggling levy on livestock, was brusquely dismissed: 'We will not render it any longer'. The German Peasants' Revolt was after all a revolt, not a debate. Nor, even in the moderation of the Twelve Articles, was a more visionary note absent, and the Garden of Eden myth of primitive equality re-surfaced in 'the Lord God created cattle for the free use of man . . . '.

Such a note is not fully representative of the Articles: for instance, the attack on the system — wasteful, degrading and vexatious — of serfdom invokes not Eden, but Martin Luther's celebrated 1520 pamphlet, *On the liberty of a Christian*. In this work, Luther, and following him, article three of the Memmingen Articles, envisaged a highly responsible, collective and non-individualistic use of freedom, won through the voluntary surrender of liberty in favour of service to the entire community.[63]

The Lutheran inspiration is never entirely absent from the Memmingen Articles, though as we get half way through them, and the quasi-religious rhetoric gives way to detailed agrarian grievances, the voice of the exasperated is heard more and more stridently: 'in the future we shall not allow a lord to oppress us further.' Since these articles as a whole emerged out of a mass meeting, we are entitled to see in them several, and possibly conflicting, voices. It has already been suggested that visions of a primitive paradise allowed for more radical possibilities of action than did the idea of preserving the *status quo* from attack or restoring a *status quo* but recently prevalent. In the German Peasants' Revolt the difference between revolution and conservation turns on another difference, as to whether the ideal situation for peasants existed in the primitive paradise, in the here-and-now, or in yesteryear. The Twelve Articles actually contain the ambivalence. References to the primitive utopia — a nostalgic eschatology — are certainly present, as in the strong egalitarian flavour of 'when the Lord God created man, He gave him dominion over all animals, over the birds of the air and over the fish of the water'. To set alongside this heady vision, we have the focus of basic conservatives on the areas in which the position of the peasants was under attack: the privatising of timber supplies in what was very much a wood-using and wood-burning society; new and inconvenient labour services and new rent levels; enclosure of common arable. All these things were evil usages because they were new, not so much because they broke with the rules of the Garden of Eden but because they broke with the customs of yesteryear, or of the here-and-now. Günther Franz usefully distinguished between concepts of divine and ancient law in the German Peasants' Revolt,[64] but it is also clear from the Twelve Articles that the peasants themselves did not distinguish too clearly between old law and God's law, and that in fact there was in their view a timeless way of doing things that was also of divine institution: as they themselves put it, 'according as our forefathers performed their services according to the tenor of the Word of God'.

There were no barons in the Garden of Eden, but the Twelve Articles did not go back as far as Eden in its nostalgia for a rural world of harmony between lords and peasants — to the extent that lords were invited to join in the Revolt. It would be well to try to relate the conservatism of the Twelve Articles to the 'condition' of the German peasant — if we could generalise at all about the material condition of so many people over such vast areas. Perhaps reverence for the recent past is explained by the fact that the fifteenth century, in the wake of the Black Death's population losses, had been something of a golden age for the German peasantry, with its relatively advantageous conditions eroded by the population recovery of the early sixteenth century.[65] On the other hand, the economic changes of the later Middle Ages continued to diversify peasants. Not only were peasants distinguished as to their formal legal condition — as to whether they were unfree, half-free or free — but there were also economic differentiations which did not always entirely overlap with the legal ones. There were certainly peasants who employed other peasants, and there is internal evidence in the Twelve Articles to suggest that the sixteenth-century German equivalents of *kulaks* — 'those of us who have farms', men already prominent in the *Gemeinde* organisations — were also to the fore in the Peasant Revolt. These might well have been the sort of energetic and ambitious farmers who felt that their hard struggle to keep afloat was being exploited by nobles and monasteries.

When we speak of 'rich peasants', however, we should be clear what we mean. The recurrent term for the peasant in the propaganda of the German Peasant Revolt is 'the poor man' or in the plural 'poor folk'.[66] For the peasants, even modest sufficiency meant careful frugality and a generally unvaried diet; the maintenance of a standard of living also required a watchful attitude towards lords and their demands, and protection of popular access to game, water and timber in waste lands and forest which were being increasingly threatened by private control. This is why the Twelve Articles contain, alongside the exalted if conservative rhetoric, much concern with the minutiae of marginal resources — though we should remember that one man's minutiae are another man's meat. Other Peasants' Revolt articles consist largely if not exclusively of routine details, as we shall see in a moment.

Before we move on from the Memmingen Articles, however, let us consider a few more features of their style. Firstly, they look rather like the lists of propositions for the agenda of the debates that were taking place in towns and cities all over Germany, to decide on the religious future of communities. In the context of the nation-wide religious debate of the 1520s, we might consider the Articles' unmistakable allusions to the man who was still, for the time being, the national hero. Indeed, in the continued failure of the imperial monarchy to live up to the visionary expectations Germany had of it, it is not too fanciful to see Luther in a quasi-kingly role: one of his pamphlets, for instance, was addressed in true regal style to 'his dear German people'. Luther had captured the national imagination at Worms in 1521 with his projection of himself as the national archetype — the German Hercules, brave, candid, reasonable, but immovably obstinate when the truth was at stake. At Worms a kind of identification had been sketched between the cause of the peasant's son, Luther, and the protest movement of the peasants: a Luther supporter reading a message of support had uttered the defiant war cry '*Bundschuh, Bundschuh*'. Luther's own message of defiance had taken the form of his stand on Holy Scripture, which it was not safe to abandon, whatever the risk: 'Unless I am convinced by the testimony of the Scriptures . . . I am bound by the Scriptures I have quoted and my conscience is captive to the word of God.'[67] The conclusion of the Memmingen Articles follows this closely:

> if one or more of the articles set forth here were not to be in agreement with the Word of God . . . these articles should be demonstrated to us to be inadmissable by the Word of God, and we would abandon them, when it is explained to us on the basis of Scripture.

The folk-hero image that attached to Luther at the time of his

91

appearance at the *Reichstag*, when the danger of martyrdom that he faced prompted publicists to liken him to Christ,[68] still clung to him in 1525. The peroration of the Twelve Articles reflected the power he still exercised over the German popular imagination, for popular culture needs its heroes. Only when we glimpse the role the peasants wanted to give Luther as a sort of heraldic supporter do we appreciate the grief caused by his brusque dismissal of the insurgent cause in 1525.

Through his work as history's first writer for a mass market, Luther had a pan-German appeal, and the Peasants' Revolt was a national phenomenon, even though it did not take in all areas of the *Reich*. However, villagers live in villages as well as in the German *Reich*, and when we turn away from the Twelve Articles to some of the less well-known manifestos of the German Peasants' Revolt, we find the typical intense peasant localism that co-existed with the national, or even universal, vision of the Memmingen Articles. A pre-occupation with the everyday annoyances of small communities in small places, the relentless practicality that is a major feature of peasant risings — even alongside the loftiest ideology — are seen in a set of German Peasant Revolt articles, with only the most abrupt introduction and hardly any conclusion, from the Swabian villages of Öpfingen and Griesingen.[69]

These numbered complaints seem far away from the relative universalism of the Twelve Articles. As their caption indicates, they are concerned with just two villages, and with their squire, a terrifying, violent and choleric *Junker* of whom his peasants were clearly petrified. He joins a cast of characters which includes a grasping abbot, harsh bailiffs and an innkeeper with a chip on his shoulder who has managed to get his convoluted complaint included in the general articles. The props are pigs, a mill, the inhabitants of a stud farm, and a most contentious manure heap — the latter being a reminder, if we needed one, of the central importance of manure in European history.[70] The inclusion of the manure heap would doubtless have convinced the peasants' enemies that they were irredeemably boorish. Indeed, the farmers of Öpfingen and Griesingen seem to have been incapable of raising their eyes above their fields and muck-heaps — certainly not to have seen avenging angels on clouds of glory. Instead of a messianic judgement awaiting the oppressor, we seem to have only timid serfs cowering before a village despot and gaining the courage to speak up only because of the stirring events going on around them. Instead of lightning flashes of the eschaton, we have only the miserable hailstorms and the heart-breaking floods and fires of the German countryside.

All in all, then, the complaints and moans of the villagers of Öpfingen and Griesingen seem far removed from any sense of justice, or from any articulation of values. Having said that, however, the action of these villagers in mobilising is itself an expression of firmly held values not always clearly expressed verbally or in writing; and towards the end of the chapter of woes of these Swabian peasants comes the statement of an idea — tentative, it must be said, but with a radicalising capacity of its own: 'We are of the opinion that the poor man is also entitled to justice.'

Having now looked at the words used in support of peasant uprisings, we may consider some of their non-verbal dimensions, such as their likely timing. Organisation, especially the welding together of separate communities, was obviously important. The individual village itself provided a basis of organisation, as a community with an institutional form, as in the French *communauté* and the German *Gemeinde* referred to earlier. For the fusion of individual villages, groups of villages and regions in revolt, there sometimes came into existence organising committees such as the shadowy *Magna Societas*, or Great Society, of the 1381 English Peasants' Revolt. There were semi-permanent, semi-clandestine leagues such as the *Armer Konrad* and *Bundschuh* and permanent leagues such as the Swiss *Grisons*. (The Swiss, by the way, were regarded as the chief ring-leaders of peasant agitation in Central Europe.)

A crucial factor in the integration of peasant unrest was permissible movement, which provided the lines of contact, face-to-face, and also cover for subversive preparation: 'if anyone asked where they were going, . . . they replied, "We are fetching Shrovetide cakes". '[71]

When the hour was at hand at which the fire of revolt was to be lit, it happened in Shrovetide (as it is called), when people are expected to visit one another, that about six or seven peasants in a village near Ulm, called Baltringen, came together and discussed many of the current troubles. As was the custom amongst peasants at that time, they travelled from one village to another as if calling on neighbours, and ate and drank together in convivial fashion; the peasants in the villages then journeyed onwards with them . . . And in such company they travelled about every Thursday and grew in numbers, until there were four hundred men.[72]

93

The passage does not, of course, tell us that peasants seldom travelled, but only that they were more likely to do so at certain times of the year, times when the rhythms of agricultural work were more relaxed, and also at consecrated or festal times, such as the eve of Lent, or Corpus Christi, as in the case of England in 1381.

The mobility of peasant risings, together with their coincidence with holy seasons, gave them something of the character of the movement of people in a pilgrimage. This flavour of a pilgrimage can sometimes be seen in the announcements of rebellions, which sound as if they might be proclamations of pilgrimages, as in the following:

> Greetings. Dear brethren in Christ, we command you in earnest that you come to us straightly and without delay to the city of Dinkelsbühl to proclaim the Holy Gospel, of which many of our brethren have been robbed by force, and to relieve certain burdens which they, and you, cannot bear.[73]

The language of religious pilgrimage — a practice deeply ingrained into popular religion — is also used in the formation of the League of Allgäu peasants:

> Actions and articles resolved, on the Monday after Invocavit, by all companies of the peasant troops who allied together in the name of the holy undivided Trinity.
>
> For the praise and honour of the almighty everlasting God and the exaltation of the Holy Gospel and God's Word, the Christian Union and alliance has been established to aid the cause of justice and divine law . . . according as the gospel and divine law teach, and especially to increase brotherly love.

These advertisements were supplemented by impassioned preaching, using the model of pilgrimage sermons, in a tradition which in Germany went back at least as far as the Drummer of Niklashausen, to whose charismatic speeches 'pilgrims' trecked in 1476. Simon Lochmeier fell into this tradition in the Peasants' Revolt: 'he assembled as many as seven thousand people and proclaimed to them that everyone should be free and have no lord but the Emperor alone.'[74]

In the English risings of the sixteenth century, most notably in the risings of the North in 1536-7 and of 1549 in East Anglia and the West, the analogy of pilgrimage is seen in the high priority given to religious issues, in the use of religious banners and songs, and above all in the choice of the word 'pilgrimage' for the Northern Rising. This was in fact also an allusion to a favourite ingredient in popular Catholicism that was under attack in the reforms and modernisations of the Henrician Reformation. A pattern of pilgrimage proclamation is also found in earlier English popular insurgency. An announcement by the Oxfordshire rebels in 1381 sounds like the declaration of a pilgrimage, albeit one filled with heavy menace: 'Arise all men and go with us, or else truly and by God ye shall be d____.'[75] Trevelyan vividly captured the atmosphere of movement and turbulence in the English Peasants' Revolt, its resemblances to a mass pilgrimage of righteous vengeance, with parish priests combining the roles of pilgrims' chaplains and rebel spokesmen: 'several parsons of poor parishes put themselves at the head of their congregations and revenged on society the wrongs that they had endured.'[76]

A pilgrimage is obviously going somewhere — Canterbury, Compostela, Rome, above all Jerusalem. A peasant revolt should also have a place to go. As early as 1381 the English rebels converged without hesitation on what was by then firmly established as the fixed seat of government. Other English revolts, on the other hand, were regional in inspiration and focused on provincial capitals such as Exeter, Norwich and York. As a militant pilgrimage to some identified place, a peasant revolt may come to resemble the medieval mass migrations that we know as crusades but which the Middle Ages were more likely to call the pilgrimage.

The German Peasants' Revolt shows its character as a pilgrimage, not so much as by being directed at a central target (Germany lacked a 'capital city') as by its inception at or near sacred time — the holy season of Lent. 'It happened in Shrovetide . . . on the Monday after *Invocavit*' (first Sunday in Lent). The German Peasants' Revolt is the classic example of a rising with a Lenten inspiration, and the season was chosen for more reasons than that the carrying of cakes facilitated secrecy. Lent implies purification and carnival, and both have something to do with peasant revolts. Indeed, the peasant revolt may even encapsulate a central theme in popular culture, celebrated by Brueghel: the battle between Lent and carnival. Lent itself was essentially concerned with purification. It was indeed preceded by a major Marian feast, that of the Purification of Mary.

Lent also included another great Marian feast, that of the Annunciation. Between them, these festivals of Mary joined with Lent itself in striking the connected chords of purification and

95

renewal. The feast of the Annunciation was especially important from the point of view of renewal because, as a sort of shadow Christmas, it marked the inception of man's redemption, which climaxed in Holy Week. The announcement of Christ's birth to Mary by the angel was vigorously promoted as a popular feast by the Franciscan Order. Known traditionally in England as Lady Day, it began the civil and financial year — for this was a time of beginnings. Popular dating in England made February the first month of Spring and the city of Venice commemorated its foundation in March.[77] Above all, Lent fell in this February-March period which was associated in popular culture with the blessedness of new beginnings, renewal, good tidings and reform — reform, above all, in the social order. The day before the peasants of the Allgäu assembled in the German Peasants' Revolt, their parish priest, in common with thousands of others across Europe, would have opened the Sundays of Lent by intoning the entrance prayer, '*Invocabit me, et ego exaudiam eum* . . . He shall cry out to me, and I will hear him: I will deliver him'. This *Introit*, with its message of deliverance, was followed by a reading from the Letter to the Corinthians announcing 'Behold, now is the acceptable time, behold now is the day of salvation.' For obvious reasons, Lent would be and would remain — even in Protestantised England — a time when disturbances could be expected.

In fact, seventeenth-century English riots were strictly speaking more likely to be touched off on Shrove Tuesday than in Lent proper. This was also the case with the serious urban rising in the French town of Romans in 1580.[78] Popular risings might have one foot in Lent — serious, religious acts of repentance and renewal — and another in carnival. The carnivalesque features in revolts were the ones that made it easiest for their enemies to discredit them and their pretensions to peace, conservatism, sobriety, chastity, religion, moderation and respect for traditional symbols. The presence of these elements dispelled tentative sympathy, or the tepid support of observers seeking any excuse to turn against insurgents. Thus Martin Luther, who had warned the German princes that they were pushing the peasants too far, confessed himself revolted by the excesses of peasants who brutally murdered a knight in full view of his wife and children.[79] Conceivably, excesses of this nature also provoked disgust on the part of some rebels. Peasant revolts failed for a number of reasons, not the least being that they encapsulated the fatal division between Lent and carnival.

Whether or not they actually took place at carnival time, all popular revolts had something of carnival about them, just as every carnival was a stylised rebellion. We can borrow from and build upon Burke's list of the main features of carnival, to see how they are to the fore in revolts. Burke considers the roles in carnival of gluttony, drink, sex and violence.[80] I would also add further themes of inversion, revenge, mockery and folly.

A German commentator, one markedly unsympathetic to the Peasants' Revolt, but one deeply familiar with popular culture, Sebastian Brant, brings out some of the features just listed. The peasants, Brant wrote,

> attacked castles, ransacked monasteries, swilled wine, looted
> treasures and assaulted clerics for no other purpose than . . .
> to get even with the clergy for the outrages and damages to
> which in the past the peasants had been subjected . . . They
> brought on nothing but disruption, injustice, murder, robbery,
> tyranny, rape . . .[81]

Brant here, like Luther in his anti-peasant pamphlet of 1525, concentrates on assault and murder in the insurrection. The means for mayhem were certainly to hand, including serviceable farms tools such as flails, pitchforks and scythes, along with weapons proper brought along by *Landsknechte*.[82] The fourteenth-century Swiss had a secret weapon, 'a lethal kind of battleaxe . . . with this terrifying weapon they could cut up even well-armoured opponents as though with a razor, slicing them in pieces . . . '.[83] The ruthlessness seen there is reflected in the Jacquerie, which became a by-word for peasant brutality, and the English Peasants' Revolt, with its cold-blooded murders.

Brant specifically linked the German peasants' violence to revenge 'for . . . outrages and damages . . . '. Now 'getting even' was part of a peasant culture in which honour and revenge played their parts; it was also an ingredient in carnival when, often under the protection of masks, and through derision and 'social blackmail', a whole year's scores might be settled against the rich and the powerful in a controlled and ritualised way. Incidentally, derision and inversion were prominent in risings. As we shall see below, the peoples' priest, John Ball, was put forward as archbishop of Canterbury in 1381, while Wat Tyler's deliberate insolence before King Richard II has the hallmark of carnivalesque inversion.

As Brant showed, those carnival keynotes, gluttony and drunkenness, were certainly present in revolts. It was largely the availability of drink and meat in carnival that had the common man living 'between the memory of the last carnival and the expectation of the next'.[84] The monotony of a peasant diet that must have centred for most of the time on bread and soup surely gave to rebellion, as to carnival, something of the allure of that enduring popular fantasy, the land of Cockaigne, in German, *Schlaraffenland*. Cockaigne was not, of course, to be taken seriously, and both Brueghel and an Italian sixteenth-century poet equate belief in its existence with the height of folly. *Schlaraffenland*-Cockaigne was a place to day-dream about, an extraordinary out-door restaurant with unusually good-service — the grilled pigeons, for instance, very obligingly flew straight into the diners' mouths.[85] For dessert, there was fruit — something for which pre-modern Europeans craved, especially out of season. On the Cockaigne menu they had iced, sugared straw-berries — surely a delicacy in anyone's language; and there was drink in abundance, as there was, of course, in the abbey cellars along the Rhine, Neckar and Mosel when the peasants raided them in 1525: 'they ransacked monasteries, swilled wine . . . ' The land of Cockaigne had arrived; in the very act and process of rebellion, peasant insurgents might live out a carnivalesque fantasy of plenty. In the German Peasants' Revolt carnival fought with Lent and won; the revolt itself was the loser.

As we saw, Cockaigne was properly regarded as a foolish idea, at least if one actually believed in its existence. The notion of folly, present in carnivals, was arguably prominent in popular revolts. When it came to folly, the peasant — our word 'clown' originally meant a countryman — entered his own domain, but it was one in which ambiguity ruled: for if the peasant was regarded as the butt of jokes involving foolish credulity, and general slow-wittedness, we should bear in mind a tradition, ranging at least from Grimmel-hausen's *Simplicissimus* in the seventeenth-century to Hašek's *Good Soldier Švejk* in the twentieth, in which stupidity affords the means of survival. We should also bear in mind the corrective value of folly in medieval and early modern European culture and in particular the religious value put upon it. In the Middle Ages, St Francis of Assisi, sometimes seeming to act in the role of a holy fool, had surely built on a tradition established by St Paul with his point about the apparent folly of the Cross. These appreciations of the positive, and especially the religious, value of folly were strengthened in the sixteenth-century by various contrasting authorities: by Luther, whose preface to the *German Theology* lauded childlike ignorance, and by the Counter-Reformation saint, Philip Neri, an accomplished preacher who used clowning as an important part of his technique. It is true, as Scribner writes, that in much German journalism of the fifteenth and sixteenth centuries, folly had a simple correlation with vice, and yet the words 'fool' and 'folly' had a two-way meaning, indicating on the one hand stupidity, and on the other, comicality with a satiric edge.

If peasants were clowns, clowns and jesters had a right of formalised impertinence that may have arisen from an original perception of them as harmless idiots whose random babblings could not be held against them. Thus, 'fools' had the important role of asking the implied question, 'who is in fact the fool?' In Shakespeare's *Twelfth Night* the comedian Feste — his very name alludes to parties, feasts and holidays — is a most important character in a comedy that takes its title from the high season of carnivalesque satire and inversion. By inversion here I mean that the job of the 'fool' is to show the Lady Olivia, whose self-indulgent grief threatens the good order of her court, that by her excesses she is the real fool of the piece: 'take away the fool, gentlemen.'[86]

On a wider front, folly was used to satirise the abuses of the social, political and ecclesiastical systems. Sebastian Brant's *Narrenschiff* (*Ship of fools*) does this, and in Erasmus's *Praise of folly*, 'Dame Folly' picks out the ills of society and the Church. Thus, when the anti-peasant pamphleteer, Thomas Murner, tried to pillory the peasants in *The Great Lutheran Fool*, his attack might well have rebounded against him, given the widespread acceptance of folly, especially at carnival time, in pointing out and righting society's ills.[87]

When the times were out of joint, what was madness and what was folly? In the English Peasants' Revolt of 1381 the role of social satirist and critic was assumed by the popular preacher John Ball, with what the hostile commentator Walsingham called his 'insane follies' and 'madness'. Ball's counter-propaganda emphasised instead the disorders of a degenerate social system which could be set to rights only by the efforts of the commons as 'prudent men', tilling England as a farm that had gone to rack and ruin.[88]

The 'prudent men' of 1381 also used the language and the stock characters of country comedy and ballads: 'John Schep . . . greets well John Nameless, and John the Miller and John Carter . . . and bids Piers Plowman go to his work and chastise well Hob the robber and take with you John Trueman and all his fellows . . . '.[89] Amongst these characters, Piers Plowman, as well as being the hero of Langland's dream-epic, is the type of the husbandmen, the equivalent of the sixteenth-century German 'Karsthans', 'Ploughjack'. The other names are those of stock types, but they are the recipients of what can only be described as a summons. Using parody, this summons is based on the conventions of a writ to a sheriff bidding him to assemble the *posse comitatus* so as to arrest some malefactors. Through this parody — a prominent feature of popular culture — the rebel peasants were implying that they were the forces of justice, even of the king's justice, against those who exploited the commons for their own benefit. One of the peasants' foremost leaders, the priest John Ball, would administer the king's justice, as chancellor, and archbishop of Canterbury.[90]

Other rebel leaders were priests, such as Jan Želivský in the Prague uprising in 1419 and the 'priests of Tabor' in that millenarian encampment in Bohemia early in the fifteenth century. Pre-modern peasants are generally said to have been anticlerical, but their anticlericalism did not cover all priests in blanket condemnation. Similarly, peasants often hated lawyers, but the leader of the English Pilgrimage of Grace was the lawyer Robert Aske. Popular entertainers sometimes emerged as charismatic leaders of mass protest movements: Hans Böheim of the 1476 Drummer of Niklashausen episode was a folk musician, and Jan Beukelson of Leyden, the dictator of the Anabaptist commune at Münster in 1535, was a former repertory actor. Individuals like this were used to moving in fairly large groups of people, knew different communities and were mobile, if not 'marginal'. These were features they shared in common with soldiers, and something has already been said about the role of mercenary *Landsknechte* in the German Peasants' Revolt. Such demobilised troops were invaluable for the tactics, organisation, weapons and physical strength they brought to the insurgent cause. Occupation alone is not the reason for a man's emergence as a recognised leader. Joss Fritz, who re-grouped the *Bundschuh* on the Upper Rhine from 1512, was indeed a former *Landsknechte* and had all the characteristics of rootlessness that we look for in the popular leader. He was also articulate, good looking, with elegant manners, and a snappy dresser.[91] He was the true type of peasant leader in that his authority was inherent only in his personality.

Because the personalities of leaders like Fritz were so heroic, rumours sometimes circulated that their origins were knightly — variants, as it were, of Robin Hood. In fact, real knights and nobles not uncommonly joined in popular revolts. This encourages the theory that such revolts were in fact 'vertical' protests of regions, grouping all social orders in those regions in acts of protest. Two other theoretical approaches can be taken in explaining the involvement of knightly 'elites' in popular causes. One is that ideological, and especially religious, affinity concealed class tensions. Thus the knight George Žižka led the rebel Hussites in the field, and squires rallied to the Pilgrimage of Grace. Another explanation is that the status difference between knight and commoner obscures a frequent identity of interest, especially at economic borderlines. The French *hoberaux* ploughing their own fields but with swords at their sides to indicate their lordly lineages, were close in terms of living standards to the better-off sort of peasant around them. The proximity in time of the German Knights' and Peasants' Revolts (1522 and 1525) tells us that in the Germany of the 1520s knights as well as peasants had acute grievances and that the knightly class felt threatened by the same forces as the peasants — the pretensions of the higher clergy, the economic challenge of the cities, and the unrelenting pressure of the territorial princes.

One might speculate that the presence of knights and nobles in popular revolts helped to give them a moderate tone of accepting the hierarchical society. The Circular Letter of the Black Forest Peasants of 1525 actually issues an invitation to 'honourable, wise and kind lords, friends and dear neighbours . . . dear lords, friends and neighbours',[92] to join in the Revolt. It is tempting to see the moderation of the Twelve Articles as a product of the participation of knights and lords. This is not satisfactory, however, and it is better to see the participation of elites as a symptom of the same lack of revolutionary vision that produced the Twelve Articles. There were knights involved in the English Peasants' Revolt[93] but their presence did not inhibit the expression of a far-reaching egalitarian ideology: 'they would obtain peace and security in the future if, when the great ones had been removed, there were among them equal liberty and nobility and like dignity and power.' Likewise, the leadership of Žižka in the Taborite Revolt in Hussite Bohemia did not repress the production of the most revolutionary concepts put forward in Europe in the Middle Ages: 'Nothing is mine and nothing thine, so everything shall be common to all forever and no one shall have anything of his own because anyone who owns anything commits a mortal sin.'[94]

There is nothing like this in the Twelve Articles, nor in any other German Peasants' Revolt articles, leaving aside the admittedly important wing led by Thomas Müntzer. One way of explaining the difference between the relative conservatism of the German Peasants' Revolt and the relative radicalism of the Taborite movement is through awareness of the prominence of eschatology in the Taborite experiment:

. . . in our time there shall be an end of all things, that is,

all evil shall be uprooted on this earth. That this is the time
of vengeance and retribution on wicked men by fire and sword
. . . In this time of vengeance only five towns shall remain
and those who flee to them shall be saved . . . everything shall
be common to all forever and no-one shall have anything of
his own . . . Debtors . . . shall be acquitted of paying their
debts . . . no king shall reign nor any lord rule on earth, there
shall be no serfdom, all dues and taxes shall cease, nor shall
any man force another to do anything, because all shall be
equal, brothers and sisters.[95]

The contrast seems startling, and all that links these ideas to the
manifestos of the German Peasants' Revolt would seem to be
opposition to serfdom and a feeling that the world needed to be set
to rights. The vision that we see in the Taborite predictions —
disappearance of the state, of property and rank, equality of the
sexes — can indeed be accounted for by the prevalence of
millenarianism in Bohemia towards the end of the second decade
of the fifteenth century, but that in itself begs a question about the
presence of millenarianism in one situation and its relative absence
in another. Some of the reasons for this millenarian pre-occupation
in Bohemia lie in the domain of ideas and feelings, without any
strong economic basis for them: for instance, the execution by the
Council of Constance of the saintly national religious leader John
Hus clearly caused a massive sense of grief and loss amongst the
Czechs. On the political front, the messianic expectation of Christ
the King was provoked by the prospect in 1419-20 of the accession
to the Bohemian throne of the ruler, Sigismund, who was alleged
to have trapped Hus into his martydom: hence 'no king shall reign'.
Conceivably, if Martin Luther had been executed after the *Reichstag*
of Worms and if in addition there was a vacancy in the German
monarchy in the mid-1520s, then the German Peasants' Revolt might
have taken a much less reassuring tone.

Manifestos echo the views of those able to capture the platform.
The quoted Taborite articles reflect the views of those with the
lightest attachment to society as it existed in their day. The fast-
growing city of Prague, for instance, contained vast numbers
permanently and chronically in debt.[96] Their plight can be heard
in their vision of a millennium in which 'debtors shall be acquitted
of paying their debts'. The difference detected between these two
great risings of the people in late medieval and early modern Europe
is the difference between those with a stake in existing society —

the most vociferous of the German peasants — and those with none — those who impressed their rejection of a world of oppression on the Taborite vision of the millennium.

Four exceptionally serious peasant revolts, or revolts with a heavy or overwhelming peasant involvement, broke out in late medieval and early modern Europe: in France, the Jacquerie of 1358; in England, the revolt of the commons in 1381; in Bohemia, the Hussite Revolution after 1418; and in Germany, the Peasants' Revolt of 1525. All were violent and all drew inspiration from themes of popular culture, especially the themes of religion in society, of carnival, Lent, pilgrimage, folly, and satire. These revolts may have been caused by deep-lying social factors, but they were actually precipitated by fractures in the political surface. The Jacquerie was triggered by the capture of King John in 1356, the English rising by the minority and youth of Richard II, the Bohemian revolt by the sudden death of King Wenceslas, and the German Peasants' Revolt by the breakdown of authority, and particularly the questioning of imperial authority consequent on the German Reformation.

It will be seen, then, that all of these revolts were involved with problems in kingship, the institution which in the popular political consciousness was the highest earthly arbiter of justice. As such, kings were the intended recipients of basically loyal peasant protests in three out of four of our 'great risings'. On the popular political level, the Jacquerie was a loud complaint against the incompetence of the nobles in losing King John to his English captors. The 1381 English Rising aimed to put King Richard at the head of a peasant commonwealth. The German Peasants' Revolt likewise called for no rulers but the emperor. Only the Hussite Reformation was 'republican', and its messianism, focused on Christ the King, confirms rather than negates the firm hold that kingship held over the popular imagination.

This popular fascination with kingship was no mere triumph of propaganda over fact: the fact was that strong rule was often in the interests of the common man. True, he was likely, notably in France, to pay the taxes that the immune classes were spared, but fiscal immunity for the privileged is best seen as a weakness in early modern states, one that might have been ended, to the mutual benefit of both, by an alliance between the state and the unprivileged. Where forceful monarchies brought an end to aristocratic anarchy in western Europe towards the end of the Middle Ages and the beginning of the early modern period, it was the peasant family that benefited most from the dawning of internal peace. Where effective rulers restrained local lords in the exploitation of peasants, territories like Bavaria in 1525 were immune from insurrection. Where royal government ordered cheap grain sales, as in England in food shortages between 1587 and 1631, a certain identity of interest between commoners and crowns might be traced. Since we more or less began this chapter by positing that peasants were not fools, we could end it by stipulating that the popular vision of monarchy was not entirely a product of mistaken consciousness. On the other hand, some of our differentiation between 'radical' and 'conservative' in peasant revolts is a little illusory, since insurgents were capable of being 'radical' about the social order — calling for an end to nobility — and 'conservative' about the political — exalting kingship: a kingship, though, that in the English and also the German Peasants' Revolts begins to look like the presidency of a peasant republic.

Notes

1. R.W. Scribner, 'Images of the peasant, 1514–1525' in Janos Bak (ed.), *The German Peasant War* (Library of Peasant Studies, Frank Cass, London, 1976), p. 39.

2. F. Grossmann, *Bruegel. The paintings* (Phaidon, London, 1966), plates 90, 91, 101, 129, 134.

3. For Louis le Nain's wretched and ragged peasants, see, for example, R.H. Wilenski, *French painting* (Boston, Branford, 1949), plates 25 a,b.

4. For the appreciation of peasant life in Italian Renaissance literature, see Jacob Burckhardt, *The civilisation of the Renaissance* (trans. S.G.C. Middlemore, Phaidon, London and Oxford, 1945), p. 213.

5. R.B. Dobson, *The Peasants' Revolt of 1381* (Macmillan, London, 1970), pp. 76–8.

6. Ibid., p. 75.

7. *Della famiglia*, p. 238.

8. Margaret Aston, 'Lollards and literacy', *History*, vol. 62 (1977), pp. 347–71.

9. Davis, *Society and culture*, pp. 243–4.

10. J.R. Hale, *Renaissance Europe 1480–1520* (Fontana History of Europe, Collins, London, 1971), pp. 200–1.

11. A.N. Galpern, *The religion of the people in sixteenth-century Champagne* (Harvard Historical Studies, Harvard University Press, Cambridge, Massachusetts, 1976), pp. 69–78.

12. William Monter, *Ritual, myth and magic in early modern Europe* (Ohio University Press, Athens, Ohio, 1983), p. 26.

13. Laurens van der Post, *Journey into Russia* (Penguin, Harmondsworth, 1971), pp. 178–9, 291.

14. Peter Blickle, 'The economic, social and political background to the Twelve Articles of the Swabian peasants in 1525' in Bak (ed.), *German Peasant War*, pp. 71–2.

15. David Underdown, *Revel, riot and rebellion. Popular politics and culture in England 1603–1660* (Oxford University Press, Oxford and New York, 1985), pp. 14–15.

16. Dobson, *Peasants' Revolt*, pp. 76, 79.

17. Guy Fourquin, *The anatomy of popular rebellion in the Middle Ages* (trans. Anne Chester, North-Holland, Amsterdam, 1978), p. 84.

18. Kate Norgate, *England under the Angevin kings* (2 vols, Macmillan, London and Edinburgh, 1887, cited here in the reprint by Haskell House, New York, 1969), vol. 1, p. 41; Josiah C. Russell, *Twelfth century studies* (A.M.S., New York, 1978), p. 250.

19. See *Bergerie dedié à la majesté de la Royne d'Escosse*, in Grahame Caster and Terence Cave (eds), *Ronsard. Odes, hymns and other poems* (Manchester University Press, Manchester, 1977), p. 179–205.

20. Dobson, *Peasants' Revolt*, p. 140.

21. Ibid., pp. 84–8.

22. A.L. Rowse, *Tudor Cornwall. Portrait of a society* (Jonathan Cape, London, 1943), ch. 11, esp. pp. 261–3; Barret L. Beer, *Rebellion and riot. Popular disorder in England during the reign of Edward VI* (Kent State University Press, Kent, Ohio, 1982), p. 52.

23. J.J. Scarisbrick, *Henry VIII* (Eyre & Spottiswood, London, 1968), pp. 470–1; Patrick Collinson, *Archbishop Grindal 1519–1583. The struggle for a reformed Church* (Jonathan Cape, London, 1979), pp. 235–42.

24. Madeleine Hope Dodds and Ruth Dodds, *The Pilgrimage of Grace 1536–1537 and the Exeter conspiracy 1538* (2 vols, Cambridge University Press, 1915, cited here in the reprint by Frank Cass, London, 1971), vol. 1, pp. 76–7.

25. Scribner, 'Images of the peasant', in Bak (ed.), *German Peasant War*, p. 36.

26. Rosario Villari, 'The insurrection in Naples of 1585' in Eric Cochrane (ed.), *The late Italian Renaissance 1525–1630* (Stratum Series, Macmillan, London, 1970), p. 321.

27. Henri Pirenne, *Histoire de Belgique* (7 vols., Lamertin, Brussels, 1953), vol. 3. pp. 424–6; John Lothrop Motley, *The rise of the Dutch Republic. A history* (3 vols., World's Classics edition, Oxford University Press, London, 1913), vol. 1, p. 408; and for the symbols of satire in the campaign against the Cardinal Granvelle, p. 398–408.

28. Philip Hughes, *The Reformation in England* (5th, revised edition, 3 vols in one, Burns & Oates, London, 1963), vol. 2, plate 2.

29. Strauss, *Manifestations of discontent*, pp. 83–4.

30. Ibid.

31. Galpern, *Religion of the people*, pp. 43–60.

32. Hans Eckhart Rübesamen, *Dürer* (Olbourne Press, London, 1963), plates XXXIV-XXXVI.

33. E.P. Thompson, 'Time, work-discipline and industrial capitalism', *Past and Present*, vol. 38 (1967), p. 58.

34. *The daily missal and liturgical manual* . . . (Laverty, Leeds, 1956), pp. 35 , 39–45, 51–2, 119, 121–2; John Julian, *A dictionary of hymnology* (Second, revised edition in one volume, John Murray, London, 1907; cited here in

the two-volume re-publication by Dover Publications, New York, 1957), vol. 2, pp. 1081–4. It is worth noting that the *Stabat Mater* acquired great popularity in a time of terrible mass distress, during the Flagellant movement in the wake of the Black Death. See also Yrjö Hirn, *The sacred shrine. A study of poetry and art of the Catholic Church* (Faber & Faber, London, 1958), ch. XIX.

35. Bernard Berenson, *The Italian painters of the Renaissance* (First published as four collected essays by Oxford University Press, 1930, and cited here in the first paperback edition by Fontana/Collins, 1972), p. 144.

36. Maurice Rheims, *19th century sculpture* (Thames & Hudson, London, 1977), p. 140 and plate 9; Michael Prestwich, *The three Edwards. War and state in England 1272–1377* (Weidenfeld & Nicolson, London, 1980), p. 242.

37. For the special devotion of Siena to Mary, see William M. Bowsky, *A medieval Italian commune. Siena under the Nine* (University of California Press, Berkeley, California, and London, 1981), pp. 274–6. For the cult of Mary in Milan, see Buratti, *et al.*, *La città rituale*, pp. 57–133. Peter Burke examines the role of Mary in insurgency at Naples in 'The Virgin of the Carmine and the revolt of Masaniello', *Past and Present*, vol. 99 (1983), pp. 3–21; however, Rosario Villari argues for a more secular and political motivation for the Naples uprising in 'Masaniello: contemporary and recent interpretations', *Past and Present*, vol. 108 (1985), pp. 117–32, and esp. p. 122.

For the whole question of Marian devotion in early modern Italy, see Massimo Petrocchi, 'La devozione alla Vergine negli scritti di pietà del Cinquecento Italiano' in M. Maccarone *et al.*, (ed), *Problemi di vita religiosa in Italia nel Cinquecento* (Editrice Antenore, Padua, 1960), pp. 281–7.

38. Victor and Edith Turner, *Images and pilgrimages in Christian culture* (Columbia University Press, New York, 1978), pp. 166–7, 175–87.

39. Phyllis Mack Crewe, *Calvinist preaching and iconoclasm in the Netherlands 1544–1569* (Cambridge University Press, Cambridge, 1978), pp. 11–12; Motley, *Rise of the Dutch Republic*, vol. 1, pp. 540–9.

40. Turner and Turner, *Images and pilgrimages*, pp. 64, 200–1. For Spain in particular, see William A. Christian Jr., *Apparitions in late medieval and Renaissance Spain* (Princeton University Press, Princeton, New Jersey, 1981), pp. 13–93.

41. Strauss, *Manifestations of discontent*, p. 88.

42. For example, *Luther's works* (56 vols, general editors Helmut T. Lehmann and Jaroslav Pelikan, Concordia Publishing House, St Louis, Missouri, Fortress Press and Muhlenberg Press, Philadelphia, Pennsylvania, 1958–75), volume 43: *Devotional writings*, II, Gustav K. Wienke (ed.) (Fortress Press, Philadelphia, Pennsylvania, 1968), p. 39–41.

43. Strauss, *Manifestations*, pp. 103, 145.

44. Scribner, 'Images of the peasants', pp. 37, 39.

45. John, 19, 26–7.

46. Strauss, *Manifestations*, p. 145; Julian Cornwall, *Revolt of the peasantry 1549* (Routledge & Kegan Paul, London, 1973), pp. 47, 99, 188.

47. Philipp Spitta, *Johann Sebastian Bach. His work and influence in the music of Germany 1685–1750* (trans. Clara Bell and J.A. Fuller-Maitland, 3 vols, Novello, London, 1889; cited here in the reprint, in 2 vols, by Dover, New York, 1952), vol. 2. p. 549; Julian, *Dictionary of hymnology*, vol. 2, pp. 989–90.

48. Scribner, 'Images of the peasants', p. 36; Siegfried Hoyer, 'Arms

and military organisation in the German Peasant War' in Bob Scribner and Gerhard Benecke (eds), *The German Peasant War 1525 — new viewpoints* (George Allen & Unwin, London, 1979), pp. 98–108.

49. Adolf Laube, 'Precursors of the Peasant War: "Bundschuh" and "Armer Konrad" — popular movements at the eve of the Reformation' in Bak (ed.) *German Peasant War*, p. 49; Motley, *Rise of the Dutch Republic*. vol. 1, pp. 499–508.

50. Scribner, 'Images of the peasants', p. 30, 39.

51. For example, Fletcher, *Tudor rebellions*, pp. 120, 128–30; Cohn, 'Peasants of Swabia', pp. 14–18.

52. For formal models of grievance literature, see, for example, 'The Great Charter' in J.C. Holt, *Magna Carta* (Cambridge University Press, London, 1965), pp. 317–37, or other specimens of the presentation of complaints in Strauss, *Manifestations*, 52–63.

53. Cohn, 'Peasants of Swabia', pp. 14, 18.

54. Ibid,. pp. 14–16; Fletcher, *Tudor rebellions*, pp. 120, 122, 124, 128.

55. Günther Lottes, 'Popular culture and the early modern state' in Kaplan (ed.), *Understanding popular culture*, p. 156.

56. Blickle, 'Economic, social and political background' in Bak (ed.), *German Peasant War*, p. 63.

57. Blickle, *Revolution of 1525*, pp. xvii, 132; Strauss, *Manifestations, passim.*

58. Dickens, *German nation and Martin Luther*, p. 107, 129, 176, 181, 211–21.

59. Cohn, 'Anticlericalism in the German Peasant War', p. 3–31.

60. The version of the Articles used here is taked from Cohn, 'Peasants of Swabia', pp. 14–18.

61. For some of the literature on this topic see: Marjorie Reeves, *The influence of prophecy in the later Middle Ages. A study in Joachimism* (Oxford University Press, Oxford, 1969), p. 211, 215, and ch. III; also Marjorie Reeves, 'Some popular prophecies from the fourteenth to the seventeenth centuries', *Studies in Church History*, vol. 8 (1972), pp. 107–34; and Emmerson, *Antichrist in the Middle Ages*, pp. 4, 6–7, 69–71.

62. In *Tithe and agrarian history from the fourteenth to the nineteenth century. An essay in comparative history* (trans. Susan Burke, Cambridge University Press, Cambridge, with Editions de la Maison des Sciences de l'Homme, Paris, 1982), p. 111. Emmanuel Le Roy Ladurie and Joseph Goy give a rather different view of tithes from this one.

63. *Luther's works*, volume 31: *Career of the reformer*: I, Harold J. Grimm (ed.) (Muhlenberg Press, Philadelphia, 1957), pp. 344 ff.

64. See John C. Stalnaker, 'Towards a social interpretation of the German Peasant War' in Scribner and Benecke (eds), *German Peasant War*, pp. 25–7.

65. For a modified, but not in the end drastically different, view of population, over-population and peasant poverty, with reference to Lower Alsace, see Francis Rapp, 'The social and economic prehistory of the Peasant War in Lower Alsace' in Scribner and Benecke (eds), *German Peasant War*, pp. 52–62.

66. Stalnaker, 'Towards a social interpretation', pp. 33–7; Cohn, 'Peasants of Swabia', p. 18–20.

67. *Luther's works*, volume 32: *Career of the Reformer*: II, George W. Forell (ed.), (Muhlenberg Press, Philadelphia, 1958), pp. 111–13.

68. R.W. Scribner, *For the sake of simple folk. Popular propaganda for the German Reformation* (Cambridge Studies in Oral and Literate Culture, 2, Cambridge University Press, Cambridge and New York, 1981), p. 21.

69. Cohn, 'Peasants of Swabia', pp. 18–20.

70. Braudel, *Capitalism*, I, pp. 116–20, 150–6.

71. Cohn, 'Peasants of Swabia', p. 24.

72. Ibid.

73. Ibid., p. 26.

74. Ibid., pp. 22, 25.

75. G.M. Trevelyan, *England in the age of Wycliffe* (New edition, Longmans, Green, London, 1909), p. 255, note 2.

76. Ibid., ch. VI.

77. Muir, *Civic ritual*, pp. 70–1; Charles Phythian Adams, 'Ceremony and the citizen: the communal year at Coventry 1450–1550' in Peter Clark and Paul Slack (eds), *Crisis and order in English towns 1500–1700* (Routledge & Kegan Paul, London, 1972), pp. 70–1.

78. Ladurie, *Carnival at Romans, passim*.

79. Belfort Bax, *Peasant War in Germany*, pp. 118–31.

80. Burke, *Popular culture*, ch. 6.

81. Sebastian Brant, 'The Great Peasant Rebellion . . . ' in Strauss (ed.), *Manifestations*, p. 167.

82. Scribner, 'Images of the peasants', pp. 33–5, 39–47.

83. Daniel Waley, *Later medieval Europe. From St Louis to Luther* (Longman, London, 1964, cited here in the revised paperback edition, Longman, 1980), p. 93.

84. For carnival, see Burke, *Popular culture*, ch. 7.

85. For peasant food, see the graphic account in Mandrou, *Introduction to modern France*, pp. 14–16. For Brueghel's depiction of the Cockaigne theme, see Grossmann, *Paintings of Bruegel*, plate 138.

In *The cheese and the worms*, pp. 83–6, Ginzburg shows how a kind of Land of Cockaigne, now sited in the New World, could be used to satirise day dreams and wishful thinking. The Land of Cockaigne had an extraordinary durability, and in nineteenth-century France a version of it was re-deployed to ridicule the folly of hoping for too much from political reforms:

> the constitution having been revised, and universal suffrage having been restricted, potatoes will grow ready cooked and tomatoes will ripen dressed with breadcrumbs and grated cheese. Streams of claret will flow on all sides. Viennese bread and sausages will hang from the branches of trees. Larks, quails and partridges — all done to a turn — will fall from the sky.

That is *precisely* the Land of Cockaigne: see T.J. Clark, *Images of the people. Gustave Courbet and the 1848 Revolution* (Thames & Hudson, London, 1973), p. 93.

86. *Twelfth Night*, Act 1 Scene 5; C.L. Barber, *Shakespeare's festive comedy* (Princeton University Press, Princeton, New Jersey, 1972), pp. 4–6 and ch. 10.

87. Scribner, *For the sake of simple folk*, p. 68; M.A. Screech, *Ecstasy and*

the praise of folly (Duckworth, London, 1980), esp. p. 63–78.

88. Dobson, *Peasants' Revolt*, p. 373–5.

89. Trevelyan, *Age of Wycliffe*, pp. 203–4.

90. Dobson, *Peasants' Revolt*, p. 86.

91. Friedrich Engels, *The Peasant War in Germany* (trans. Moissaye J. Olgin, George Allen & Unwin, London, 1927), pp. 81–4.

92. Cohn, 'Peasants of Swabia', pp. 26–7.

93. Dobson, *Peasants' Revolt*, p. 16.

94. Macek, *Hussite movement*, p. 114.

95. Ibid., pp. 112–14.

96. R.R. Betts, *Essays in Czech history* (Athlone Press, London, 1969), pp. 269, 275, 192; R.R. Betts, 'The social revolution in Bohemia and Moravia in the later Middle Ages', *Past and Present*, vol. 2 (1952), pp. 26–31.

4

Preachers, Popular Culture and Social Criticism in Late Medieval Europe

So far in this study some mention has been made of the influence of preachers, especially as bridges between the ideas of the medieval Catholic Church and the attitudes of the mass of Europeans. In this chapter, by selecting as random examples three figures, John Hus (c. 1373–1415), San Bernardino of Siena (1380–1444) and Girolamo Savonarola (1452–98), we will examine further the impact of preachers on social criticism and also the way in which preachers both adopted and added to the assumptions present amongst their auditors. We shall find that in their various ways the individuals we have chosen were cultural intermediaries. In their style, they used vernacular speech, and the ideas they purveyed were widely shared amongst their audiences.

Savonarola, in particular, was as much influenced by as influencing the ideas which Florentine audiences held about their city. Preachers such as the fifteenth-century Flemish Carmelite Thomas Conecte articulated puritanical hatred of upper-class extravagance found in plebeian congregations.[1] Incidentally, we shall not accept automatically or invariably that the imposition of strict morals, and in particular demands for frugality in society, were necessarily part of the implementation of 'social control', with elites dictating the behaviour of the lower orders. Popular culture is more complex than simply bucolic disorder, and popular puritanism, revealed especially in mass attacks on upper class luxury, has been a major strand in European social history from the Middle Ages onwards.

Of the three figures chosen, two were burned for heresy or disobedience to the Church and the third — San Bernardino — was investigated for heresy. Yet all these men taught broadly orthodox doctrines. Their cases show that the line between heresy and orthodoxy in the Middle Ages was often an arbitrary one.

Indeed, heresy and orthodoxy were usually two sides of the same coin. There was indeed radical heresy in late medieval Europe: some English Lollards of the fifteenth century denied the Church, and even Christianity itself. Many Lollards were ferocious critics of Catholic practices, focusing on superstition and clerical abuses.[2] Yet their ecclesiastical criticisms, like those of the Continental Waldensians,[3] were hardly more savage than those of Hus, San Bernardino and Savonarola.

It will be argued that Hus, San Bernardino and Savonarola were relatively egalitarian social critics, using, applying and developing the accepted norms by which the Church assessed the justice of social and economic conditions. As preachers, they both confirmed and enlarged popular social values. Their outstanding prestige, together with the authority of countless other preachers, helped to form and vindicated some of the attitudes that we see in popular protest: for example, attacks on undue exploitation by landlords, unequal tax burdens, low wages and exploitation of the poor in pricing and money-lending.

In addition, the individuals in the trio we have selected represented and adapted themselves to popular cultural forms of expression, as well as popular values. Hus in Bohemia spoke for a Slav peasantry and proletariat, in the common Czech tongue, against a wealthy, German-speaking upper bourgeoisie. After his martyr's death, a popular cult grew up around his memory, using the Czech folk song tradition. San Bernardino worked within the genre established by his predecessors in the preaching orders. He used vivid visual symbols, especially the logo of the Holy Names of Jesus, but above all his preaching — practical, earthy, anecdotal, witty, totally arresting — formed what was almost a kind of street theatre. Savonarola was no less vivid, if more sombre, than San Bernardino. In addition, he was a conscious cultural populist who repudiated, and for a while even managed to repress, the elitist ethos of the Italian Renaissance.

Both Savonarola himself and many of the followers of John Hus took up an important theme of medieval religious culture — messianism, and the hope of renewal in society through direct divine intervention. Such eschatological doctrines were by no means restricted to heretical and underground groups: they were at the heart of Catholic teaching and had been emphatically restated by the influential Abbot Joachim of Fiore in the late twelfth century.

A major question addressed in this chapter concerns the ways in which popular culture and popular social and political ideas formed and changed in our period. My argument is that preachers were constantly influencing and helping to direct the evolution of popular culture, constantly adding new strands, new cults, new emphases. San Bernardino invented a new motif, the sign of the Name of Jesus, one that was soon to be seen on the walls of peasant farmhouses wherever he had preached. On the other hand, if he needed a cautionary tale to illustrate, say, the follies of gambling, he would take it and adapt it from folk stories.[4] At the same time, as the foremost cultural communicators of the medieval period, famed preachers quite consciously trod in the footsteps of their predecessors and reiterated the ideas and actions that those predecessors had earlier implanted in the popular consciousness. Thus, for example, San Bernardino repeated, in Siena, Bologna and Florence, those spectacular demonstrations of puritanism, the burning of the vanities, that had been promoted by Conecte and were later to be mounted by Savonarola.

One recurrent set of ideas emphasised by the major popular preachers I have selected was anticlerical criticism. As we have seen, selective anticlericalism had well before 1400 become an essential ingredient in popular ideology. Whether it was an entirely indigenous ingredient in the thinking of the masses is an interesting question: for instance, there is evidence as far back as the eleventh century that lay criticism of the clergy was fostered, if not implanted, by the Church's papal leadership as part of a campaign to raise clerical standards.[5] Hus, San Bernardino and Savonarola took up this theme of anticlerical criticism and, in their so doing, it is not always easy to know when they were forming, or being influenced by, the assumptions already present in the minds of their audiences. Again, San Bernardino and Savonarola were of upper-class origin, yet they made remarkably successful efforts to speak the language (in the widest sense of the word) of their audiences.

All three of our typical representatives of the medieval art of mass preaching, Hus, San Bernardino and Savonarola, continued to uphold and to adapt to particular circumstances the medieval Church's social teachings, addressing it to the largest audiences that could then be reached at one time — a packed congregation listening to a sermon. (Hus claimed at one time to have preached to ten thousand.)[6] The social teaching in question was egalitarian within limits, stressed social justice and was critical and reformist rather than destructive and revolutionary — though, partly because of the Church's mishandling of the Hus case, a more revolutionary messianic movement arose after his death. The 'moderation' that we have detected in late medieval and early modern popular protest was arguably influenced by those preachers of whom we are about to study a small group of outstanding individuals, who were none the less surely typical of countless men, especially from the 'professional' preaching orders, who preached sermons more or less as a full-time job.

We begin our selection, however, with a secular priest rather than a mendicant friar, John Hus of Bohemia. We need in the first place briefly to consider the native reform tradition that helped to produce him. We shall review his social teaching, which largely consisted of championship of the Czech poor against a privileged clergy and a comfortably-off German-speaking upper class. Our discussion of Hus will also include his tragic death and the mass reaction to it, a reaction that was intensified through using some of the resources of popular culture that Hus himself had developed, notably vernacular songs. We shall then move on to look at one of Hus's spiritual heirs, the monk Želivský, and to look at the balance between conservatism and radicalism in his social outlook.

In studying Hus, it is helpful to be aware of two streams of influence working on an individual like him who, in common with so many 'professional' medieval preachers, was deeply grounded in the intellectual culture of his Church. With Hus, therefore, we can distinguish between a learned religious culture and intellectuality that were international in currency, and a more popular piety that in Hus's case was native and Bohemian in character, even though it bore comparison with other movements of lay piety in other lands. The predominant 'international' influence upon Hus was that of the most famous (and notorious) theologian working in Hus's youth, the Englishman John Wyclif (1326?–84).[7] Wyclif was a masterly practitioner of the medieval Church's system of theology known as scholasticism.[8] His influence on the University of Prague where Hus first studied and then taught stemmed not only from his accomplishments as a theologian but also from extraneous, largely political, factors. Wyclif's immense impact on Hus, on questions such as the membership of the church, made up a great part of Hus's theoretical system — a largely borrowed one.

The other, less theoretical, side of Hus derived not from Wyclif at Oxford but from a Bohemian reform tradition with strong popular roots, extending back to the later fourteenth century.[9] A religious revival in Bohemia can be traced back to the reign of the Emperor Charles IV (d. 1378). In conditions of economic prosperity engendered by silver mining and in a realm that had largely escaped the Black Death, Charles IV patronised a cultural flowering which included the setting up of the University of Prague and which embraced a religious revival.[10] Intense, fiery preachers entered the Bohemian capital including the Emperor's protegé, the German Konrad Waldhauser, who preached in Prague between 1362 and 1369, bringing to Bohemia the vogue for sermons that was a prominent feature of popular lay piety in the later Middle Ages in German towns.[11]

Waldhauser was the step-father of the Czech Reformation in that his preaching pointed to some of its major themes, later summarised in the 1417 Four Articles of Prague. He drew attention to the moral issues confronting a Christian society shaken by its yawning economic contrasts and its new but selectively distributed luxury. The targets of his puritanism were acquisition and display, and the self-indulgence of a corrupt clergy. If this was anticlericalism, then as has already been suggested, anticlericalism is indeed a complex phenomenon, propagated by clerics like Waldhauser himself and later by the priest Hus and the monk Želivský.

Waldhauser preached in German but already Czech vernacular preaching was emerging in Prague. Jan Milič (d. 1374), a former civil servant under Charles IV, experienced a dramatic religious conversion to a life of poverty and extreme asceticism, and preached in the Bohemian capital in Latin and German, as well as Czech, taking up Waldhauser's themes of social puritanism and anticlericalism. In addition, Milič, a prophetic visionary, adopted and passed on to the Czech Reform of the fifteenth century an intense apocalyptic tone.

This apocalyptic note was taken up by Thomas of Štitný (d. 1401), a layman and a writer (rather than a preacher) in Czech. A member of the lower nobility, Štitný, like the former courtier Milič, shows the deep conversionist religiosity of sections of the later medieval European elites, a trait seen in the anguished piety of a group of English 'Lollard knights'.[12] The advocacy of frequent communion for all repentant Christians which Štitný shared with Milič, along with Štitný's origins in Hus's own South Bohemian countryside, paved the way for Hus himself, whose last major forerunner was the scripturalist and Prague university teacher, Matthew of Janov (d. 1394). The Charles University of Prague also provided a platform for John Hus, as did his pulpit at the Bethlehem Chapel, founded by two laymen in 1391 expressly for sermons in Czech.

Until the arrival on the scene of Janov and Hus, the most

creative elements in Bohemian religious life were Germans and members of the upper classes. Hus himself, born in around 1373, came from an unmistakably Czech and commoner background in the deeply religious terrain of peasant South Bohemia. As was mentioned earlier, Hus operated in two fora, the Bethlehem and the University, but in both he was a spokesman for the identity and aspirations of the Czech majority in Bohemia — a Slav-speaking peasant and plebeian mass maintaining a partly Germanised nobility and an upper bourgeoisie largely of ethnic German origin.[13] As spokesman for the Slav majority, Hus conducted bitter attacks on the German monopoly of office, wealth and privilege in the Bohemian lands. His xenophobia in a country in which 'foreigners' seemed to have all the advantages — not least in university politics — had strong class notes, Hus representing especially young Czechs struggling for recognition in their own country. Poverty was characteristic of many, as it had been for Hus who laid claim to it proudly: 'When I was a poor student I used to make a spoon out of a piece of bread till I had done eating my pease porridge, then I ate the spoon.'[14]

The scriptural doctrine that poverty was a virtue had been emphatically reasserted by the Franciscans, whose influence was still strong; and in Bohemia, it was the poor Czechs, especially the peasant masses, who laid claim to this virtue — especially in contrast to well-off German burghers. If poverty was a virtue, since Wyclif, Hus's mentor, had taught that 'dominion' (power, wealth, privilege) belonged to the virtuous, it followed that poor Czechs should enjoy dominion in their own land. The equation between Czech nationality and moral virtue was probably confirmed by a national myth according to which the ancient Bohemians lived in a primitive paradise of simplicity and equality — an idea that may have helped shape the messianic commune at Tabor.

As an official censor of clerical morals, Hus was obliged to direct his strictures at the moral failings of his fellow clerics, though these failings — luxury, pride, exploitation, avarice — were also classic 'social sins', sins against the poor whose champion Hus undoubtedly was.[15] Indeed, Hus castigated luxury, fashion, avarice, usury and all forms of exploitation, wherever he found them: it is little wonder that his candour began to embroil him with the establishment, especially from around 1409. A typical treatise by Hus — his *On simony*[16] — is on the face of it a straightforward attack on an abuse peculiar to the clergy; yet Hus's themes in this work could readily be turned into a wider ranging social critique — as they were by the monk Jan Želivský.

In *On simony*, Hus lashes out against the proto-capitalist policies of monasteries in swallowing up countless benefices. He attacks the profusion of servants and of luxury goods amongst prelates, who oppress the poor: they 'force the poor to pay for it . . . they rob the poor of their alms'. He praises 'poor priests, poor laymen and women (who defend the truth more bravely than doctors of Holy Writ) . . . '. He condemns 'kings, princes, lords' who permit priestly simony and who are themselves 'guilty of it'. It is hardly surprising that Hus came to be regarded in Prague as the champion of the poor. His observations on simony in fact make up a disturbing critique of social ills — gross inequality and exploitation — and it was left to Želivský to draw out even more fully the social implications of Hussian doctrine.

His anticlerical tirades mounting in intensity, with an attack in 1412 on an indulgence promoted to finance a papal war, Hus was identified as a disruptive demagogue in Prague and was expelled from the city, so as to head off a papal interdict depriving the Bohemian capital of all religious services and sacraments. Hus spent the next two years of his life in his native country of south Bohemia. In that period, his impending tragedy became caught up in urgent attempts to heal the Church's disabling Schism, to end the scandal that had been going on since 1378 of popes, anti-popes and pseudo-popes and to restore unity to the Church's leadership on earth. It seemed to some that the most damaging side-effect of the Schism in the papacy had been the proliferation of heresy and of disobedience to the Church: after all, the 'errors' of the English heresiarch Wyclif had sprung up and spread at the start of the Great Schism. It followed that the clearest expression of the Church's recovery of unity would be the prosecution of such heretics. Hus himself certainly upheld some of Wyclif's ideas — though not the obviously heretical ones. In its sessions between 1414 and 1415 the Church's Council of Constance tried, condemned and executed Hus for the heresies of Wyclif, and the Bohemian nation rose in an explosion of grief and resentment.

Following the execution, we can see how the resources of Czech demotic culture, some of which had been developed by Hus himself, were tapped so as to broadcast a readily acceptable image of Hus as people's champion, as national hero and as religious martyr. The promotion of Hus, whose way of life was indeed holy, might provide an example of how saint cults — in this case an 'alternative' saint — are popularised. The verbal medium for projecting Hus as a saintly national hero was the same one that Hus had excelled in — the Czech language of the mass of the people, and it was developed not only in further sermons and in manifestos, but above all in a series of popular songs, building on the already established Czech tradition of vernacular hymnody and having simple, forceful tunes and inflammatory or anguished lyrics.

Before we examine these verbal and musical media of mass propaganda, we should consider briefly other, visual means of communicating the message about Hus: for example, the walls of the Bethlehem Chapel, Hus's main forum, were covered, some time after Hus's death, with frescoes attacking the papacy and the Council of Constance.[17] These pictures prefigure the greater use, facilitated by printing, of pictures to convey polemical messages to mass audiences in the German Reformation.[18] The Bethlehem wall paintings adapt the convention of using wall paintings to teach religious instruction,[19] but they now use the pictures to put over a partisan, albeit a national, version. Whether the messages were for an illiterate public is a moot point. Their references to Antichrist were fairly technical, though we should never underestimate the religious knowledge of even illiterate audiences exposed to generations of skilled preaching, as was the congregation of the Bethlehem. The cartoons were accompanied by verses written in Czech. These could be read, of course, by those who could read their own language, and perhaps read out the jingles to others less educated.

Other surviving elements in the popular visual propaganda of the Hussite Reformation, such as depictions of the martyrdom of Hus, tend to come from later periods of Czech history and we shall not take them into account here. The popular currency of Hussitism was enlarged, though, in the more immediate sequel to Hus's death by popular songs, deliberately designed, whoever wrote them, to create or intensify a martyr cult of Hus, who had himself vigorously promoted congregational hymn-singing as part of his programme of teaching piety to the uneducated.[20] The Czech song, *Ó Svolánie Konstantské*, for example, contrasted Hus's integrity and candour with the cruelty and corruption of the Council fathers at Constance:[21]

O, ye Council of Constance
Which do call yourself holy,
How did you with great carelessness,
With great unmercifulness
Destroy a holy man!

Has he been thereto guilty
That he showed many their sins
Moved thereto by divine grace,
So that they could do penance
Without any stratagem?

Both your pride and lechery,
Gluttonous parsimony
Did he seek to take away
And to guide you on the road
Of your truthful dignity.

The Council fathers were not the only villains, however. Their treatment of the national martyr would have been impossible without a safe conduct issued to Hus by the Holy Roman Emperor, Sigismund, brother of Bohemia's King Vaclav, who tried to put the breaks on reform, especially in Prague, by installing a religiously conservative set of councillors in the city government. In 1419 these councillors were ejected and killed in a popular coup led by Jan Želivský. The news of the town-hall revolution literally killed the childless King Vaclav, his throne now to be claimed by his brother Sigismund.

Czech Hussite opinion, still incensed at what the Council of Constance had done to Hus, now faced the prospect of having as Bohemia's king the man whose duplicity had apparently made Hus's judicial murder possible. A moral and dualistic alignment of forces was set up, and depicted in the language of eschatological polarisation which had been used in Bohemia since the time Milič had identified Sigismund's father, Charles IV, as the Antichrist. Now in the song, *Slyšte, rytieři Boží*, 'Hear, you knights of God', the enemy of the Bohemian people was identified as *Antikristus*. Extending this language of eschatological drama, the popular song *Povstaň, Povstaň, veliké město Pražské*, 'Rise up, rise up, you great city of Prague', contrasted Prague, now identified as Jerusalem, with the evil 'Babylonian' empire of Sigismund whose claim to the Bohemian throne would necessitate his capture of Prague: 'Rise up against that king of Babylon who is threatening the city of Jerusalem'.[22]

Since the town-hall coup of 1419, this 'Jerusalem' of Prague was dominated by the messianic monk Jan Želivský, who was in many ways Hus's authentic successor in the Prague ministry. True, Želivský's preaching seems even more overtly social — and inflammatory — than Hus's. The attacks on the wealthy — and not just wealthy clerics — seem less restrained, the social programme more radical. This had come about partly because of the more polarised, and indeed beleaguered, atmosphere in Bohemia and in Prague after 1415, and especially after 1419. Želivský seems to speak, even more clearly than Hus, for Prague's Czech artisans struggling against the high taxes, rents and interest rates levied by a German *rentier* patriciate:

> Every Christian should earn his living through work . . . All courtiers and lackeys, ladies-in-waiting, wealthy priests, chaplains and canons, yearn for an idle life . . . Toiling people fall less readily into sin . . . The wealthy have no excuse for their luxury and their precious jewelry . . . If any would not work, neither should he eat . . . Only those who work can rightly say: 'This is our daily bread' . . . they are unworthy of [sacramental] bread that in their deeds have no care for the common weal, be they kings and princes, sworn judges or other idlers of the court, who shun work and flaunt themselves in luxury for which others have toiled and sweated . . .[23]

Želivský does indeed seem to have taken moral and religious criticism to its limits, though it should be pointed out that he does not single out only the rich for attack but also, in the tradition of preachers pointing out the characteristic faults of all the social orders, he attacks dishonest workers as well: 'the craftsmen, goldsmiths, painters, stone masons, carpenters, shoemakers, butchers, bakers'. Also, even in one of his seemingly most revolutionary sermons, on Dives and Lazarus, Želivský shows, with his profusion of quotations from both the Old and New Testament, that his impassioned calls for justice in society come from the very core of Christianity. Linked to that point, Želivský's condemnations of great wealth confronting extreme poverty could be paralleled in sermons delivered by perfectly orthodox preachers throughout Europe: for instance, the manual for priests drawn up by the fourteenth-century English parish priest and writer William of Pagula (who took King Edward III to task for the oppressions of forced labour and purveyance) reminded parish priests to censure usury, false weights and measures, injustice by royal officials and the withholding of wages.

Another fourteenth-century English writer, the anonymous author of the priests' handbook, *Memoriale Presbiterorum*, dealt with the examination of penitents' sins in the Sacrament of Penance. He advised confessors that knights should be interrogated about the oppression of their tenants 'and especially poor villeins with undue tallages and exactions'. Lords should be grilled about their dispensing equal justice in manor courts and were condemned if they extorted 'many goods by violence, whence it sometimes happens that such tenants being reduced to poverty have scarcely enough to provide themselves and their families with victuals'; the author of the *Memoriale* shared with John Hus an insistence that poor rustics have the right to their meagre property: of the *Memoriale*, Pantin says that its 'orthodox criticism' contains 'a strong sympathy for the underdog, for the poor and weak who are the victims of officials or powerful neighbours . . . '.[24]

Želivský in his sermons, then, hardly went beyond proposals for society found both in Hus and in the tradition of social criticism exemplified in medieval orthodox sermons. Having emphasised the relative conventionality of Želivský, we do not need to make of him a totally safe and emollient character, nor to minimise the militantly radical Hussite millenarian revolution of which he was a major leader until his assassination at the hands of conservative burghers in 1422. Macek rightly speaks of him as the refuge of the Prague poor, the fierce critic of patricians and nobles.[25] Away from Želivský's Prague, a disused fortress renamed Tabor became a spearhead for the defence of the Czech Reformation. Beginning its life as a prayer camp, Tabor was much more than just a military bastion. An extraordinary experiment, a new-made society, Tabor's population of uprooted peasants, craftsmen, priests and minor gentry formed an armed monastery of Hussite *perfecti* who, freed from the constraints of traditionalistic communities, could live out the highest ideals of the national reformation: property-less communalism, the New Testament's vision of a world without possessive pronouns, a terrifying conviction of crusade and a strident puritanism.

Above all, Tabor represented adventism, eschatology.[26] It has been said that a messianist recourse to supernatural agents for solving temporal problems becomes more likely when secular mechanisms for removing difficulties fail to operate.[27] As we have already seen, medieval kingship has a crucial role in at least holding out the hope of deliverance from crisis through this-worldly means. In Bohemia, however, even before the death of Vaclav, the kingship was largely inoperative, and the collusion of Sigismund in the judicial murder of Hus made the Holy Roman Emperor unacceptable to Hussites as king of Bohemia; the monarchy fell into abeyance. The Taborite dream of a messianic kingdom must therefore be seen against the background of the suspension of temporal monarchy in a period in which Bohemia became what Florence became under Savonarola, a godly republic. Taborite millenialism in part turned to Christ the King out of disenchantment with actual kings. This millenial recourse also stemmed from the social problems which have been examined by R.R. Betts.[28] These were: the large-scale migrations of population into the towns, especially Prague; the instability of employment, particularly in the building industry; the prevalence of debt and destitution; and the enthronement of the profit motive in the countryside, and especially on noble domains.

At first sight, it might appear that this list of social grievances, lying behind the messianic movement which got under way in Bohemia in the second decade of the fifteenth century, implies that messianism, focused on Tabor, would appeal primarily if not exclusively to the poor. Yet once again we find that a single-class explanation of an ideology like messianism is inadequate. This is because it equates a sense of social protest only with lower-class destitution. It leaves out of account the emotional and intellectual appeal of messianism as an integral part of the Christian, and indeed of the Judeo-Christian-Islamic, corpus of ideas. Christianity is, after all, a faith that proclaims: 'Christ has died, Christ is risen, Christ will come again'. There have been phases in Christian history when the last part of that sequence has been obscured, and yet Christianity, above all scriptural Christianity, *is* an apocalyptic faith, and that apocalypticism has been particularly to the fore in renewal movements, such as the Hussite Reformation and the second English Reformation in the seventeenth century, when biblical awareness has been acute.

Even if we relate, as we should, Christian apocalypticism to social distress and dissatisfaction, those traits need not be the monopoly of the poorest of the poor. If millenarianism is a response to stress and to awareness of decline in one's standing and standard of living, then in early fifteenth-century Bohemia, there were others apart from peasants and urban plebeians who might have experienced such feelings of crisis and resentment. Such included lesser nobles and gentry, who played an indispensable role in the Czech Reformation, above all on the military side and in the leadership of George Žižka. Žižka was not only a brilliant general but also a powerful orator. In his speeches — or rather lay sermons — he whipped up the already existent anti-German feelings of his audiences, inflamed the intense religious nationalism of the Hussite Reformation, appealed to the potent, if vague, example of the 'ancient Czechs' and directed the anger of his followers against their foes as the apocalyptic symbol of evil, Antichrist.[29] The popular Hussite marching songs of the period make a strong appeal to the social stratum which Žižka represented, for example *Slyšte, rytieři Boží* ('Hear, ye knights of God') and *Povstaň, Povstaň* ('Rise up, you great city of Prague'):

> All the truthful empire of the Bohemian land,
> All you knighted people, all you powers that be, ... [30]

The couplet just quoted alludes to support by the nobility and knights for the Hussite cause. Klassen has pointed out the enormous importance of the baronage in the Czech Reformation, and R.R. Betts has shown that before the end of the fifteenth century a major social effect of the Bohemian Reform was the advancement of the titled nobility and the legal depression of the peasantry.[31] None the less, the Czech Reformation has important features of a 'vertical' revolt, such as we see also in the English Rising of 1381 and the German one of 1525. We may indeed describe the Hussite movement in Bohemia as a religiously inspired peasant and plebeian revolt with leadership, both ideological and military, provided by socially alienated squires and priests.

The presence, or even leadership, of gentry and priests, the essential moderation, in the tradition of Hus himself, of so much of the Hussite Reformation should not be allowed to mask the advanced radicalism of Tabor which we considered in Chapter 3: 'Prague . . . together with all other towns, villages and hamlets, shall be burnt and destroyed . . . in Tabor nothing is mine and nothing thine, but all is in common . . . Christ himself shall rule . . . .'.[32] The passionately militant and destructive mood caught in these Taborite articles of 1420 could obviously not be sustained indefinitely. They are the product of an intense millenarian excitement such as is found in societies in which millenarian speculation has already been widespread and which are suddenly shaken by major political upsets, such as England in the 1650s or Iran in the 1970s. In the speeches, or political sermons, of Žižka and his successor Procop the Shaven, it is possible to read something of the retreat from total radicalism which Macek sees happening to the Hussite Reformation after 1421.[33]

The same decade that saw the death of the radical Hussite Revolution also witnessed the height of fame of one of fifteenth-century Italy's best-known and most powerful preachers, San Bernardino of Siena. We will be considering San Bernardino in a tradition of the popularisation of the medieval Church's social teaching, especially its teaching on social justice, and we need also to consider the way that San Bernardino, building on the earlier work of his predecessors in the preaching orders, captured and developed the resources of popular culture.

Circumventing the limitations of mass illiteracy, San Bernardino used popular culture's essential form, vernacular speech. He also employed visual symbols, in particular his emblem of the Name of Jesus, so as to foster popular religious devotion. As with the Hussites' use of the sacred chalice as a symbolic icon, San Bernardino's use of the logo that he made his own — the initials of the Holy Name — became suspect for a time to the ecclesiastical authorities. In the event, San Bernardino escaped serious trouble over this apparently innocuous issue. Unlike Hus, he had friends, not enemies, in high places, but the cases of the two men show that prosecution for heresy in the medieval and early modern periods could depend on the drawing of fine lines, and on more or less fortuitous circumstances.

The resemblances between Hus and San Bernardino, and indeed between these two and our third figure, Savonarola, are close. All these three popular communicators and popular heroes show a fundamental problem of the Catholic Church's leadership in the fifteenth century: traditionally, social and ecclesiastical criticism was the task of preachers and was included in sermons which might be delivered to large audiences, especially in cities. There was, though, a line, all too easily crossed, between reformist criticism and a challenge to the Church leadership. In the fifteenth century, the Church's papal leadership, absorbing a family-centred Renaissance ethic that was at heart non-Christian, became increasingly intolerant of the kind of moral scrutiny that had traditionally been aimed — even against the papacy — by such saintly charismatics as St Catherine of Siena in the fourteenth century.

Some of the tension, overt or implicit, between the Church leadership and its puritanical Catholic critics arose over the question of the imitation of the poverty of Christ, and of all the destitute — the holy poverty that was central to the Christianity of San Bernardino. On economic issues — 23 of his Latin sermons were on such issues[34] — San Bernardino, in a world of increasingly complex economic activity, remained *essentially* wedded to the Church's traditional and strict teaching — the teaching of San Bernardino's mentor, St Thomas Aquinas — on such matters as the just price. San Bernardino condemned all forms of avarice, denounced widespread market practices, in particular the hoodwinking of simple peasants, and attacked all forms of acquisition for its own sake, especially money-lending and foreign-exchange dealings.[35] San Bernardino's attacks on the practices that created wealth — for some — were accompanied by his championship of the poor, the unemployed, the hungry. There was withal an unmistakable threat of social revenge, hardly less disturbing than Želivský's fulminations:

> How many are the cries of your poor, oppressed by your officials! They rise up to heaven . . . Do you know what the moth of the spirit is! It is avarice. All day you [the rich] shake and hang up your clothes, whilst that beggar is shivering with cold. Could you but hear, you would hear his shivering cry, 'Vengeance, vengeance!'[36]

As a characteristically medieval moralistic economist, in common with Želivský before him and Savonarola after him, San Bernardino believed that the manufacture and acquisition of luxury items deflected resources from the poor: hence the ceaseless puritanical attacks on display that we find in these preachers has to be seen as part of a strong social message. Whether or not we regard this message as economically naive, we must acknowledge San Bernardino's detailed knowledge of widespread, but from the Christian point of view, reprehensible practices in Renaissance Italy. These included the payment of starvation wages to weavers and spinners and payment of wages in kind, along with imprisonment for debt for small sums.[37]

In line with established Church teaching, San Bernardino seems to have thought it hardly if at all sinful for a hungry man to steal, but instead considered as theft great wealth that did not recognise the demands of justice and charity — charity to be given regardless of the moral character of the claimant.[38] The threats to the rich that we have already glimpsed in San Bernardino, the forceful presentation of a Christian social ethic, is best seen in his own words:

> The poor call for alms and only the dogs reply . . . You men, who have so much wheat in your granary that your attics are filled and all your shelves laden, so much that you cannot even

keep it clean and it goes bad, the worms eat some of it and
even the sparrows have their share, but the poor go hungry
— what do you think that God will do to you? Let me tell
you that this wheat is not yours but belongs to the poor man
who lacks it.[39]

Traditional as they were — echoing St Augustine — it might
be supposed that San Bernardino's warnings that surplus property
was theft by-passed their intended auditors, that the rich simply
disregarded what San Bernardino, in common with countless other
preachers of social justice, wanted them to hear. To set against this,
we have some evidence of the effect of Christian social teaching on
its intended recipients: anecdotes like that of the financier renouncing his way of life under San Bernardino's influence or of the firms
that set aside funds for alms — 'God's account'.[40] Yet perhaps the
real impact of the preaching of popular spokesmen like San Bernardino was on the lower orders and the poor, and though we cannot prove it with absolute certainty, it seems clear that social teaching
like his was fed into the popular consciousness — the 'collective
memory'[41] — and helped to inspire popular complaint, protest and
insurgency.

The fourteenth and fifteenth centuries are important — for Italy
and for Europe at large — in that they depict a clash of value
systems, a conflict of which we need to be aware as we come to consider at some length the third of our trio of critics and dissidents,
Savonarola. The clash came as received Catholic attitudes — to
wealth and poverty, to family and community, and to learning and
culture — were coming to be questioned by newer assumptions.
First of all, the economic outlook that the medieval Church inherited
ultimately from the gospels — the preference for poverty over wealth,
the distrust of acquisition — was being called into question. It was
indeed inevitable that the continued development of a sophisticated
international economy based on cash would be facilitated by, and
would call forth, a viewpoint that frankly accepted the glories of
wealth, that despised the shame of poverty. The Italian humanist
Poggio Bracciolini — significantly, an opponent of the preaching
orders — in his *On avarice* actually celebrated as a productive virtue
what had traditionally been considered a vice. Bracciolini, a minor
if typical figure in the evolution of a humanist culture, rejected the
exaltation of poverty, praised wealth and rich men and equated
civilisation with riches: 'Money is a necessary good for the state,

and men who love money must be considered its basis and foundation.'[42]

More disturbingly still, views in some ways similar to Bracciolini's, in deeds if not in words, had permeated to the highest Church leadership. In addition, between its absorption with Italian politics and artistic patronage from the mid-fifteenth century and its capture by the Catholic Reformation in the mid-sixteenth, the papacy fell prey to a new ethos whose main features were avarice, aestheticism, power-hunger and nepotism. As early as 1322, the way was prepared for the new outlook in a papal doctrinal statement of John XXII to the effect that Christ and the Apostles were not poor. The pope thereby questioned reverence for poverty and the poor and the distrust of wealth that had been so emphatically reasserted by St Francis and his Order. Yet the new values, including an altered economic outlook, did not go unresisted. Indeed, we see the counter-challenge issued by guardians of the medieval Church's own earlier official attitudes such as San Bernardino and Savonarola.

In Chapter 2 we saw the Church using the concept of peace so as to assert the primacy of the wider community over fragmentary forces, especially assertive families. The quest for peace in the community, prevailing over the various egoisms of factions and clans, filled the whole career of San Bernardino; anathema to him was the current slogan, 'my house was never wont to forgive'.[43] Attitudes like that were the outcome of a view of the individual family as having absolute primacy, making demands on the members of the family to which all other loyalties — to community, to Church — took at best second place. It seems likely that the 'absolutist', or self-centred, family underwent a revival in Europe at the end of the Middle Ages, along with factions, especially sub-feudal factions based on the model of the family, which could offer protection and assistance to individuals within them. It was a period of widespread decline in government, and hence of public order, before the recovery of governmental competence in countries such as France, Spain and England from the end of the fifteenth century onwards. In such conditions, the family and the clan seemed to be the individual's safest refuge. We saw something of the cult of the family in our look at Alberti's *Della famiglia* in Chapter 2. Throughout his life, from the time of his vocation onwards, Savonarola encountered and resisted the demands of the egocentric family.

In our examination of Savonarola, we shall also see him in opposition to a culture, esoteric, neo-pagan and partly secular, which had captivated most of the leaders of Italian society, and of the Church. At a time when worship of the classics and a cult of beauty for its own sake threatened to swamp Italian Catholicism, Savonarola led a populist but also widely supported revivalist reaction in favour of the more exclusively Christian values of the previous centuries.

We shall not in this brief study try to offer anything like a complete picture of him. For this purpose, there are fine studies to which the reader can turn, both in English and Italian.[44] We shall try only to highlight four themes in Savonarola's career. Firstly, distinctively old-fashioned — 'medieval' in his style and attitudes — he represented a backlash against the threatening merger of Christianity into a neo-pagan synthesis. (We shall see something of this when we come to examine Ficino and Politian.) Secondly, in the tension in fifteenth-century Italian life between family and community, Savonarola unmistakably stood for the latter. Thirdly, he championed an inherited Christian economic code of justice and charity against the newer frank exaltation of acquisition. Finally, he championed traditional republicanism against the onward march of the princely state.

We begin this section on Savonarola with an attempt to appreciate the upsurge or revival in the cult of the family in Renaissance Italy, since in part it was against this that Savonarola set his face. With some exaggeration, we might say that the medieval Church did not really get on with the family. It tried to ban the feud, one of the main ways in which the family asserted itself; in baptism, it sought responsible adults as godparents, rather than young cousins whose acting as baptismal sponsors would help weld together branches of a clan.[45] The Church tried to insist on free choice in marriage, and also on free choice as between marriage and holy orders or the religious life. In a way, the medieval Church can be said to have freed the young individual from parents and the dictatorship of the family, if only so as to accept the close embrace of the Church.

In such a caste-ridden society as that of the Middle Ages, the Christian Church held out options of social choice and mobility. Who could obstruct a decision that had been prompted by God? For the real justification of the theory of vocation developed by the Church in the Middle Ages (and inherited by the Protestant Reformers) was that in exercising a choice of life, the individual was not expressing merely his or her will, but that of God. The free choice of a way of life, particularly a religious way of life, often in defiance of parents and customary superiors, was made possible by linking vocation and religious conversion — the sudden in-pouring

of the dictates of God. One of the most dramatic and irresistible
of such conversions and vocations was undergone by St Francis of
Assisi, whose call to holy poverty from the assured life of a central
Italian bourgeois was strongly opposed by his parents.[46]

In addition, through its control over marriage as a sacrament
and through its long-standing preference for virginity over marriage,
the medieval Church preserved some freedom of choice over
marriage partners or indeed over the choice of the married state
itself. The supremacy of a religious vocation allowed the English
dévote Margery Kempe virtually to suspend her own marriage.[47]
Savonarola went so far as to advocate the freeing from marriage
bonds of women who wished to take up the religious life. The long
struggle of the Catholic Church in favour of individual free choice
against the subordination of individuals to the advancement of their
families achieved some of its greatest victories at the time of the
Counter-Reformation. The Church then demanded further
guarantees for the liberty of marriage — imposed decisions could
lead to annulment — and for the choice of the religious life and
of holy orders.[48]

However, before, and even during, the Counter-Reformation the
family principle threatened to overwhelm the Church itself, though
as we shall see Girolamo Savonarola, a herald of Italy's sixteenth-
century Catholic Reformation, represents a strong protest against
encroaching dynasticism in the Church's leadership. The clash
between Savonarola and the papacy has been represented as a
personal struggle between the friar and Pope Alexander VI.[49] Yet
we need to realise also that the egoism of Alexander VI was subord-
inated to a dynastic motive, aimed perhaps at carving out a
hereditary Borgia domain in the papal states. Alexander VI's
ambitions for his family were frankly imperial. Not only did he
assume the papal name Alexander because it was that of a
Renaissance hero of *virtù*, the Greek military genius, but in addition
Alexander's son's name, Cesare, was the Italian version of the title
given to the heirs of the Roman emperors.[50]

Indeed, a significant shift may have taken place around this time
in the conventions of papal nomenclature, indicating the way in
which the worship of the family was squeezing the spiritual life out
of the Church's leadership. When the Sienese humanist Enea
[Aeneas] Silvio Piccolomini was elected pope in 1458, he assumed
the then little used papal name of Pius. The choice arose from a
recondite pun, typical of the dawning triumph, against which
Savonarola was to protest so vigorously, of literature and the arts

over piety in the Christian Church. The allusion was to the recurrent epithet for the hero in Virgil's *Aeneid: pius Aeneas* — dutiful Aeneas, devoted to parents and native land. Required by convention to take on a papal name part of whose purpose was to lose the individual personality in the papal office, it looks as if Piccolomini was cleverly cheating the convention by keeping his former name under an elegantly contrived disguise, thereby clinging to the individualism that historians used to see as lying at the heart of the Italian Renaissance.

However, the focus of ambition in fifteenth-century Italy was not so much the individual as the family, outside of whose protective framework it seemed that the individual had little chance of surviving, let alone immortalising his achievements. That is why the family machine demanded the individual's highest allegiance. If there was egoism, it was the egoism of the clan. Thus, behind the covert allusions of Pius II's name there may perhaps lie an even deeper level of meaning: *Pius Aeneas* — Aeneas the ancestor-worshipper, Enea Piccolomini, devoted to his clan. When this cardinal attained to the glory of the papacy, it was the Sienese house of Piccolomini which was placed there, just as later with the Medici popes in the 1520s and 1530s it was the Florentine dynasty that occupied the papacy. The dynasticisation of the papacy even survived the Counter-Reformation, certainly after its first heady puritanism had subsided: the architrave of St Peter's celebrates the building's completion in the pontificate of 'Paulus V. Burghesius' — 'Paul V of the family Borghese' — while inside the great church fascination with family on the part of Bernini's patron, Urban VIII, is perpetuated in an insistent marmoreal murmuration of Barberini bees.[51]

Before the Counter-Reformation, and in Savonarola's lifetime, such family motivation seems to have been virtually unchallenged as a guiding principle in papal policy and diplomacy. Sixtus IV (della Rovere) threw Italy into turmoil to promote the territorial interests of his nephews, and his successor in 1484, Innocent VIII (Cibo), openly acknowledged his illegitimate children.[52]

Neither Pius II (1458–64), nor Sixtus IV (1471–84), nor Innocent VIII (1484–92), nòr Alexander VI (1492–1503), nor Julis II (della Rovere, 1503–13), nor Leo X (de' Medici, 1513–21), nor Clement VII (de' Medici, 1523–34), nor Paul III (Farnese, 1534–49), nor even, for all his Counter-Reformation fanaticism, Paul IV (Carafa, 1555–9), could ever have thought to heed Christ's call to renounce family.[53] The total allegiance demanded by the Italian Renaissance family precluded altruistic service to society or commune, hid the face of Christian charity, made of blood revenge a supreme manly virtue, exalted conspicuous consumption and extravagance into laudable forms of family self-advertisement, and, with disastrous consequences for the Church, imposed chronic misfits on the clergy, from the highest to the lowest, all for the sake of family finance and family prestige.[54]

The dramatic collision between Alexander VI and Savonarola is one of history's great duels, but it was a clash between two sets of values and attitudes. For Pope Alexander, ruthlessness, simony, and the systematic exploitation of the Church were dedicated to the advancement — albeit frustrated — of the family. In Savonarola's case, and in his own early life, the Church protected the individual from the heavy demands that the family might make upon him. Later, in his mature career, he played his part in the temporary eclipse of the House of Medici in Florence and reasserted the primacy of the whole commune of Florence as a single entity. From the very beginning of his life in religion, Savonarola struggled to resist the claims of family which, as we have seen, had become so insistent, especially in the highest circles, in Renaissance Italy. His choice of the priesthood, in the preaching order of St Dominic, was made in the teeth of parental objections. For the young Savonarola — as earlier for St Francis and for St Thomas Aquinas, and as later for Martin Luther — the Church functioned as a sanctuary of personal liberty. It provided choice for the young in the face of parental dictation over marriage and careers, decisions made in the light of what was considered best for 'the family' as a whole.

Savonarola was aware of what his parents had in mind for their 'house' through him: honour, ennoblement. In rebuking them for their objections to his vocation, he used a metaphor of the classic type of liberated solitary, the knight. Distancing himself from his family, he drew a contrast between 'me', the individual who had made a free choice of the Church, and 'you', the family with its collective ambitions for its future, focused on Girolamo, now thwarted:

> if some temporal lord had girt me with a sword, . . . you would have regarded it as an honour to your house and rejoiced; yet now the Lord Jesus Christ has girt me with His sword and dubbed me His knight, you shed tears of mourning.

The knightly analogy carried distant echoes of St Francis who had also struggled free of family plans. Yet that kind of romanticism must have seemed antique in the hard-headed, family-centred world of fifteenth-century Italy.[55]

In our earlier sketch of conflicting value systems, we said that Savonarola challenged the values represented in what we know as the Renaissance. These values were essentially elitist, anti-popular and aristocratic, the cultural accompaniment of the aggrandisement of great families that we have been considering and also the cultural underpinning of aristocratic and courtly royal states. It is true that conflict between 'Renaissance' and Christianity has often been overstated. Nevertheless, there was between these two systems of thought and of values — two systems assembled here with some over-simplification — a collision over priorities.

There were marked tendencies in Italian humanism towards a new synthesis between Christianity and pre-Christian artists, philosophers, writers and values. Medieval Catholicism had to a degree been capable of assimilating 'outside' influences, notably much of the philosophy of Aristotle. However, Italian, and especially Florentine, Catholicism in the second half of the fifteenth century was arguably faced with the formidable intellectual challenge of a syncretic amalgam in which Christianity would be not so much assimilating as assimilated. Threatened with absorption into Platonism — and even with merger into a revived polytheist pantheon — pre-Counter-Reformation Italian Catholicism found in Savonarola the champion of the faith of the medieval past. His traditional, even reactionary, Catholicism was in intellectual terms relatively exclusive, but for that reason it was more extensive in the range of its popular appeal. Essentially, Savonarola spoke primarily to large numbers of people whose concepts, culture, social attitudes and piety pre-dated the Renaissance which, even in its capital, Florence, excluded the mass of craftsmen, workers and most of the 'middle class' from its essentially elitist reach.

Savonarola, with his deep spirituality, combined with social commitment to the poor, and his somewhat narrowly Christian set of ideas, was in many ways a throwback to the Middle Ages. The religious emphases he represented — the austerity, the anti-eroticism, the passionate commitment to working in and for the social world — raised the curtain on a religious revival — almost a neo-medieval reaction — which reached its climax in the Catholic Reformation of the sixteenth century. Some of the attitudes we detect in later fifteenth-century Italy — the relative optimism, the confidence in man, the obsessive aestheticism, the occasional oblivion about the eternal in favour of a sometimes secular here-and-now

— rested on insecure psychological foundations. As a philosophy, 'humanism', in the sense of belief in man, burst like a bubble in the sixteenth century, with a revival, in both Protestant and Catholic Churches, of the God-centred system of St Augustine. When they peeked through a pervasive, long-term anxiety, the glimpses of optimism of which we catch sight, for instance, in Erasmus[56] were made possible by ephemeral factors as far as Italians were concerned. These were an economic leadership that would eventually pass to non-Italians and a relative but unstable peace enshrined in the 1454 Peace of Lodi — a peace shattered by the French invasion of Italy 40 years later. Even in the years before the invasions, the weakness and division of Italy, presaging disaster, made sensitive observers like Savonarola incapable of any merely human optimism. Ultimately, Savonarola would re-build a scheme for the future on the foundation of the Christian virtue of hope, but in the 1470s and 1480s his initial position was one of confronting human optimism with a sterner realism.

This is evident in Savonarola's early poem of 1472, *Canzone de ruina mundi*, 'Lines on the world's ruin'.[57] The poem seems to reveal a personality in the throes of acute depression — rather like the young Martin Luther — and perhaps, like Luther, taking to the cloister for refuge. It is important, however, to realise that Savonarola left home and family not for the monastery but for the active commitment to the world of the Dominican preaching mission. We will also need to bear this point in mind when we come to consider a slightly later work by Savonarola, his *Dispregio del mondo*. As for *De ruina mundi*, its evident gloom does not indicate an abandonment of the world but rather an impassioned critique — like that of Savonarola's model, San Bernardino — of the world's departure from Christian ethics, especially in the field of social justice:

> Seeing the whole world overcome
> All goodness and virtue entirely spent,
> I see only complete darkness.

> Happy now the man who lives by theft
> And feeds on others' blood,
> Who exploits widows and children in his care
> And brings the poor to the brink of ruin
> . . . To such goes the world's honour.

'I see only complete darkness.' In the *Canticle of the sun*, St Francis had seen only light.[58] Italy's situation, though, certainly by the end of the fifteenth century, was to be very different from what we see as the glad, confident morning of St Francis's day. The country was to become first a war zone and then, relinquishing all its erstwhile leadership of a whole civilisation, merely a set of dependencies of a foreign power. The very brilliance of Italian politics had arrested the peninsula's political development and had deepened the fragmentation that would allow other European nations to make Italy their victim in the period of the Italian Wars. As we move closer to the crisis year of 1494 — the year in which, for later Italian historiography, most of the nation's misfortunes were born — we see fatal internal divisions, easily exploitable by France and other powers, between some of the foremost Italian states, especially Milan, Naples and the papacy. It did not require a Joachimist prophet to understand that balkanised Italy in the 1470s and 1480s was in the midst of the prelude to a tragedy. It was an unstable equilibrium of competitive states, in shifting alliances, whose squabbles were likely at any moment to bring into the peninsula the vast, predatory, destructive forces of the highly organised transalpine or transmediterranean national monarchies. The unleashing of these forces into Italy as a consequence of Italy's internal quarrels was a peninsular nightmare until 1494 when the nightmare became reality.

In 1486 Savonarola conducted a preaching tour in the Lombard country of the North which would be the first in line for any invasion of Italy from beyond the Alps. Addressing the people of the foothills town of Brescia, he predicted that they would see rivers of blood in their streets, the rape of wives and maidens, the murder of children before their parents' eyes, terror, fire and bloodshed. Now as Pasquale Villari tells us, in 1512 Brescia fell to the French troops of Gaston de Foix, and six thousand were massacred. In the 1470s, 1480s and early 1490s, Savonarola's chilling predictions presented an eerie, exact and entirely realistic vision of a calamitous future, a vision — not that of 'Renaissance optimism' — which many Italians doubtless shared.[59]

Yet like our other case studies, Hus and San Bernardino, Savonarola was a severe critic of a world which he ultimately accepted. Thematically linked to the *Ruina mundi* from earlier in the same decade, his treatise *De contemptu mundi*, in Italian *Dispregio del mondo*, apparently composed just on the eve of his entry into the Bologna priory of the Preaching Order, had a fitting subject for someone ostensibly about to leave this world behind. The theme and title seem to have been in a familiar genre, to which, for example, Pope Innocent III contributed. It was no doubt fitting that a friar about to begin his training as a practitioner of sacred rhetoric should compose an essay, eloquently, even hyperbolically, expressed, signalling his departure from the world. Yet that impression misses the point. Savonarola's *Dispregio del mondo* is not a work of a would-be contemplative but of someone whose order and profession would necessarily involve him in daily work in the world. Therefore, *Dispregio del mondo*, like Pope Innocent's *De contemptu mundi*, is a work of moral criticism by a reformer. Critical of the present, it looks to a drastic *reformatio*, though not through human agencies but through apocalyptic divine intervention in human affairs so as to restore justice.

Savonarola's intellectual biography seems to fall into two parts, characterised in the first phase by pessimism and in the second by optimism. Yet the two parts are knit, as we see from *Dispregio del mondo*. This, as early as 1475, already contained the message of collective salvation through moral renewal — the message that Savonarola was to proclaim in Florence from 1494. The treatise has a triple time-scheme, a division of present ills, future but transient punitive crisis and final deliverance, at least of the elect. All that is missing is the identification that Savonarola made after 1494 of the elect with the Florentines. His triple scheme can be indicated numerically, using a passage from the Italian version:

(1) not one, not a single righteous man is left; . . . the good are oppressed, and the people of Italy become like the Egyptians who held the people of Israel in slavery.
(2) but already famine, flood, pestilence and many other signs betoken future ills, and herald the wrath of God.
(3) Divide, O Lord, divide once again the waters of the Red Sea and let the impious perish in the flood of Thy anger.[60]

His use of such a scheme enables us to fit Savonarola into a tradition of prophecy that was a major ingredient of popular culture and popular religion in late medieval Europe.[61] As his Brescia sermon indicates, his Scripture-based predictions, recalling San Bernardino's threats of revenge against the rich, promise a hope of deliverance to the virtuous, to the poor.

In these years of his apprenticeship as a preacher, Savonarola was developing his style and approach which were, as was the convention of the Order of Preachers, clearly aimed at a socially inclusive audience. He used no allusions that a popular audience could not grasp, unlike the modish practitioners of a Renaissance pulpit rhetoric which was replete with recherché references to classical poets and philosophers. The 1486 Brescia sermon gives us an early glimpse into his characteristic approach — one that would have been deeply familiar to audiences, especially urban audiences for whom sermons formed a cultural staple, a source of information, poetry and history, a way of making sense of the world and of trying to grasp its future. Savonarola used historical references and *exempla* derived almost exclusively from a familiar and oft-quarried source, Scripture. In 1475 his allegorical reference comes from an episode that would have been well known to most of his audience, the story of Israel in Egypt. Later, in Florence, Savonarola would turn to an even more familiar scriptural story — one repeated not only in countless sermons but also in street plays and in paintings — the story of Noah's Ark, which he would tell so as to illustrate the same theme of crisis and deliverance.

This was of course entirely in line with the well-established preachers' technique of treating Scripture imaginatively and as an inexhaustible treasury of divine meanings. Savonarola's allegorical approach was ingrained in the consciousness of sermon audiences through the accumulated efforts of generations of preachers: San Bernardino, for instance, constantly used this method.[62] The method was based on an adaptation of the preachers' style to the anecdotal tastes and educational limitations of the average lay audience. Savonarola's use, albeit imaginative, fresh and inventive, of a number of well-thumbed Bible stories is one of the traits that allows us to place him, like Hus and Bernardino before him, firmly in the domain of popular culture. That was in fact why his first preaching ventures in Florence were despised by those who had come to value a more polished and classical style. Such a style integrated topics from classical mythology into sermons — though such an approach meant little to one of Savonarola's favourite stock types, the pious unlettered old woman to whom Plato was a closed book.

Ignorant if devout old women notwithstanding, a sustained attempt to weld Christianity and classicism, or even, it may be, to supersede Christianity by classicism can be seen in a passage from the Platonist Marsiglio Ficino, who after a period of apparent empathy with Savonarola eventually identified the friar, posthumously, with Antichrist.[63] Savonarola was a prophet, and one who revered the Old Testament prophets who had foretold the coming of Christ. Ficino, in his anxiety to incorporate pre-Christian writers in a kind of revised Christian scheme, tried to show how Christ was predicted by a different sort of prophet, Greek and Roman writers. Ficino's efforts are strained, affected and ultimately absurd, but they indicate a major Renaissance trend. It was one that Savonarola attacked bitterly — an attempt to incorporate Christ and Christianity into classicism and paganism, or even to subjugate the former pair to the latter: as Ficino wrote:

> The coming of Christ was frequently prophesied by the Sybils; the verses in which Virgil foretold it are known to all . . . The gods declared Christ to be highly pious and religious, and affirmed that he was immortal, testifying to him very benignantly.[64]

This sort of nonsense can be paralleled by Renaissance writers who avoided using New Testament terms since these were not in Cicero's vocabulary. There is however another point about Ficino's remarks: 'the verses in which Virgil foretold it are known to all . . .'. What Ficino meant here was that Virgil's verses were known to all members of a highly restricted circle of the educationally and socially privileged. That restrictedness was the most direct challenge to the popular, and indeed, universal, preaching mission that Savonarola inherited from his Dominican tradition.

In common with San Bernardino, Savonarola eschewed the showier tricks of the preacher's trade, but he was none the less unmistakably a popular artist, and the Christianity that he promulgated was suffused with traditional popular (rather than elite) culture. The friar was in total opposition to major traits of the classical Renaissance, above all its preference to beauty above all else which, like the cult of the family, had taken over the leadership of the Church:

> Go to Rome and throughout Christendom; in the mansions of the great prelates and great lords, there is no concern save for poetry and the oratorical art. Go there and see, thou shall find them all with books of the humanities in their hands telling one another that they can guide men's souls by means of Virgil, Horace and Cicero. . . . [The clergy] tickle men's ears with talk of Aristotle and Plato, Virgil and Petrarch, and take no concern in the salvation of souls.

And again [Plato, Aristotle] 'and other philosophers are now in hell.

An old woman knows more about faith than Plato. It would be good for religion if many books that seem useful were destroyed'.[65] It sounds ferociously anti-intellectual, though Savonarola was far from being that. Yet there surely was a kind of populist class appeal, perhaps to those of lower or middling social class, and those of little or modest educational attainment. These might take some comfort from the promise that as they were Christians, they were saved from the damnation that was held out by the preacher for Plato — and perhaps even for the fashionable Platonists too.

There was another fashionable characteristic which was missing in Fra Girolamo — eloquence, or at least eloquence of the polished kind employed by the most favoured preacher in Florence in the early 1480s, Fra Mariano Genazzano, of the Augustinian Order. Of this Platonist and Virgilian rhetorician, the humanist Politian, again exalting beauty above all else, wrote: 'I am all ears to his musical voice, his chosen words, his grand sentences. I note the clauses, recognise the periods, am swayed by their harmonious cadences'. It is an extraordinary, but in many ways typically humanist eulogy, concentrating entirely on style — the style of rediscovered Ciceronian rhetoric — and failing to give any clue that the object of this tribute was professedly a Christian preacher. Now in contrast with the elegant pulpit stylist Fra Mariano, Savonarola, on his first hesitant, and indeed disastrous, foray into preaching to Florentine audiences, must have seemed a country bumkin, a crude provincial tub-thumper, lacking refinement of declamation or gesture, lacking even a proper Tuscan accent in his Italian. The Lenten course of sermons that Savonarola gave during his second-ment to Florence in 1482 was not a success. However, the friar undertook a much more successful preaching campaign in the perhaps more old-fashioned and empathetic area of San Gimignano near Siena in 1484-5 and in the North from 1486 to 1489.[66]

It is a mistake, however, to see Savonarola's appeal exclusively in terms of class, regional or cultural orientation. In 1490 Savonarola was recalled to Florence by Lorenzo de' Medici, the city's prince in all but name and the magnificent patron of humanists and artists. The friar's crusade against vice, luxury, human learning, political corruption and civic discord won him adherents from the highest intellectual, artistic and social reaches of Florentine life. Exponents of Burckhardt's 'Renaissance culture' flocked to the friar from Ferrara, although when they did so they had to abandon some or all of the values summed up for us in the word 'Renaissance'. Under Fra Girolamo's influence, the painter Botticelli renounced the neo-pagan themes which had inspired such works as the Birth of Venus and turned to Savonarolan and Joachimist subjects.[67] Pico della Mirandola, the vaunted prince of linguists and an outstanding ornament of the new scholarship, became an ardent Savonarolan. As we saw earlier, even Ficino the Platonist can be counted amongst the friar's disciples, at least for a time. This reminder is necessary because Savonarola's revival was not simply a class-based reaction, or one linked *simply* to a populist appeal to the educationally deprived. Of course, the elite's vogue for Savonarola could be dismissed as just another of those passing fashions to which Dante believed his ever-changeable fellow-citizens were addicted.[68] Yet Savonarola evoked values deeper than fashion in the hearts of Florentines and Italians.

This is why his revivalist campaign, brief as it was, can be described as a foretaste of the massive Catholic revival, affecting all social classes, that we witness in sixteenth-century Italy. The values that Savonarola reawakened were those of traditional Italian and European Catholicism in general, and of Florence in particular. Firstly, there were the patriotism and deep-seated civic republicanism that Medici rule had not succeeded in eradicating. Secondly, he called for moral renewal and Christian social justice. Finally, he recalled a real or imagined golden age of liberty, simplicity, fraternity and frugality in the city republic.[69] This return to older values was facilitated by a new sense of crisis. Just as war and catastrophe in the sixteenth century created the conditions for Italy's Catholic revival, so the country's impending disasters of the late fifteenth century gave Savonarola his audience.

If in this next section we spend some time considering the political development of Florence in the immediate pre-Savonarolan and Savonarolan periods, it is not by any means because we wish to claim Savonarola as a political democrat.[70] Democratic constitutions were not on his agenda, and, as we shall see, his policy for Florence, which he saw as a single entity, was to subordinate the competing interests of factions, guilds, districts, classes and families in a holistic view of the interests of the commune, with a stress on the *economic* (if not political) rights of the poor. We have also been concentrating, and will be continuing so to do, on Savonarola as a spokesman for a democratic culture, eschewing the exclusiveness and semi-secularism of so much of the Italian Renaissance.

In terms of political development, in the fourteenth and fifteenth centuries Florence, with its formal republican constitution, was

being gradually and informally converted into the Medici principality that it eventually became in the sixteenth century.[71] It should be
stressed that, as we saw earlier, Savonarola was invited back to
Florence by the Medici, after his less than successful preaching visit
in 1482. This extraordinary family owed its prominence and fortune
to banking, though the best of the Medici were no mere bank
managers: they were men of learning, political shrewdness, wide
culture and, in the case of Lorenzo de' Medici, artistic creativeness.
The supremacy of the family in Florence was largely the achievement of the patriarch, Cosimo de' Medici (d. 1464) and of his grandson, Lorenzo, called the magnificent (d. 1492).

Yet in the fifteenth century the Medici never occupied a formal
princely position, and if they were advancing towards such a
position, they were doing so by stealth. The old constitution, with
its oligarchic and suspicious republicanism, remained in being under
the slow growth of Medici rule. Though the Medici guided the policy
of the republic, they held no regal titles. Their position rested on
party management, loans to prominent families, the cultivation of
republican affability and the avoidance of princely pretensions, the
pursuit of popularity with the lower classes through the sponsor-
ship of popular culture, and the patronage of the arts and of religion.
So many Florentines — Savonarola included — were in one way
or another their clients, and they took so much care not to offend
the prickly republican susceptibilities of their fellow citizens, that
it was not until after the temporary fall of the house in 1494 that
the Florentines realised that they had conspired in the inexorable
establishment of a proto-monarchy whose arrival was all the more
menacing in that its ascent had been covert.

After the death of Lorenzo the family came to be blamed for
the arrival of the French in 1494 and the consequent catastrophic
loss of Florentine territory to them. In addition, Lorenzo's son and
successor, Piero de' Medici, lost much of the secret of his family's
earlier political success — republican dissimulation, political charm.
Savonarola then became the mouthpiece for a return to the
traditional Florentine virtues of civic puritanism, simplicity and
'popular' government, so that under republican forms Florence
could become a holy city, the messianic kingdom of *Jesus Christus
Rex noster.* When Florence emerged as the kingdom of Christ after
1494, Savonarola discovered that the Medici had been tyrants,
perhaps in the technical sense of being the usurpers of some other
rulers' realm, in this case Christ's. This was when Savonarola
discovered politics and its enormous ethical potential. In his

'pre-political' period before 1494, Savonarola depended on Medici influence to further his plans for the reform of the Dominican Order. Thus, although it is the argument of this chapter that Savonarola espoused republican politics in and after 1494, it is important not to overstate the argument by reading that political position back into his career before the crucial year of 1494. The events of that year persuaded Savonarola of the possibilities of republican institutions as a vehicle for virtue, if not for theocracy: Jesus Christ might become ruler in a republican state just as the Medici had ruled under republican forms.

In the period between the death of Lorenzo and the French invasion of 1494, Savonarola continued to preach his fiery, terrifying, predictive sermons, vivid, concrete and aimed at the widest audience possible. By 1494 his apocalyptic scenario had evolved. Italy was to be punished by God for her sins through the invasion of a great king, likened by the friar to the Old Testament Persian ruler, Cyrus. For Savonarola, all forms of temporal disturbance — preparations for war, civil unrest, epidemics, natural disasters of all kinds, the deaths of great men — were warning signs of even greater disasters to come. His interpretation of signs and portents was part of the popular culture of his time.[72] His programme was also profoundly biblical, derived from the Hebrew prophets, from the Book of Revelations and from the many medieval commentators on it, including Abbot Joachim and the writers on Antichrist.[73] Savonarola's Joachimistic predictions would have been particularly appreciated by popular audiences in Florence. In this city, where the Joachimist-inspired dissidents known as Fraticelli had established themselves in the fourteenth century, audiences were well prepared for Savonarola's message. It echoed an important element in popular culture — important because, as we saw in the case of Tabor, messianic prophecy brings a message of hope for the despairing.

Between 1492 and 1494 Savonarola was preaching his sensational series, *Prediche sopra l'Arca di Noè*, Sermons on Noah's Ark.[74] The story, as well as having the status of a universally familiar folk tale, was a well-established metaphor of suffering and deliverance, as well as providing a simile for the Church. Savonarola gave fresh allegorical meaning to the popular story by reading into it a prospect of divine punishment for sins, exempting a saved remnant of the virtuous. As we saw in our earlier study of Savonarola's use of the Exodus story, he always held out the prospect of deliverance even after the most terrible 'messianic woes', and even if the saved remnant was not identified.

Within his preaching work in 1492–4, a particular point of interest came in 1492 itself, a year indeed of great interest from the prophetic point of view.[75] The death of Lorenzo in April made this year one of obvious importance in Florentine history, while the passing of Pope Innocent, followed by the simoniac election of Cardinal Borgia as Alexander VI, made it a turning point in the history of the Church. These mortalities, predictable though they may have been, were, the friar claimed, foretold by Savonarola; this lent additional allure to his growing status as a seer. North of the Alps, the death of Louis XI and the accession of Charles VIII as king of France would soon have vast consequences for Italy in general and for Florence and Savonarola in particular. In this momentous year Savonarola preached a group of sermons which encapsulated his prophetic system and its dramatic alternation of crisis and hope.

We can see in these sermons important aspects of Savonarola's popular, vivid, sensational and almost pictorial manner. In the sermons the friar related two visionary dreams he had had. The first, taking place in the previous Advent, was a vision of menace and choice. In this vision a hand appeared in heaven, carrying a sword described as 'The sword of the Lord upon the earth, swift and speedy'. In this announcement of divine wrath to the wicked, the sword of the Lord pointed to the earth, bringing war, starvation and plague. The vision, reproduced in popular medallions, became the mainstay of the new Savonarolan iconography that replaced secular art during the friar's heyday. The vision, or a version of it, also influenced Sandro Botticelli in a work of lamentation art after the death of Savonarola.[76]

For all its power, the vision of the 'sword of the Lord' was only a part of Savonarola's prophetic scheme. The sword of wrath was followed by a second vision, in two parts, taking place on Good Friday 1492. Fittingly for that day, it was a vision of the Cross. In the first part of this Good Friday vision, a dark cross arose out of Rome. In shape and meaning, this cross, 'the cross of the wrath of God', was an obvious repetition of the 'sword of the Lord'. Against a black stormy sky announcing a verdict against Rome, the cross of wrath was, however, succeeded by a golden cross rising out of Jerusalem, 'the cross of God's mercy'. This second vision reflects the alternation of depression and elation in Savonarola's personality. It shows, however, that his prophecy, while harsh and menacing in the short term, was in line with all Christian apocalyptic literature and preaching, from the Apocalypse itself onwards: it was ultimately optimistic, because the Cross was the seal of God's mercy to mankind.

Savonarola's identification of Rome and Jerusalem probably indicates his reliance on Joachimist and sub-Joachimist sources, as well as on the Prophets and the Book of Revelations.[77] As for Rome, with its tyranny, its privilege, luxury, sensuality, ease and corruption made possible through the exploitation of the Christian people, it could be compared with the sinful city of Babylon, a powerful symbol of evil: 'this is the city of Babylon, my brethren', Savonarola thundered out in 1493, 'the city of the foolish and the impious, the city that will be destroyed by the Lord'.[78] In fact, Fra Girolamo had in his sights the whole of Italy and its royal and aristocratic courts, the papacy above all because it was bringing to a high point the patronage of the arts for their own sake and for the sake of dynastic propaganda: 'Go to Rome . . . there is no concern save for poetry . . . '. What made Rome and the other courts 'Babylonian' was their worship of beauty. This was the aestheticism that Savonarola denounced so emphatically in his great mass pageants, the burnings of the vanities of 1495 and 1497.

The typological opposite to Babylon was Jerusalem. The actual place fascinated medieval and early modern Europeans: Savonarola's plan of reforming the Tuscan Dominicans was designed to qualify them to preach a mission in the Holy Land.[79] However, Jerusalem and its temple were also types of the Church. Between 1492 and 1494 Fra Girolamo was speaking of the arrival in Italy of a 'new Cyrus'[80] whose triumphant progress through the country would encounter no opposition and who would do what the original Cyrus had done in the Old Testament, renew 'Jerusalem'. Once he had arrived in Italy in 1494, 'Cyrus' could be identified: Savonarola recognised him in Charles VIII of France.

In August 1494, at the head of an army estimated to number sixty thousand and advancing various dynastic claims to Italian territory, Charles entered Italy, bringing with him a chill blast of efficiency and atrocity. The new style of warfare came as a brutal shock to Italians, though Italian writers tended to exaggerate the docility of their own warfare before 1494. The French methods, however, especially the massacres ordered by Charles VIII so as to induce garrisons to surrender promptly, had a deliberate cruelty about them. They were designed to persuade people of the folly of resistance. The tactic seems to have worked. When the French entered Tuscan territory, Lorenzo's son, Piero de' Medici, left the city to negotiate with — or rather capitulate to — Charles VIII. He ceded large sums of money and key blocks of territory to the

French, thereby not only failing to head off a French descent upon Florence but also giving away the resources that would make it possible for the commune to resist. It is little wonder, then, that after making this humiliating and dangerous surrender, Piero was barred from retrieving his position in Florence. The rule of the House of Medici was, to all appearances, over.[81]

What was Savonarola's position during this crisis? We cannot explain the hold he was to exercise solely in terms of his fulfilled predictions. As we have seen, his jeremiads were only part of his prophetic system. A vision of the ultimate apocalyptic triumph of the just was a vital ingredient in his prophecies, from 1475 to the essential optimism in his vision of the cross of God's mercy in 1492. He was about to inherit the authority of a popular leader who alone can promise security in crisis — a security, moreover, which he was to be credited with achieving.

Charles VIII had no dynastic interest in Florence and, deeply impressed with the friar who had given a higher meaning to the French descent on Italy, fell in readily with Savonarola's pleas that he leave Florence quickly. Though the arrival of the French had caused deep fear in the city, in the event their stay was brief and relatively untroubled. To the Florentines, this was almost a miracle, and one brought about by the same friar who, little less miraculously, had originally predicted the calamity from which he had now rescued his adopted commune.

At the height of his prestige, Savonarola was called upon to deal not only with the immediate difficulties caused by the French invasion, but also with Florence's longer-term social, economic, political and moral problems. His successful 'embassy' to Charles VIII showed that, like Lorenzo before him, he was fit to assume leadership in Florence. His role also corresponded to the established role of the members of the religious Orders in Florentine life, especially those of them who came from outside the city as impartial arbitrators, peace-makers and professional experts on economic and other questions.[82]

The four-year ascendancy of Savonarola constituted a revolution in Florence in seven areas. Firstly, the rise of a Medici monarchy, through the extinction of communal government, was interrupted, though the constitution supported by Savonarola was the least democratic or revolutionary aspect of his message.[83] Next, Savonarola temporarily dissolved what had been a developing socio-cultural division in Florentine life between a cultivated elite and a populace still wedded to an older, more Christian, more communal culture. Thirdly, his economic measures and his attacks on 'vanities' made up a moral crusade against the divisive conspicuous consumption of the rich. Fourthly, his popular puritanical campaign created something of a mass party, and a counter-party, both of which were to some extent class-based. Fifthly he tried to include in public life categories hitherto excluded, especially youth. Next he was a spokesman for, and adopted the resources of, popular culture. Finally, in economic, political and cultural life, he sought to re-direct the Florentines away from their obsession with family and faction and towards concern for the commune, especially its poor and unemployed. To sustain his campaign, he orchestrated what we would recognise as the theatre of a revolution, with great public rituals, including his own sermons, mass processions and, of course, the 'burnings of the vanities'.[84]

With the safety of the commune apparently secured upon the departure of the French, Florence's most pressing problem was the form of government of the state, which the fall of the Medici had pushed to the foreground. The city sought a constitutional settlement that would prevent the restoration of a Medici, or any other one-family 'tyranny'. The label *governo popolare* is misleading to us, since the word 'popular' referred to the avoidance of autocracy rather than the introduction of democracy. What mattered was not so much Fra Girolamo's advocacy of a constitution — a modified version of the much-acclaimed Venetian model — as his persuasion to the Florentines to drop the inter-family and inter-faction feuds which had disfigured their recent history. It was surely their obsession with family that had driven the Medici to establish their 'tyranny' in the first place, just as it was the mania for family, creating vendetta, that had caused one of the most shocking episodes in Florentine history, the Pazzi conspiracy of 1478, when the victim, Giuliano de' Medici, was murdered at Mass.

Along with the stilling of faction, Savonarola's attempts to suffuse Florentine life with an ethical revival took in proposals for introducing social justice. Given the restricted nature of the 'middle-class democracy' that Florence adopted, the poor could have little part to play in ending their own distress.[85] The distress existed and was long-standing. Though there is some dispute over the matter, the city seems to have undergone industrial contraction in the late Middle Ages, its population falling from nearly 100,000 before the Black Death to perhaps 55,000 in Savonarola's day.[86] While there was decline in the woollen industry, there was expansion in silk manufacture, along with a widespread concentration of capital and proletarianisation of labour. Many inhabitants knew debt, cramped, sub-standard housing, unemployment and extremely poor diet. This was alongside spectacular wealth and expenditure, much of it devoted to luxury, prestige building and the intense, competitive artistic patronage that Savonarola decried. These are, of course, the sorts of conditions that have fed popular messianic movements in cities from Prague in the early fifteenth century to Tehran in the late twentieth.

While announcing a messianic future, Savonarola and his programme of reconciliation faced a more immediate challenge in the form of the polarisation of the social classes. His campaigns against luxury, above all the burnings of the vanities, have to be seen as part of an attempt to reclaim social resources for the poor. Behind his active Christian commitment to social justice lay a tradition going back through Florence's fifteenth-century archbishop, San Antonino, to the Fraticelli and Spiritual Franciscans of the Middle Ages. To solve an endemic problem of poverty, chronic debt, Fra Girolamo resurrected the *monti di pietà*, low-interest credit banks that had been launched earlier in the city's history by the Franciscan Bernardino da Feltre.[87] His proposal of a ten per cent real estate tax, which was adopted, was probably intended to favour industry and thereby revive employment.[88]

Put at its simplest, Savonarola's concentration on expenditure was designed to cream off the surplus wealth that the rich spent on luxury and display, and to put that wealth at the disposal of the poor. The avarice of the wealthy and the destitution of the poor, the latter brought about in part by tax incidence, was part of Savonarola's depiction of Italy's moral crisis: 'Think well, you rich, for affliction shall smite you . . . the poor are oppressed by grievous burdens . . . when the poor complain, they are told to pay and pay again'.[89] The words of warning strongly recall San Bernardino's 'How many are the cries of the poor . . . They rise up to heaven'.[90] The theatrical climax of Savonarola's crusade to recall the Florentines to their real or imagined ancestral frugality was the pair of burnings of 'vanities'.

The first of these, in 1495, took place in Florence's most important area for public spectacle and ceremonial, the Piazza della Signoría. On a vast bonfire — fires were to play a major part in the career and downfall of Girolamo Savonarola — were set cosmetics, mirrors, hairpieces, perfumes, veils, ornaments, jewellery, paintings of beautiful women, chess pieces, playing cards and all objects of personal pleasure or sensuality. If this was 'social control', it was certainly not the control of the disorderly poor by the elite, but, if anything, the direct opposite of that. A key figure was an effigy or portrait of a Venetian merchant surmounting the bonfire, the real character having reputedly offered the commune a fortune for the items consigned to the blaze:[91] the Florentines were supposed now to have other priorities than profits alone. That the burnings were a celebration of, and an aspiration towards, concord is shown in their choreography. There was dancing by three circles made up of monks and boys dressed as angels, young laymen with priests, and old men and leading citizens with priests. Savonarola was not noted for his sense of humour.

He was, however, as skilled in the use of carnival themes as Lorenzo de' Medici had been. An important aspect of his work in Florence was a kind of youth crusade. Youth in medieval and early modern popular culture had a special part to play, particularly at times of carnival, in reasserting social values through the use of derision and mild, or not so mild, brutality against dissidents and eccentrics.[92] Savonarola adapted from popular culture the roles that youth played in carnival and charivari to extend his work of diverting wealth from rich to poor. Traditionally at carnival time boys in Florence were allowed to extort money for party food and drink from passers-by. Savonarola harnessed this system of rough begging, getting young people to demand money for the poor. Such efforts reached a high point in the transformed Florentine carnival of 1496 when rich citizens gave their costliest goods for poor relief.[93]

Through such actions Savonarola hoped to set Florence firmly on the path of virtue that would lead it to its providential and messianic destiny which had been revealed in the deliverance of 1494. This destiny was threefold: firstly, the recovery and enlargement of Florentine territory; secondly, the leadership of Italy; and thirdly, the reform of the Church. Acting as one in a moral renewal under the direction of Savonarola as the prophet of God, the Florentines would at last accomplish the glorious destiny traced for them in their already existent civic myth.[94]

For the Florentines, the recovery of territory came to be a condition of Savonarola's continued ascendancy. Florence was an empire in miniature, but by 1494 had lost a string of strategically vital fortresses and its dependent city of Pisa, a grain centre whose loss resulted in food shortages in Florence. Savonarola's survival in the city came to depend on alterations and manipulations in

Italian and European balances of power between 1494 and 1498, because diplomatic and military factors dictated whether or not the Florentines would recover their territory. Savonarola was inevitably involved in foreign politics; in the event his downfall was brought about by his inability to control foreign affairs in such a way as to return to the Florentines their lost empire. At the same time, Savonarola lost his influence and position because his theatre of unity was an illusion. In this city of faction, the friar's search for concord was vitiated by divisions of class and party which in the event his campaign against luxury exacerbated. As another Christian civic reformer of morals, John Calvin, was to discover, a drive to make citizens better may create opposition threatening the cause, or even the life, of the reformer.

Savonarola himself created polarities: the good, the simple and the poor against the corrupt, the sophisticated and the rich, the young against the old.[95] His enrolment of youth on his side gave rise to a powerful, violent organisation of young *anti*-Savonarolans, *Compagnacci* or *Arrabbiati*. Underlining the increased polarisation of Florence, despite all his efforts, Savonarola's supporters were enrolled in a party, the *Piagnoni* or *Colletorti*. Like all the best party labels, these latter were pejorative nicknames connoting woeful and puritanical religiosity. There clung to the party something of the atmosphere of an anti-aristocratic grouping, with a middle- or lower-class puritan ethic. With their cavalier style, and the silks and scents that the friar had made his special targets, the *Arrabbiati* had the appearance of an aristocratic party.

Throughout the period of his dominance in Florence, Savonarola continued to condemn the papacy of Alexander VI. Though Pope Alexander cared nothing for the friar's moral criticisms in themselves, he was concerned that Savonarola's sway in Florence was keeping the republic out of the grand coalition which the pope was building in order to drive the French out of Italy. The pope's ultimately successful campaign against the friar was part of a diplomatic offensive. As early as 1495, Pope Alexander tried to silence Savonarola, but in 1496 the friar defied prohibitions and in his cycle of sermons on Amos attacked the immorality of the papal court. The 1497 burning of the vanities was an attempt, using a characteristically Florentine public ritual, to reassert his authority. Yet with the recovery of Pisa as far away as ever and famine and plague in the city, the elections of 1497 went in favour of the *Arrabbiati* and the new, anti-Savonarolan *Signoria* obtained a bull of excommunication against Fra Girolamo. Like Hus before him, Savonarola was to be the victim of politics — international, ecclesiastical and domestic' politics, but above all of the electoral politics that Savonarola had helped to rebuild.

In Lent 1498, in open defiance of the excommunication, Savonarola resumed preaching, an action which, as in the case of Hus, threatened an interdict — a complete stoppage of religious services in a city that could hardly exist without religious rituals.[96] To rescue the friar's position would need a repetition of the miracle of 1494, or of the dramatic successes of the burnings of the vanities, or a combination of both — a miraculous drama, featuring fire, and ending in vindication. The Ordeal by Fire of 1498 was an extraordinary event, even in a city familiar with the sensational. A fanatical supporter of Savonarola, his fellow-Dominican Fra Domenico da Pescia, issued a challenge to an anti-Savonarolan Franciscan, Fra Francesco di Puglia, to take part in a primitive test of truth by fire. The intended drama got off to a tedious start, with much convoluted argument about the propriety of carrying sacred objects into the flames through which the contestants were to walk to prove or disprove Savonarola's claims to have divine backing. Finally, a dismal rain put an end to argument, drama and fire. The following day, an *Arrabbiati*-led mob attacked the convent of San Marco and arrested Fra Domenico and Fra Girolamo, who was brought before a Church court, tried and sentenced on a charge of heresy. The Florentines finally got the bonfire of which they had been cheated in the fiasco of the ordeal. The burning of Savonarola for heresy was singularly gruesome, even by the standards of such events, and some went so far as to liken it to the Crucifixion. The *Signoria* ordered the friar's remains to be carefully destroyed because, as the following years showed, he had a strong following amongst the poor and the pious.[97]

Girolamo Savonarola was a visionary, a Joachimist prophet, a Catholic civic reformer, a critic of social abuses, a preacher of justice, a spokesman of popular culture and a protesting voice against the imminent descent on Italy of an absolutism that would extinguish what was left of the free institutions of the Middle Ages.

Notes

1. Jean Wirth, 'Against the acculturation thesis' in von Greyerz (ed.), *Religion and society*, pp. 68–9.
2. For example of Lollards' attacks on important features of late medieval

orthodox religious practice, see Margaret Aston, 'Lollards and images'; this is Chapter 5 of Dr Aston's collection of essays, *Lollards and reformers: images and literacy in late medieval religion* (Hambledon Press, History Series, 22, London, 1984), pp. 135–92. For examples of Lollard anticlericalism, see Aston's 'Lollardy and the Reformation'; this article was originally published in *Past and Present*, vol. 30 (1951), pp. 23–51 and is reprinted in *Lollards and reformers*, with particular reference here to pp. 222–3. A typical Lollard preacher's attack on the Catholic clergy, using a gospel incident involving Pharisees, can be read in Anne Hudson, *English Wycliffite sermons* (4 vols, University Press, Oxford and New York, 1983 and in progress), vol. I, p. 316. A full account of fifteenth- and early sixteenth-century Lollard beliefs can be found in J.A.F. Thomson, *The later Lollards 1414–1520* (Oxford University Press, Oxford, 1965).

3. Euan Cameron, *The reformation of the heretics. The Waldenses of the Alps 1480–1580* (Oxford Historical Monographs, Oxford University Press, Oxford and New York, first published 1984, reprinted (with corrections) 1986), pp. 78–9, 84–5, 87, 92–4, 100–1.

4. Iris Origo, *The world of San Bernardino* (Jonathan Cape, London, 1963), pp. 149–50.

5. For the interaction between lay and papal criticism of the clergy, see, for example, the complaints of Sigebert of Gembloux to Pope Pascal II (1099–1118), in J.B. Russell, *Religious dissent in the Middle Ages* (John Wiley, London, 1971), pp. 37–9. Ramihrd was a 'Hildebrandine' reformist in Cambrai, killed as a heretic. For him, see Erik van Mingroot, 'Ramihrdus de Schere, alias Ramihrd d'Esquerchin (+1077)' in R.Lievens *et al.*, *Pascua mediaevalia. Studies voor Prof. Dr. J.M. de Smet* (University Press, Leuven, 1983), p. 76 ff.

6. For Hus's claim see *The letters of John Hus*, Matthew Spinka (ed.) (Manchester University Press, Manchester, 1972), p. 46. For urban preaching, see the following: C.N.L. Brooke, 'The missionary at home: the Church in the towns, 1000–1250' in G.J. Cuming (ed.), *Studies in Church history*, vol. 6: *The mission of the Church and the propagation of the faith* (Cambridge University Press, Cambridge, 1970), pp. 59–83; also D.L. D'Avray, 'Sermons to the upper bourgeoisie by a thirteenth-century Franciscan' in Derek Baker (ed.), *Studies in Church history*, vol. 16: *The Church in town and countryside* (Basil Blackwell, Oxford, 1979), pp. 187–99; and Barbara Rosenwein and Lester K. Little, 'Social meaning in monastic and mendicant spiritualities', *Past and Present*, vol. 63 (1974), esp. pp. 16–32.

7. Something of the intellectual relationship between Wyclif and Hus can be seen in John Hus, *Magistri Johannis Hus Tractatus De Ecclesia*, S. Harrison Thomson (ed.) (University of Colorado Press, Boulder, Colorado, 1956), pp. xxxii–xxxiv, 8, 10, 15–18, 20–1, 23–4, 26–8, 34–42, 44, 47, 49–50, 53–5, 64–6, 68–70, 73–8 and *passim*. Matthew Spinka deals with this topic in *John Hus at the Council of Constance* (Records of Civilisation: Sources and Studies 73, Columbia University Press, New York, 1965), pp. 167, 169, 171–4, and Howard Kaminsky examines it in his *History of the Hussite Revolution* (University of California Press, Berkeley and Los Angeles, California, 1967), pp. 35–8.

8. The standard biography of Wyclif is still Herbert Workman, *John Wyclif. A study of the English medieval Church* (2 vols, Oxford University Press,

Oxford, 1926, cited here in the reprint, in one volume, by Archon Reprints, Hamden, Connecticut, 1966), vol. I, pp. 119-20 for Wyclif and Hus. More recent studies of Wyclif include K.B. McFarlane, *John Wycliffe and the beginnings of English nonconformity* (English University Press, London, 1952) and Anthony Kenny, *Wyclif* (Past Masters series, Oxford Paperbacks, Oxford University Press, Oxford and New York, 1985).

9. For the predecessors of Hus, see, for example, A.H. Wratislaw, *John Hus. The commencement of resistance to papal authority on the part of the inferior clergy* (SPCK, London, 1882), p. 50 ff.

10. Betts, 'Social revolution', p. 31; A.H. Hermann, *A history of the Czechs* (Allen Lane, London, 1975), pp. 23-8; Kamil Krofta, *A short history of Czechoslovakia* (Williams & Norgate, London, 1935), pp. 32-5.

11. Bernd Moeller, 'Religious life in Germany on the eve of the Reformation' in Gerald Strauss (ed.), *Pre-Reformation Germany* (Stratum Series, ed. J.R. Hale, Macmillan, London, 1972), p. 25.

12. K. B. McFarlane, *Lancastrian kings and Lollard knights* (Oxford University Press, Oxford, 1972), chs. 5 and 6.

13. Hermann Schreiber, *Teuton and Slav. The struggle for Central Europe* (trans. James Cleugh, Constable, London, 1965), p. 197, and in contrast, Roger Portal, *The Slavs* (trans. Patrick Evans, Weidenfeld & Nicolson, London, 1969), pp. 21, 86; H.A.L. Fisher, *A history of Europe* (Edward Arnold, London, 1936), p. 357.

14. Wratislaw, *John Hus*, p. 76.

15. F. Graus, 'Social utopias in the Middle Ages', *Past and Present*, vol. 38 (1967), p.12; W.T. Waugh, 'The Councils of Constance and Basle', in C.W. Previté-Orton and Z.N. Brooke (eds), *The Cambridge Medieval History*, vol. VIII (Cambridge University Press, Cambridge, 1936, cited here in the reprint by Cambridge University Press, Cambridge, 1964), p. 47.

16. Matthew Spinka, *Advocates of reform. From Wyclif to Erasmus* (SCM Press, London, 1953), esp. pp. 192, 206, 220-1, 235.

17. Macek, *Hussite movement*, following p. 90.

18. Scribner, *For the sake of simple folk*, esp. ch. 3.

19. W.A. Pantin, *The English Church in the fourteenth century* (Cambridge University Press, London, 1955, cited here in the reprint by University of Notre Dame Press, Notre Dame, Indiana, 1962), pp. 239-42.

20. Waugh, in Cambridge Medieval History, VIII, p. 47.

21. From the recording, *The oldest monuments of Czech monody* (Musica Antiqua Bohemica, Aria, Prague), Supraphone 59453.

22. Ibid.

23. Macek, *Hussite movement*, pp. 99-103.

24. Pantin, *English Church*, pp. 196, 200, 207, 208, 210.

25. Macek, *Hussite movement*, p. 50.

26. Howard Kaminsky, 'The free spirit in the Hussite Revolution' in Sylvia Thrupp (ed.), *Millenial dreams in action: Essays in comparative study* (Mouton, The Hague, 1962), pp. 168-73; Howard Kaminsky, 'Chiliasm and the Hussite Revolution' in Sylvia Thrupp (ed.), *Change in medieval society. Europe North of the Alps 1050-1500* (Peter Owen, London, 1965), pp. 249-78; see also the interesting Marxist comparative study by Ernst Werner, 'Popular ideologies in late mediaeval Europe: Taborite Chiliasm and its antecedents', *Comparative Studies in Society and History*, vol. 2 (1959-60), pp. 344-63,

and esp. pp. 345-6.

27. David F. Aberle, 'A note on the relative deprivation theory as applied to millenarian and other cult movements' in Thrupp, *Millenial dreams*, p. 212.

28. Betts, 'Social revolution', pp. 26-30.

29. Macek, *Hussite movement*, pp. 105-6.

30. *Oldest monuments of Czech monody.*

31. J.M. Klassen, *The nobility and the making of the Hussite Revolution* (East European Monographs, No. XLVII, Columbia University Press, New York, for East European Quarterly, Boulder, Colorado, 1978), *passim*; R.R. Betts, 'Social and constitutional developments in Bohemia in the Hussite period' in his *Essays in Czech history*, pp. 272-3, 280.

32. Macek, *Hussite movement*, pp. 112-15.

33. Ibid., chs. 6, 7 and pp. 107-9.

34. Origo, *San Bernardino*, p. 77.

35. Ibid., ch. III

36. Ibid., p. 116.

37. Ibid., pp. 102, 113.

38. Ibid., p. 114.

39. Ibid., pp. 115-16.

40. Ibid., pp. 96, 104.

41. M. Halbwachs, quoted by Martin Scharfe, 'The distance between the lower classes and official religion: examples from eighteenth-century Württemberg Protestantism' in von Greyerz (ed.), *Religion and society*, p. 168.

42. Origo, *San Bernardino*, pp. 86-7.

43. Ibid., p. 137.

44. For example, Michael de la Bedoyère, *The meddlesome friar. The story of the conflict between Savonarola and Alexander VI* (Collins, London, 1957); Romeo de Maio, *Savonarola e la Curia romana* (Edizioni di storia e letteratura, Rome, 1969); Roberto Ridolfi, *The life of Girolamo Savonarola* (trans. Cecil Grayson, Routledge & Kegan Paul, London, 1959); Giacinto A. Scaltriti, OP, *L'ultimo Savonarola. Essame giuridico-teologico del carteggio . . . intercorsi tra Papa Alessandro VI e il frate Girolamo Savonarola* (Paoline, Turin, 1976); Villari, *Life and times of Girolamo Savonarola*; Donald Weinstein, *Savonarola and Florence. Prophecy and patriotism in the Renaissance* (Princeton University Press, Princeton, New Jersey, 1970).

45. Bossy, 'Counter-Reformation and the people', pp. 57-8.

46. For sources on St Francis, see: Marion A. Habig, *St Francis of Assisi. Writings and early biographies. English omnibus of the sources for the life of St Francis* (SPCK, London, 1979), and esp. pp. 230, 635-7, 890-2; also John R. Moorman, *The sources for the life of St Francis of Assisi* (Manchester University Press, Manchester, 1940); and Rosalind Brooke (ed.) *Scripta Leonis, Rufini et Angeli Sociorum S. Francisci* (Oxford University Press, Oxford, 1970).

47. *The Book of Margery Kempe 1436, a modern version by W. Butler-Bowdon*, with intro. by R.W. Chambers (Jonathan Cape, London, 1936), ch. 11.

48. Bossy, 'Counter-Reformation and the people', pp. 56-7. The freedom of vocation on which the Counter-Reformation Church tried to insist features (with particular reference to the religious life) in: Raimondo Creytens, 'La riforma dei monasteri feminili' in *Il Concilio di Trento e la Riforma Tridentina* (2 vols, Herder, Rome, 1965), vol. 1, p. 50, and also in Franco

Molinari, 'Visiti pastorali nei monasteri feminili' in ibid., vol. 2, p. 697; but for a famous story illustrating devious attempts (with tragic consequences) to obstruct these Tridentine aims, see Alessandro Manzoni, *The betrothed* (trans. Archibald Colquhon, Dent, London, 1983), pp. 137 ff.

49. De la Bedoyère, *The meddlesome friar*, esp. ch. IV.

50. Michael Mallett, *The Borgias. The rise and fall of a Renaissance family* (Bodley Head, London, 1970), esp. pp. 180–2. For speculation about Pope Alexander's name, see Orestes Ferrara, *The Borgia pope. Alexander VI* (trans. F.J. Sheed, Sheed & Ward, London, 1942), p. 110.

51. Cecilia M. Ady, *Pius II. (Aeneas Silvius Piccolomini) The humanist pope* (Methuen, London, 1913), p. 151; and see the Sienese and Piccolomini tributes on Pius's tomb, reproduced facing p. 340. Piccolomini's choice of 'Pius' may also have referred to his Sienese patriotism and his taking up, as *Pontifex Maximus*, responsibility for the Roman state, the ultimate focus of the original Aeneas's selflessness. These points were suggested to me by Fr Aidan Turner.

For the Barberini motif in St Peter's, see Roloff Beny and Peter Gunn, *The churches of Rome* (Weidenfeld & Nicolson, London, 1981), pp. 247, 255.

52. See, for example, Henri Marc-Bonnet, *Les papes de la Renaissance* (Presses Universitaires de France, Paris, 1953), pp. 29–39. For discussion of the possible conversion of the papacy into a della Rovere 'secular, hereditary kingdom', see John Addington Symonds, *Renaissance in Italy. The age of the despots* (Smith Elder, London, 1901), pp. 307, 316.

53. For example, Leopold von Ranke, *The history of the popes during the last four centuries* (trans. Mrs Foster and G.R. Dennis, 4 vols, George Bell, London, 1907, based on the 6th edition, 1874), vol. 1, p. 227 ff.

54. Harold Acton, *The Pazzi conspiracy: the plot against the Medici* (Thames & Hudson, London, 1979), esp. pp. 72–3; Symonds, *Renaissance in Italy*, pp. 306–7.

55. Umberto Cosmo, *Con madonna povertà. Studi francescani* (Laterza, Bari, 1940), p. 46; Trexler, *Public life in Florence*, p. 34.

56. Alberto Tenenti, *Il senso della morte e l'amore della vita nel Rinascimento (Francia e Italia)* (Einaudi, Turin, 1977), pp. 229–43.

57. Girolamo Savonarola, *Poesie*, Mario Martelli (ed.) (Angelo Belardetti, Rome, 1968), pp. 3–4.

58. Pascal Robinson, OFM, *The writings of St Francis of Assisi* (Dent, London, 1906), pp. 152–3.

59. For summaries of the Italian situation, see, for example, Cecilia M. Ady, 'The invasions of Italy' in G.R. Potter (ed.), *The new Cambridge modern history*, vol. 1 (Cambridge University Press, Cambridge, 1961), ch. 12, or Peter Laven, *Renaissance Italy 1464–1534* (Batsford, London, 1966), p. 113 ff.; Villari, *Life*, pp. 84–5.

60. Robert Kees Bolle, 'Structures of Renaissance mysticism' in Robert Kinsman (ed.), *The darker vision of the Renaissance* (University of California Press, Berkeley and London, 1974), pp. 119–45. Pope Innocent's actual title was *De miseria conditionis humane*; for the Latin version of *Del dispregio del mondo*, see Girolamo Savonarola, *Operette spirituale*, Mario Ferrara (ed.) (Belardetti, Rome, 1976), pp. 3–7, 293–4; Villari, *Life*, pp. 17–18.

61. Marjorie Reeves, 'Some popular prophecies from the fourteenth to the seventeenth centuries', *Studies in Church History*, vol. 8, pp. 107–34; Robert

E. Lerner, 'Medieval prophecy and religious dissent', *Past and Present*, vol. 72 (1976), pp. 3–24.

62. Origo, *San Bernardino*, p. 37.

63. Weinstein, *Prophecy and patriotism*, p. 186.

64. Villari, *Life*, p. 60; The removal of Christian material from Renaissance neo-classical religious literature can be seen (to take a random example) in Politian's *Oratio ad Deum*, which appears to begin as a Christian prayer — 'O pater noster' — but which develops into a deistic hymn in praise of creation, featuring 'aethere Pan': *Prose volgari inedite e poesie latine e greche edite e inedite di Angelo Ambrogini Poliziano*, Isidoro del Lungo (ed.) (G. Barbèra, Florence, 1867, cited here in the reprint by Georg Olms Verlag, Hildesheim, 1976), p. 181 — though it should be said that Politian could preach fervently on such subjects as the Eucharist, the Passion, and Christ's humility: *Prose volgari*, pp. 3–16. Ficino tried to classicise as much as he could, including the Marriage Feast of Cana which became a Platonic *convivium*: *The letters of Marsiglio Ficino* (3 vols, Shepheard-Walwyn, 1978), vol. 2, p. 54.

65. Villari, *Life*, pp. 179, 183; in Savonarola's convoluted analogy of the plagues in Exodus, philosophy is presented as the plague of water turned to blood, with Plato and Aristotle in 'the devil's house': Girolamo Savonarola, *Prediche sopra Amos e Zaccaria*, Paolo Ghiglieri (ed.) (3 vols, Belardetti, Rome, 1972), vol. 3, p. 192.

66. Villari, *Life*, pp. 79, 82–5.

67. Weinstein, *Prophecy and patriotism*, pp. 100–1, 240, 334–8 — though the Birth of Venus may be interpreted as an allegory of Christian love.

68. *Purgatorio*, VI, 143–151 (*Le opere di Dante Alighieri*, E. Moore (ed.) Oxford, 1963), p. 61

69. Charles T. Davis, 'Il buon tempo antico' in Nicolai Rubinstein (ed.), *Florentine studies. Politics and society in Renaissance Florence* (Faber & Faber, London, 1968), pp. 50–3, 64–7.

70. For Savonarola's politics, there is a summary, with the right degree of ambiguity, in Domenico di Agresti, *Sviluppi della riforma monastica Savonaroliana* (Olschki, Città di Castello, 1980), p. xi: 'a republican government having a democratic base of a certain breadth'.

71. Studies of Florence include: Arnaldo d'Addario, *La formazione dello stato moderno in Toscana* (Adriatica, Lecce, 1976); Rudolf von Albertini, *Firenze dalla repubblica al principato* (trans. Cesare Cristolfini, Einaudi, Turin, 1970); Gene Brucker, *Renaissance Florence* (John Wiley, London, 1969), esp. ch. 7; Umberto Dorini, *I Medici e loro tempi* (Nerbini, Florence, 1982); Giovanni Fanelli, *Firenze* (Laterza, Rome, 1980); D.V. and F.W. Kent, *Neighbours and neighbourhood in Renaissance Florence: the district of the Red Lion in the fifteenth century* (J.J. Austin, Locust Valley, NY. 1982); Francis William Kent, *Household and lineage in Renaissance Florence. The family life of the Capponi, Ginori, and Rucellai* (Princeton University Press, Princeton, New Jersey, 1977).

For Cosimo de' Medici, see Dale Kent, *The rise of the Medici faction in Florence 1426–1434* (Oxford University Press, Oxford, 1978). For Lorenzo, see, for example, Sara Sturm, *Lorenzo de' Medici* (Twayne, New York, 1974). In her recent biography (Hamish Hamilton, London, 1984), Judith Hook argues that there was certainly an implied collision between Savonarola and Lorenzo but that it must not be exaggerated (pp. 181–2). For the Fraticelli etc., see John L. Stephens, 'Heresy in medieval and Renaissance Florence',

Past and Present', vol. 54 (1972), pp. 25-60.

72. For example, Kaspar von Greyerz, 'Religion in the life of German and Swiss autobiographers (sixteenth and early seventeenth centuries), in von Greyerz (ed.), *Religion and society*, p. 229 ff.

73. Emmerson, *Antichrist in the Middle Ages*, p. 56.

74. Villari, *Life*, pp. 185-6.

75. For example, Marcel Bataillon, 'The idea of the discovery of America among the Spaniards of the sixteenth century' in Roger Highfield (ed.), *Spain in the fifteenth century 1369-1516* (Stratum Series, ed. J.R. Hale, Macmillan, London, 1972), pp. 451-4.

76. Girolamo Savonarola, *Prediche sopra i salmi*, (Vicenzo Romano (ed.) (3 vols, Belardetti, Rome, 1969), vol. 1, p. 59; Weinstein, *Prophecy and patriotism*, pp. 70-1, 203 and between 226 and 227.

77. Villari, *Life*, pp. 154-5; E.R. Daniel, 'Apocalyptic conversion: the Joachimite alternative to the Crusade' in Delno C. West (ed.), *Joachim of Fiore in Christian thought. Essays on the influence of the Calabrian prophet* (2 vols, Burt Franklin, New York, 1957), vol. 1, pp. 306, 308, 320; Emmerson, *Antichrist*, pp. 61, 260, note 72, 267, note 16.

78. Savonarola, *Poesie* p. 4; the fact that Rome — 'Babillonia Roma' — (cf. Emmerson, *Antichrist*, p. 267, note 16) was 'full of pride, lust, avarice and simony' announced the renovation of the Church: *Prediche sopra i salmi*, vol. 1. pp. 44, 52; yet the more than conventional reverence that Savonarola was capable of expressing for Rome and the papacy — *Poesie*, pp. 13-14, and *Le lettere di Girolamo Savonarola*, Roberto Ridolfi (ed.) (Olschki, Florence, 1933), pp. 55-8 — indicates an ambivalence, perhaps arising out of Joachimist expectations of an 'angelic' pope: *Lettere*, p. 102.

79. Villari, *Life*, pp. 181, 183.

80. 2 Chron., 36, 22-3.

81. Acton, *Pazzi conspiracy*, p. 104; Piero Pieri, *Il Rinascimento e la crisi militari Italiana* (Einaudi, Turin, 1968), pp. 304-19; Villari, *Life*, pp. 207-8.

82. Weinstein, *Prophecy and patriotism*, ch. 8; Trexler, *Public life*, pp. 37-9; Savonarola himself alluded to the traditional peace-making role of his Dominican Order: *Prediche sopra i salmi*, vol. 1, pp. 108-9.

83. On Savonarola as a 'democratic champion' (in a democracy of about 3,000 voters), see Ferdinand Schevill, *History of Florence, from the founding of the city through the Renaissance* (Harcourt Brace, New York, 1936, cited here in the 3rd reprinting, by Frederick Ungar, New York, 1976), p. 439; for Savonarola's ideas on avoiding both tyranny and disorder through entrusting the citizens' rights to a 'certain number of citizens who exercise the authority of the whole people', see his tract, *Della instituzione e modo del governo civile* in *Prediche sopra Aggeo*, ed. Luigi Firpo (Belardetti, Rome, n.d.), p. 474.

84. Bruce Lenman, 'The limits of Godly discipline in the early modern period with particular reference to England and Scotland' in von Greyerz (ed.), *Religion and society*, p. 130.

85. Trexler, *Public life*, p. 11; Savonarola certainly did advocate the inclusion of artisans in public office: Weinstein, *Prophecy and patriotism*, p. 156.

86. Samuel Kline Cohn, *The laboring classes in Renaissance Florence* (Academic Press, New York, 1980), pp. 10-11, 14-15, 67, 69, 124; Trexler, *Public life*, pp. 475, 78-9.

87. Umberto Cassuto, *Gli Ebrei a Firenze nell' età del Rinascimento* (Olschki,

Florence, 1918), pp. 66-7.

88. For Savonarola's 'equitable' tax proposals, see Weinstein, *Prophecy and patriotism*, p. 254, and Villari, *Life*, pp. 275-7, 482-3; note also plans to regenerate the woollen and silk industries, and the efforts at poor relief through charity: Ridolfi, *Life*, pp. 91, 128; see also d'Addario, *La formazione dello stato*, pp. 86-7.

89. Villari, *Life*, p. 126.

90. Origo, *San Bernardino*, p. 102.

91. Trexler, *Public life*, p. 41.

92. Natalie Zemon Davis, *Society and culture in early modern France*, ch. 4.

93. Villari, *Life*, pp. 368-9, 419, 485.

94. Villari, *Life*, p. 379.

95. Trexler, *Public life*, pp. 420-1, 474-82.

96. Ibid., pp. 488-9.

97. C. Vasoli, 'Une secte hérétique Florentine à la fin du 15ᵉ siècle: les "Oints" ' in Jacques le Goff (ed.), *Héresies et sociétés dans l'Europe pré-industrielle 11ᵉ-18ᵉ siècles* (Communications et débats du Colloque du Royaumont, 27-30 Mai 1962; École Pratique des Hautes Études — Sorbonne, VIᵉ Section: Sciences Économiques et Sociales, Civilisations et Sociétés, 10, Mouton, Paris, 1968), pp. 259-71.

5

Conclusion: Social Control and Popular Culture in Early Modern Europe

In terms of the periodisation of history, the sixteenth and seventeenth centuries have traditionally been regarded as the opening of the modern era. The consolidation of great states, the Protestant Reformation, the great discoveries and the scientific revolution marked major shifts away from the medieval order. However, in many ways the sixteenth and seventeenth centuries can be regarded as the last medieval rather than the first modern centuries: the leading American historian of the Pilgrim Fathers stressed their scholastic and Augustinian intellectual roots.[1] The centuries in question saw little progress towards modernisation in the sense of improvement in western man's material standard of living — at least not until after mid-way through the seventeenth century. If anything, these centuries witnessed a deterioration for most, reaching a nadir in the first half of the seventeenth century.

Despite scientific progress, there were few improvements in technology, either industrial or agrarian, to assist European man's mastery over what had always been a challenging environment. True, there were impressive drainage schemes in Holland and England in the seventeenth century. Yet there was one cosmic factor over which man could have no control, one he did not even understand. Although its ultimate causes are still something of a mystery, it is clear that there was a long-term weather crisis — a 'little ice age' — causing food shortages and famine.[2] Despite this, and despite recurrent plague, over much of Europe an upward demographic trend continued into the seventeenth century. In countries such as France, the level of population taxed to the limit or exceeded available food resources.[3]

A vital difference between our modernity and the pre-modernity of our period is that we tend to resort to scientific, technological

156

and administrative solutions to material and social questions and problems. Such solutions indeed form much of our 'magic' and our 'religion'. Pre-modern Europeans looked instead for supernatural answers to questions and supernatural solutions to problems. This meant that 'religion' did not in any way lose its grip — in favour of rationalist approaches — between the Middle Ages and the sixteenth century. Far from it: the grip was tightened. The religion in question — for most Europeans, Christian religion — was still heavily social and instrumental: it was concerned with the social order, the community and with influencing nature.

Religion remained a mass force. A volcanic series of religious revivals continued to rumble across Europe during these centuries. England and Scotland seemed in particular to be in the grip of an almost continuous religious reformation. Messianism and millenarianism exerted an even greater fascination than they had in the Middle Ages. They were the antidotes to a pervasive and entirely understandable anxiety. There were, it is true, large pockets of religious ignorance and indifference. There were spectacular blasphemers who set out, with considerable success, to shock, such as the Elizabethan playwright Christopher Marlowe. There were people who constructed their own intricate cosmological systems, like the Italian miller Menocchio. Many Europeans — not necessarily from the lowest social strata alone — knew or cared little of or for Christianity. For all that, it will be argued that Christian religion remained a major part of the mental world of the great mass of Europeans. Many rejected the over-dogmatising of professional theologians. The old anticlericalism remained strong. Yet Christian religion was a *popular* force, and the religious renewals that we know as the Reformation and the Catholic or Counter-Reformation were not simply imposed by clerics and elites on an indifferent or recalcitrant populace.

The hold exerted by religion in the sixteenth and seventeenth centuries was related to the insecurity of life. As a salvationary religion dealing with life after death, Christianity offered an escape from damnation in the all too likely event of a sudden or early death.

Between the first invasion of the Black Death in the mid-fourteenth century and its retreat, country by country, in the seventeenth, Europe was seized by a massive anxiety focusing on death. Death was a personality, one of the most forceful in the universe. A major talking point in the theological and political thought of late medieval and early modern Europe was the degree of authority inhering in sovereign forces. Was God, for instance, an absolute or a limited power? Or was the power of kings arbitrary or limited? Whatever answers were given to those questions with regard to God and kings, it was clear that Death accepted no constraints. Death's triumph was total and the marks of his victory were contempt for all men and unpredictability. Death came 'prematurely' to vastly more Europeans in the period we are considering than is the case today. Infant mortality was appallingly high and, for many, birth and death were effectively simultaneous. Childhood mortality was horrific in all families from the highest to the lowest.[4]

A warrior caste such as the nobility in early modern Europe tends to be heavily suicidal — and I dwell somewhat on sudden death among the great ones because of its psychological effect on society at large, in convincing all of death's invincibility. Great families such as the Guises were bled away in revenge killings in the French Wars of Religion. The vogue for sectarian assassination in the second half of the sixteenth century made power and regality dangerous. Jousting, before its imminent demise, still took its toll in accidents and deaths. The prestige diet of the leading classes could itself be lethal — too much meat, too much drink.[5]

An outstanding victim of power and the courtly lifestyle — prematurely aged, dead at 58 — was the Emperor Charles V. I select Charles because, as the most powerful man in Europe, he seems to have exemplified a theme repeated in European art since the Black Death, the *danse macabre*. In this depiction of a dance, Death set a tempo and led all men and women, from pope and emperor, to peasant and pauper, to their certain end. Brueghel's *Triumph of Death*[6] is a late adaptation of the theme. In the foreground of this horrifying work lies Death's highest-ranking victim, a king or perhaps an emperor. Death's caprice was endless and his power infinite — levelling even the rigid hierarchical divisions of society ordained by God Himself.

All Europeans knew death's power. War, international and internecine, filled the greater part of the periods 1494–1558, 1562–98 and 1618–48. For those on its path, a distinction between combatants and non-combatants was virtually meaningless. Apart from the activities of marauding troops, including the massacres of populations in great cities such as Rome (1527), Antwerp (1576) and Magdeburg (1631), armies probably kept plague active in Europe for longer than it would otherwise have survived. Another source of sudden mortality was fire: housing was generally of wood, fire prevention inadequate and towns heavily at risk. Burnings for another reason — deliberate execution by fire for religious dissent

— took place all over Europe, with high spots in areas such as the Netherlands and Spain. In these centuries of the 'witch craze', thousands, generally women, were burnt.

As for deaths by violence, the question whether or not pre-modern Europeans were in some way temperamentally more prone to violence than are modern Europeans cannot be answered here.[7] What is certain is that with poor policing everywhere the individual had largely to defend himself, his kin and their precious 'honour' against insult, assault, theft and murder. People carried knives to eat with — and to stab with. Urban murder rates — in sixteenth-century Artois, to take one example[8] — were especially high.

Nature conspired with one's fellow man to shorten life. Speaking very roughly, we could say that the plague came in waves on average every ten to fifteen years, winnowing population, and perhaps taking two million out of France's seventeenth-century population.[9] The question, much debated amongst historians of plague, of the impact of official action in stemming plague in the seventeenth century, is of interest to us here since it concerns a matter of attitude to man's control over the environment and over death. Any success of quarantine measures in checking plague would certainly have given a fillip to psychological confidence in man's mastery over forces that had hitherto mastered him. Any such conquests, as also with the victory over famine, would have to wait until after the crucial mid-seventeenth century watershed.[10]

How did death's insistence and omnipresence affect the attitudes, the psychology, the unspoken assumptions, of Europeans in a period — the sixteenth, and the first two-thirds of the seventeenth centuries — before European man had gained any tolerable measure of control over his environment? I suggest that their lives and thinking were affected in three major ways: stoicism; disorganisation; and religion.

Stoicism is the philosophic face of indifference, and indifference is not far removed from callousness. Were sixteenth- and seventeenth-century Europeans callous? Their acceptance, perhaps their enjoyment, of brutal legal punishments and of executions suggest that they were. The view has been put forward that in the mass they were hardened and indifferent to the deaths of their spouses and children, that the age of family affection had not arrived and that people tended to be cold and incapable of much love. In particular, it has been claimed that since they were virtually sure that many of their children were going to die young, they avoided 'investing' much affection in them. Such views as these raise questions which cannnot be answered here about how innate to human nature are such features as love of children over time and space. There is certainly evidence of heart-rending lamentation at the deaths of children, though it may be that very young infant mortalities were accepted more calmly. [11]

Stoicism was a more philosophically derived way of coping with tragedy — and with happiness. Originally a Roman set of ideas, it enjoyed great vogue in our period and was built into the code of the Spanish gentleman. The realisation of that ideal was Philip II, who would show as little grief at a great defeat like that of the Armada as he would joy at a great victory like that of Lepanto. How much such traits were found throughout the social scale must be an open question. Perhaps it is no accident that a favourite passage of Scripture — for Luther, for instance — was Job. [12] One has an impression of a mass of Europeans capable of enduring — and, it must be said, of inflicting — much pain. Hard times produce hard people.

It may be that the imminent presence of death affected the psychology of Europeans in the ways in which they organised, or did not organise, their lives and activities. The sixteenth century in particular was an age of heroic enterprises. Yet for all their importance, these were often rushed and botched in planning and preparation. The Armada, for instance, set out with massive gaps in elementary provisions: the water barrels would not hold good water. The logistical impulsiveness of the Armada suggests uncommon urgency. Now the man designated to lead the Armada to victory, the Prince of Parma, was dead of a wound, aged 47, within four years of the campaign. Much of the human effort of the period suggests a frantic attempt to rush things through before death stepped in to cancel the effects of all endeavour. [13]

In our period, Christian religion offered the only real existing resistance to the triumph of death: hence its undimmed, indeed its increased mass appeal. Ignoring for the moment the important distinctions of Catholic and Protestant, I wish to argue that in the sixteenth and seventeenth centuries, Christian religion was an inherent mass ideology: that is to say, the European masses were not simply dragooned by their rulers and dictated to in the matter of religious direction. Coercion certainly happened but it tended to be uphill work. Over a lengthy period, England's Tudor governments secured religious reformation, but they were forced to adopt for popular consumption a hybrid between Protestantism and the past. Peasants and urban lower orders tended to have strong

160

religious preferences of their own and they were capable of promoting, or obstructing, or modifying the nature of religious change. Whether these lower strata adopted or opposed religious innovation would depend on the nature and extent of the innovation in question, and upon different political and social factors operating in different parts of Europe.

Over much of Germany in the 1520s, plebeians, including miners and peasants, seemed to be enthusiastic for the Reformation — though it is worth noting that the Reformation in question was the most conservative of the Continental Reformations. This mass enthusiasm was assisted by social factors. Popular anticlericalism was particularly bitter in the German lands and it fuelled patriotic hatred of Rome. Lutheranism seemed to give support to a movement of national reform that climaxed in the Peasants' Revolt. In cities such as Strassburg plebeians set the pace of religious change.

In other countries, however, religious change fared less well with the common people. The French peasantry was largely unsympathetic, as we shall see later. In England major sixteenth-century popular risings — the 1536-7 Pilgrimage of Grace and the 1549 Western Rising — evinced the articulate conservative religious preferences of the common people, along with their economic grievances. In South Germany, the retention of pilgrimages helped to keep Catholicism genuinely popular in Bavaria.[14] In Spain ardent popular Catholicism was fostered by racism and by a kind of inverted snobbery amongst the lower orders. The best-selling 'green books' purported to show that the highest families in the country had Jewish or Moslem ancestors — a stigma in this frankly racist society. In contrast, the very poorest could claim, through their undeviating Catholicism and for want of evidence to the contrary, that of their ancestors, a kind of nobility — that of 'purity of blood': 'in Spain there is more esteem for a pure-bred commoner than for a *hidalgo* who lacks this purity.'[15]

Clearly, a mass attachment to one religious form or another in early modern European societies has to do with more than strictly religious factors in the narrow, modern sense of the word. The majority of the French urban masses in the sixteenth century was, or at least became after about 1570, fanatically Catholic, expressing their bigotry in ferocious massacres. Their actions were prompted by the fear that Protestants in their midst 'polluted' their communities.[16] Such attitudes were encouraged by indoctrination, especially revitalised preaching, as the Counter-Reformation and its new Orders made their presence felt. This was not, however, simply a case of manipulative propaganda on the part of elites, but something more complex and two-way: for instance, mob attacks on Protestants in France during the Wars of Religion were replicas of mass attacks, encouraged by the preaching of religious Orders, on Jews in medieval towns. Violent hatred of religious minorities and their use as scapegoats in times of trouble were, or had over time become, built into mass culture, and were given a new direction in the France of the Wars of Religion. Catholicism had become indigenous to a French popular culture that had been in the process of being assembled — preachers taking a major part in its slow construction — throughout the medieval centuries. In the sixteenth century, Catholicism continued to embrace and be embraced by popular culture, though its devotional intensity could dwindle, as it seems to have done between c. 1540 and c. 1570.

The saint cult was particularly strong amongst the masses.[17] Some of its imaginative wealth was about to be sacrificed to Counter-Reformation hagiographic scholarship. Does this represent an attack by a learned elite on an important religious ingredient in popular culture? In some ways it does: popular wonder-workers such as St Christopher, St Uncumber (who had the useful trick of ridding women of unwanted husbands) and St Blaise (who was almost a complete religion in his own right) won short shrift from the humanist-inspired critical historical scholarship of the Catholic Reformation.[18] Yet not all of the traditional saints were swept away. As part of its abiding traditionalism, the Counter-Reformation firmly restated the usefulness of invoking the saints. Well-authenticated medieval saints, such as the much-loved Antony of Padua, were recommended for veneration, especially at pilgrimage sites. Although in the Counter-Reformation period Urban VIII forbade spontaneous popular canonisations, there was still official responsiveness to popular recognition of saintliness. With some existing saints, the cult might be altered or stepped up. St Joseph, for instance, now came to be regarded as the patron saint of marital restraint. Devotion to Mary, which we considered in Chapter 2, hardly altered in character and if anything increased in intensity. Some of the new saints of the Counter-Reformation itself emerged as well-documented popular hero figures. Francis Xavier represented the exotic adventures of the foreign mission, Vincent de Paul exemplified compassion for the poor, orphans and prisoners, and Carlo Borromeo stood for personal asceticism and service to the poor, especially in plague epidemics.[19]

As part of his incessant work in his Milan archdiocese, Carlo

Borromeo put in hand a schedule of the genuine relics in his cathedral. The relic cult, a major and to us extraordinary feature of medieval mass piety,[20] undoubtedly had curbs placed upon it in the Counter-Reformation period. The curbs did not always work. As late as the nineteenth century, at the internment of the saintly Calabrian Fra Egidio, a surgeon tried to cut off a toe from the deceased's foot. The incident recalls the earlier events allegedly surrounding the internment of a popular saint when 'one of the deceased's toes was bitten off with a most regrettable excess of devotion by the teeth of a man in the crowd, who wished to preserve it as a relic'. Possession of the milk of Mary, sometimes liquefying, was still claimed in some places — again as late as the nineteenth century.[21] Despite these sometimes bizarre manifestations, there is no doubt that the relic craze which loomed so large in medieval popular religiosity was much less prominent in approved Counter-Reformation spirituality.

Do we read into this another attack by learned elites on popular religious culture? — not necessarily. Upon the dethronement of discredited, albeit popular, saints, new saintly heroes were installed: the saint cult itself, so important in popular piety, was not diminished. In the same way, the playing down of saints' relics led to a further development of popular devotion to the greatest 'relic' of all, the eucharistic Host. The Council of Trent emphatically approved worship of the reserved Host:

> And so no place is left for doubting that all Christ's faithful should in their veneration display towards this most Holy Sacrament the full worship of adoration which is due to the true God, in accordance with the custom always received in the Catholic Church.[22]

'Always received in the Catholic Church': it is arguable that the Church's clerical leadership 'received' the worship of the eucharistic Host in large part from lay people and religious sisters. The feast of Corpus Christi was of such popular origin, as was the practice of elevating the Host in the Mass, which medieval priests began to do in response to lay promptings. Having argued that reverence for the Host as God was largely a popular cult adopted by the clerical Church, we should also try to see how the popular 'groundswell of eucharistic piety' can be related to Innocent III's official acceptance of Transubstantiation as dogma.[23] The exchange between 'popular religion' and 'elite religion' is clearly complex and not one-way.

The clergy evolve a dogma, there is a popular paraliturgical response to the doctrinal development, and the clergy incorporate, and may further elaborate upon, the devotional responses. An example of the last phase in the sequence of initiative, response and counter-responses is the way the Counter-Reformation clergy, especially the Jesuits, extended eucharistic devotions, such as the forty-hour exposition, *Quarant' Ore*, outside the Mass so as to cater for lay eucharistic piety.

The idea that the Counter-Reformation — and also the various forms of the Protestant Reformation — represented the religious front of a massive attack on 'popular culture' has become widely received.[24] The thesis has been deeply documented and is in many respects unanswerable. Yet it rests on the assumption that there existed a single, homogeneous popular culture — largely equated with pre-literacy, with play, carnival and pleasure — at the mercy of a single elite culture, largely equated with a work ethic, with self-restraint, education and rationality. According to this thesis as applied to the Counter-Reformation, seminary-educated priests, of urban middle and upper-class origin and trained in the classics, imposed an alien discipline on the peoples of Catholic Europe, in particular from about 1600. They attacked charivari, carnival and the popular burlesque groups known in France as '*royaumes*' or '*reinages*'. Dancing, drinking, and 'profanisation' of the church building all came under attack from these Tridentine Malvolios. Sociable religion was to become private piety. Autonomous lay religious societies became clerically controlled sodalities. The 'new priests' were austere, cold and aloof: far removed from the gregarious ordained peasants of yesteryear, these were frightening cadres broken and re-made by long training in distant, urban seminaries. Imposed on the countless villages of Catholic Europe, they were missionaries of the all-conquering city, the absolutist state and its ally, the Tridentine Church.

To repeat, much — and more — of the model is indeed valid. Religion *was* to be interiorised, behaviour in church was to be restrained, and cases of conflict between villages and *curés* over lifestyle are too well documented to be ignored. Yet some questions still remain. Firstly, was there only one popular culture and did all peasants and all urban workers subscribe to it? With reference to Protestant England, Eamon Duffy shows that there was a 'popular' culture that was also a 'godly' culture.[25] Its archetype would be

John Bunyan whose vastly popular writings adapted themes such as burlesque and disguised satire from popular culture: the influence of the picaresque novel *Guzmán de Alfarache* has been traced in his *Mr Badman*.[26] In Counter-Reformation Europe, the Catholic equivalent of 'godliness' — devotion, self-discipline — was no preserve of elites. On the contrary: Borromeo in Milan faced just the same kind of opposition in reforming the city as Calvin had in Geneva from 'highly placed lay people whose disorderly lives he used the strongest measures to curb'.[27]

Popular culture was of course no more monolithic than was elite culture. The culture of the lower strata was itself subject to change. Perhaps part of it was even spontaneously moving towards the rationality, literacy and modernity that would eventually overtake the whole civilisation of the continent. To some extent, any simple confrontation of two homogeneous cultures is crossed and complicated by distinctions of age and gender rather than of class alone. The Pre-Reformation male domination of villages was challenged by the Tridentine clergy who were supported by many peasant women and opposed by many peasant men.[28] 'Women', says Hoffman, 'made some significant gains during the Counter-Reformation' — a point that might be confirmed by Bossy's analysis of women's important roles in the English Catholic community after 1570.[29] Again, youth, the custodians of so much of medieval village popular culture, often seemed hostile about the Counter-Reformation. However, not all aspects of the 'old' culture came under attack from the Catholic Reformation, or the attack was muted: for example, in France the satirical '*royaumes*' were not always to be abolished under Tridentine auspices; they were not to be held until *after* parish High Mass.[30] The Counter-Reformation's attack on confraternal worship has been identified as part of a campaign against independent lay culture. Yet the Council of Trent's heavy concentration on parish worship surely strengthened the identification of parish and community which we examined in Chapter 2.

Counter-Reformation priests' alienation from their rural parishioners has sometimes been commented upon. Bourgeois 'urban intellectuals', subjected to years of dehumanising indoctrination at seminaries, the new priests are unfavourably contrasted with the matey and 'jovial country *curés* who drank and played with laymen'. Undoubtedly, such Friar Tuck figures must have existed in medieval villages, but there is no guarantee that drunks, and seducers like Montaillou's Clergue, were much liked: Dr Hoffman gives as an example of the 'old style' parish priest an obnoxious drunkard who tried to seduce parishioners' wives.[31] Aloof though they may have been, parish priests who conformed to a Tridentine norm conformed also to long-standing popular lay ideas of what a priest ought to be like:[32] chaste, sober, exemplary and liturgically effective because he was virtuous. On the other hand, the extent to which 'Tridentine' priests were severed from rural communities by lengthy and rigorous seminary training has sometimes been exaggerated: seminaries took a long time to set up and the important diocese of Paris did not get one until 1696.[33] When they were established, seminaries, at least in France, seem to have taught many entrants only short courses or brief refresher courses. Their intended harsh, dehumanising disciplines were impracticable and had to be relaxed.[34]

While it is true that over 60 per cent of ordinands in the diocese of Lyon in the late seventeenth and eighteenth centuries were of middle-class origin, over 20 per cent in the mid-eighteenth century were from the popular classes, with the priesthood proving especially attractive, as was the case throughout Europe, to peasants' sons.[35] The typical European parish priest of *Ancien Régime* Europe was less of a cultural alien to his flock than has sometimes been claimed.

The Counter-Reformation and the Reformation undoubtedly helped to bring new, post-medieval cultural influences to European villages. An older, pre-literate, collective and entirely rustic culture could not survive unchanged indefinitely. No-one in the sixteenth, seventeenth or eighteenth centuries thought of converting European villages into folk museums. Only in the nineteenth and twentieth centuries, when the 'old culture' was extinct, did anyone bother to collect the remains — the proverbs, folk tales and songs. Yet a new popular culture overlaid the old in pre-modern Europe. Literacy in such countries as Sweden, Scotland and England made major strides amongst the populace at large in the seventeenth century. Whether this represented a victory for 'dominant ideology' is arguable. Much of the dissent, the protest, the demand for social justice survived from medieval into early modern popular political culture. The newly literate might of course use their skill only to read works that upheld the *status quo*, but the printed word is not subservient to political establishments. Men and women who could read could use that priceless accomplishment to read the highly subversive Leveller and Digger tracts that poured off the presses in seventeenth-century England, or the four thousand printed attacks on Mazarin in France.[36] States were not so powerful that they could ignore the populace, especially one often surprisingly well-informed.

There is evidence of political authorities both paying close attention to, and altering policy to take account of, mass opinion. This was particularly the case in that field of religion in which large masses of people had, as we have seen, a major stake. Of course, states that claimed to be absolute were not likely to admit that they were deflected from a course by anything approaching 'public opinion'. So it is only a guess, but it might have been the case that Henry VIII's deceleration, or reversal, of religious change in the last ten years of his reign was influenced by large-scale resistance, shown most clearly in the Pilgrimage of Grace, to religious alteration. As far as Germany is concerned, students may be familiar with the Latin tag used to sum up the settlement reached in the 1555 Peace of Augsburg: *cujus regio, ejus religio*. It was supposed to mean that a ruler could impose his religious preferences quite arbitrarily on the people of his state. Rothkrug rightly rejects its applicability regardless of the popular will in sixteenth-century Germany.[37] German ruling houses making changes of faith after the first Lutheran Reformation sometimes even gave up trying to bring over their subjects with them: this was the case in Brandenburg-Prussia.[38] Rather than dynasties always being able to dictate to populaces over the vital matter of religion, it was as common for mass opinion to dictate to princes: the religion of the prince must be the religion of his subjects. Thus, to make good his strong dynastic claim to the throne of France towards the end of the Wars of Religion, Henry of Navarre had to accede to the unbending popular Catholicism of Paris and much of France — the highly politicised, indeed revolutionary, Catholicism that had been clearly evident in popular support for the duke of Guise as a Catholic tribune.

Looked at from another point of view, in an age of dawning statism, although as we saw above, the poor needed some of the strength yielded by the state, religion protected the subject from leviathan. It was, for example, Calvinist Christianity, the mainstay of Scots nationality, which gave the signal for the northern kingdom to resist its incorporation in a Stuart mega-state in 1638. It was Christian religion and only Christian religion that could provide the Quakers with a pacifist answer to the almighty state as a war machine. It was Christian religion which gave Gerrard Winstanley's Diggers a communitarian and egalitarian voice much like that of John Ball. Neither Reformation nor Counter-Reformation resulted in the extinction of the European popular consciousness.

Notes

1. Perry Miller, *The New England mind: the seventeenth century* (First published by Harvard University Press, Cambridge, Massachusetts, 1939, and cited here in the second printing of the 1954 re-issue, Harvard University Press, Cambridge, Mass., and Oxford University Press, London, 1967), pp. 1–5.

2. For an excellent summary, see Geoffrey Parker, *Europe in crisis 1598–1648* (Fontana History of Europe, ed. J.H. Plumb, Fontana paperbacks, London, 1979), ch. 1.

3. Robert Muchembled, *Popular culture and elite culture in France 1400–1750* (trans. Linda Cochrane, Louisiana State University Press, Baton Rouge, Louisiana, 1985), p. 26.

4. Stone, *The crisis of the aristocracy 1558–1641*, pp. 167–8.

5. Ibid., pp. 254–7.

6. Max J. Friedlaender, *From Van Eyck to Bruegel* (edited and abridged by F. Grossmann, trans. Marguerite Kay, 2 vols, Phaidon, London, 1956, and cited here in the third edition, Phaidon, London, 1969), vol. 2, plates 283 and 284. Shakespeare dwelt on this same theme in, for example, *Hamlet*, Act 4 Scene 3, and Act 5 Scene 1.

7. Stone, 'Interpersonal violence in English society 1300–1980', pp. 22–34; J.A. Sharpe and Lawrence Stone, 'Debate: the history of violence in England', *Past and Present*, vol. 108 (1985), pp. 206–4.

8. Muchembled, *Popular culture*, p. 96.

9. Parker, *Europe in crisis*, pp. 23–4.

10. P. Slack, 'The disappearance of plague: an alternative view', *Economic History Review*, 2nd. ser., vol. 34 (1981), pp. 469–76.

11. Stone, *The family, sex and marriage*, pp. 247–9; Alan MacFarlane, *Marriage and love in England 1300–1840* (Blackwell, Oxford, 1986), pp. 52–3, 54–6.

12. For example, *Luther's works*, vol. 42 (ed. Martin O. Dietrich) (Fortress, Philadelphia, 1969), p. 32 ff.

13. Garrett Mattingly, *The defeat of the Spanish Armada* (First published by Jonathan Cape, London, 1959, and cited here in the Pelican edition, Harmondsworth, 1965), pp. 267–8. To be fair, the English had destroyed usable barrels, and the commander of the fleet was 'impressed by the perfection of organisation he and his staff had achieved': ibid., p. 265.

14. Lionel Rothkrug, 'Popular religion and holy shrines. Their influence on the origins of the German Reformation and their role in German cultural development' in James Obelkevich (ed.), *Religion and the people 800–1700* (University of North Carolina Press, Chapel Hill, North Carolina, 1979), esp. p. 66. For France, see J.H. Elliott, *Europe divided 1559–1598* (Fontana History of Europe, ed. J.H. Plumb, Fontana paperbacks, London, 1968), p. 34, showing that despite their massive preponderance in the overall population, peasants made up only fewer than five per cent of a Calvinist congregation — even in Languedoc; however, we should recognise the strength of peasant Calvinism in the Cévennes, issuing later in a millenarian revolt following Louis XIV's Revocation of the Edict of Nantes.

15. Marcellin Defourneaux, *Daily life in Spain in the Golden Age* (Daily Life series, 13, George Allen & Unwin, London 1970), p. 40.

16. Zemon Davis, 'Rites of violence', pp. 51–91.

17. Galpern, *Religion of the people*, pp. 45–8, 103–7.

18. Ladurie, *Carnival at Romans*, pp. 102–3, 173–4.

19. G.L. Mosse, 'Changes in religious thought' in J.P. Cooper (ed.), *The new Cambridge modern history*, vol. IV: *The decline of Spain and the Thirty Years War* (Cambridge University Press, Cambridge, 1970), pp. 171, 182.

20. Rothkrug, 'Popular religion', p. 34 ff.

21. Norman Douglas, *Old Calabria* (First published by Martin Secker, London, 1915 and cited here in the Peregrine edition, Harmondsworth, 1962). pp. 263–4, 276.

22. Edward McNall Burns, *The Counter-Reformation* (Anvil Original Series, ed. Louis L. Snyder, Van Nostrand, Princeton, New Jersey, 1964), p. 140.

23. Rothkrug, 'Popular religion', p. 36.

24. For example, Philip T. Hoffman, *Church and community in the diocese of Lyon, 1500–1789* (Yale Historical Publications, Miscellany, 132, Yale University Press, New Haven, Connecticut, and London, 1984), ch. 4.

25. Eamon Duffy, 'The godly and the multitude in Stuart England', *The seventeenth century*, vol. 1 (1986), pp. 31–55; see also Margaret Spufford, 'The social status of some seventeenth-century rural dissenters' in G.J. Cuming and Derek Baker (eds), *Studies in Church history*, vol. 8 (1972), pp. 203–10.

26. Parker, *Europe in crisis*, p. 310.

27. Donald Attwater,*The Penguin dictionary of saints* (Harmondsworth, 1973), p. 84.

28. Hoffman, *Church and community*, p. 145.

29. John Bossy, *The English Catholic community 1570–1850* (Darton, Longman and Todd, London, 1975), pp. 152–60.

30. Hoffman, *Church and community*, p. 187.

31. Ibid, pp. 82–98.

32. R.I. Moore, 'Family, community and cult on the eve of the Gregorian reform', *Transactions of the Royal Society*, 5th ser., vol. 30 (1980), pp. 49–69. For a view of the Counter-Reformation as a spontaneous popular movement in France (rather like Rothkrug's interpretation of its popular acceptance in Bavaria), see Philip Benedict, 'The Catholic response to Protestantism. Church activity and popular piety in Rouen, 1560–1600' in Obelkevich (ed.) *Religion and the people*, esp. pp. 184–90.

33. Michael Mullett, *The Counter-Reformation and the Catholic Reformation in early modern Europe* (Lancaster Pamphlets, Methuen, London, 1984), p. 5 (citing Delumeau).

34. Hoffmann, *Church and community*, pp. 77–9.

35. Ibid., p. 158.

36. Parker, *Europe in crisis*, pp. 300–4.

37. Rothkrug, 'Popular religion', p. 65.

38. Ibid., p. 66.

Select Bibliography

This brief bibliography concentrates generally (but not exclusively) on more recent works and on books not mentioned in the endnotes to the chapters.

Bernard Guenée, *States and rulers in later medieval Europe* (trans. Juliet Vale, Basil Blackwell, Oxford, 1985) itself contains an exhaustive bibliography, and also incorporates stimulating theoretical and historiographical surveys.

From numerous surveys of economic history, I have selected Catharina Lis and Hugo Soly, *Poverty and capitalism in pre-industrial Europe* (trans. James Coonan in *Pre-industrial Europe 1350–1850*, ed. G. Parker, Harvester, Hassocks, Sussex, 1979). This is an ambitious long-range treatment, extending from c. 1000 to the mid-nineteenth century, and emphasising poverty and the poor. See also Thomas Riis (ed.), *Aspects of poverty in early modern Europe* (Publications of the European University Institute, 10, Klett-Cotta, Stuttgart, 1981), a collection of essays with a special focus on England.

A major work on medieval insurgency is Michel Mollat and Philippe Wolff, *The popular revolutions of the later Middle Ages* (trans. A.L. Lytton-Sells, George Allen & Unwin, London, 1973). Mollat and Wolff say they are 'struck . . . by the absence of any heresy in numerous revolutionary movements . . .' . By contrast, Rodney Hilton in *Bond men made free. Medieval peasant movements and the English Rising of 1381* (Methuen, London, 1977) writes that 'Heresies became the basis of mass movements'.

Reflecting the reawakening of interest in the German Peasant Revolt following its 450th anniversary, together with the fascination of East German historians with the subject, Europe's greatest rural rising continues to attract major studies. See, for example, P. Blickle, *The revolution of 1525: the German Peasants' War from a new perspective* (trans. Thomas A. Brady and H.C. Erik Midelfort, Johns Hopkins University Press, Baltimore, Maryland, 1981). Note also: P. Blickle, H.C. Rublack, and W. Schulz (eds), *Religion, politics and social protest. Three studies on early Germany* (German Historical Institute/George Allen & Unwin, 1984). A major work — taxing and rewarding — on peasant culture in early modern Germany, with an emphasis on the interaction between villagers and authority, is David Sabean, *Power in the blood. Popular culture and village discourse in early modern Germany* (Cambridge University Press, London and New York, 1984).

The enhanced authority of post-medieval states is dealt with in Theodore Rabb's seminal work, *The struggle for stability in early modern Europe* (Oxford University Press, New York, 1975). See also the social study of the establishment of state power in a major French province, William Beik's *Absolutism and society in seventeenth-century France. State power and provincial aristocracy in Languedoc* (Cambridge Studies in Early Modern History, eds. J.H. Elliott *et al.*, Cambridge University Press, Cambridge and New York, 1985).

French historians and historians of France such as Natalie Zemon Davis have pioneered the study of popular culture and mentalities. One major work was by a Russian, Mikhail Bakhtin's *Rabelais and his world* (trans. Helene Izwolsky, Massachusetts Institute of Technology, Cambridge, Massachusetts, 1968). Earlier, in *Rabelais and the Franciscans* (Oxford University Press, 1963), A.J. Krailsheimer dealt with the vernacular style of the Mendicants and their influence on Rabelais — a classic 'cultural amphibian'. N.Z. Davis has added *The Return of Martin Guerre* (Penguin, Harmondsworth, 1985) to her portfolio of works on French popular culture and assumptions. Moving into the eighteenth century, R. Darnton, in *The Great Cat Massacre and other episodes in French cultural history*, offers a collection of half a dozen essays which, *inter alia*, examine the roots of folk tales in the peasant condition and study the strong survival of ritual cruelty to animals.

On religion, society and culture, I have already mentioned in the footnotes John Bossy's *Christianity in the West 1400–1700* (Opus paperback, Oxford University Press, 1985), a condensed and deeply thoughtful study. In *The German Reformation* (Macmillan paperback, 1986), R.W. Scribner has done an impressive job of compression and clarification. On the Counter-Reformation, Jean Delumeau, in *Catholicism between Luther and Voltaire* (trans. Jeremy Moiser, Burns & Oates, 1977) shows us that the Catholic Reformation only *began* in the sixteenth century and was essentially a long-term process. Whether the process involved the imposition of Catholicism on masses of Europeans is open to debate. In *Local religion in sixteenth century Spain* (Princeton University Press, Princeton, New Jersey, 1981), William A. Christian reveals the genuine popularity of a Catholicism sensitively integrated with local needs.

Index

Index

San Bernardino of Siena 133
  and faction 126
  and popular culture 135
  economic teachings 123-6, 132,
    134, 145
  preaching of 18, 44, 110-12,
    136
San Gimignano 137
Savonarola, Girolamo 123, 125-48
  passim
  and Florence 14, 20-1, 29, 121
  and popular culture 110-12
  and Scripture 44
Scandinavia 19
Schlaraffenland 98
Scotland 10, 166, 167
  Queen Margaret of 82
Seville 57
Shakespeare, William 8, 99
Siena 82, 112, 137
Sigismund, Emperor 83, 102, 118,
  120
Simplicissimus 98
Sixtus IV, Pope 129
Smith, Adam 10
Spain 11, 32-3, 53, 126, 159,
  161
Spenser, Edmund 34
Speyer 83, 84, 87
Štitný, Thomas of 114
Stoicism 159-60
Strassburg 20, 54, 161

Tabor, Taborites 50, 101-3, 115,
  120-2, 140
Tasso, Torquato 36
Terling 19, 39
Titian 35
Toulouse 11, 21-2
Trent, Council of 163, 165
Tyler, Wat 97

Urban VIII, Pope 129, 162

Vaclav, King of Bohemia 103, 118,
  120
Venice 9, 13-14, 19-20, 34, 54-5,
  96
Virgil 129, 136

Waldensians 15, 73, 111
Waldhauser, Konrad 114
Winstanley, Gerrard 167
Worms, *Reichstag* of 102
Wren, Christopher 8

Wyclif, John 15, 29, 13, 115,
  116

Xavier, St Francis: *see* St Francis
  Xavier

York 95
Ypres 16, 17 , 20

Želivský, Jan 50, 100, 113, 116,
  118-20, 124
Žižka, George 101, 121-2
Zürich 18, 20, 54
Zwingli, Ulrich 18, 41